W9-ADD-623

WHY WE BELIEVE

IS VOLUME

107

OF THE

Twentieth Century Encyclopedia of Catholicism

UNDER SECTION

IX

*THE CHURCH AND THE MODERN WORLD*

IT IS ALSO THE

15TH

VOLUME IN ORDER OF PUBLICATION

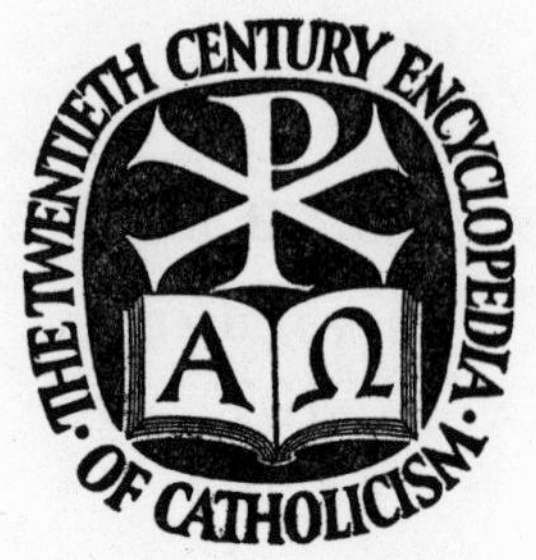


*Edited by HENRI DANIEL-ROPS of the Académie Française*

# WHY WE BELIEVE

*By MSGR. LÉON CRISTIANI*

***Translated from the French by DOM MARK PONTIFEX***

HAWTHORN BOOKS · PUBLISHERS · *New York*

 This book was manufactured in the United States of America and published simultaneously in Canada by McClelland & Stewart, Ltd., 25 Hollinger Road, Toronto 16. Original French edition, *Nos raisons de croire* © F. Brouty, J. Fayard et Cie, 1956. The Library of Congress has catalogued The Twentieth Century Encyclopedia of Catholicism under card number 58–14327. Library of Congress Catalogue Card No. for this volume: 59-8202.

*First Edition,* April, 1959
*Second Printing,* June, 1959

NIHIL OBSTAT

Hubertus Richards, S.T.L., L.S.S.

*Censor Deputatus*

IMPRIMATUR

E. Morrogh Bernard

*Vicarius Generalis*

Westmonasterii, die II JANUARII, MCMLIX

# CONTENTS

I. The Reason for Apologetics 7
Creative Action 7
Respect for the Human Person 9
Our Divided Hearts 12
Nature and Limits of Apologetics 14
Basic Principles 16

II. Apologists of the Second Century 20
Large Number of Apologists 20
The Charges against the Christians 21
St. Justin (100–10 to 163–7) 22
Other Apologists 24
The *Epistle to Diognetus* 27
The *Octavius* of Minutius Felix 30
The Apologetics of Tertullian 32

III. The Apologetic of the Christian Centuries 38
Changes in Form 38
St. Augustine's *City of God* 38
Analysis of the *City of God* 39
The Apologetic of the Middle Ages 44
Apologists of the Renaissance 47
The Apologetic of Pascal 48
The Apologetic of Bossuet 51

IV. Classical Apologetics 54
The Determining Fact 54
The Key Points 55
Jesus Christ, God's Representative 56
Signification of Jesus' Claim 60

The Miracles 62
Jesus and Miracles 64
The Purpose of Miracles 65
The Witness of History 67
The Argument from Prophecy 70
Strength of the Argument in History 71
Conclusion 73

V. THE CHURCH IN CLASSICAL APOLOGETICS 75
The Church and Jesus 75
Institution of the Church 76
Origin of the Church 77
The Ultimate Proof of the Church 78
Christ's Plan 79
Fulfilment of the Plan 82
The Coming of the Holy Ghost 85
Pentecost, the Birth of the Church 87
A New Society 89
The Church as Visible 90
The Marks of the True Church 91

VI. MODERN APOLOGETICS 96
Lawfulness of Other Forms of Apologetics 96
Method of Transcendence 97
Blondel's Method of Immanence 102
Teilhard de Chardin's Method of Evolutionary Convergence 109

VII. A FULL, LIVING APOLOGETIC 116
Continuity 116
Apologetics and Faith 118
Living Apologetics 120
Conclusion 122

SELECT BIBLIOGRAPHY

## CHAPTER I

# THE REASON FOR APOLOGETICS

### *CREATIVE ACTION*

"And now the eleven disciples took their journey into Galilee, to the mountain where Jesus had bidden them meet him. When they saw him there, they fell down to worship; though some were still doubtful. But Jesus came near and spoke to them; All authority in heaven and on earth, he said, has been given to me; you, therefore, must go out, making disciples of all nations, and baptizing them in the name of the Father, and of the Son, and of the Holy Ghost, teaching them to observe all the commandments which I have given you. And behold I am with you all through the days that are coming, until the consummation of the world" (Matt. 28. 16–20).

These are the closing words of the first of our Gospels, St Matthew's. We must also read the last lines of the Gospel of St Mark: "And he said to them, Go out all over the world, and preach the gospel to the whole of creation; he who believes and is baptized will be saved; he who refuses belief will be condemned" (Mark 16. 15–16).

These two texts deal with the same subject and are complementary, nor has anything more impressive ever been said. We cannot be too attentive to every syllable of Christ's utterances.

What he puts in the forefront of his teaching is the divine origin of his authority: "all authority in heaven and in earth has been given to me". Manifestly he is not speaking of political authority or of military authority, but of something far greater, of all *spiritual authority*. What Jesus claims is lordship over souls; he will be the one master of minds and hearts. And it is in the name of this lordship and of this universal mastership that he introduces a new work, hitherto unknown, the work of an apostle. From the beginning of his public life he had chosen his apostles, and had said to them: "I will make you fishers of men." Now, before leaving the earth, he sends them forth. What kind of work does he entrust to them? That of teaching *all nations*. Thus he takes charge of all souls. While the creation of man had been the crown of creation, the salvation of man will be the crown of Christ's mission.

It is hard for us to realize how supernatural, how revolutionary, these words are. *All nations*—there had never before existed so vast an outlook, and in religion less than in any other domain. By degrees Rome had been able to form the plan of extending its rule over the whole known world, but it had never dreamt for a moment of imposing its gods and culture upon the conquered peoples. Religion of course existed everywhere, but everywhere it was centred around the city. So thoroughly did it inspire all local institutions that it seemed inseparable from them. In the words of Bergson only the religion of the "closed city" was known. Jesus was the first and only one to proclaim the religion of the "open city", a religion which was to be neither that of a people, nor of a race, nor of a time, but the one religion of mankind, the one way to salvation.

And what an immense stake is involved! "He who believes and is baptized will be saved; he who refuses belief will be condemned."

A clear-cut, categorical, choice with no middle course;

either salvation, and eternal salvation, or condemnation and irrevocable condemnation.

### *RESPECT FOR THE HUMAN PERSON*

If the commands of Christ are plain, if the way he opens is obligatory upon all and the only way, if he takes into his hands, as I have said, the destiny of the whole of mankind, and of each individual soul, and if he speaks in the name of God himself, it is of supreme importance for us to see how he means to reach each one of us. Is it by the power of the omnipotence which he has assumed? Is it by constraint? Is it by force?

That no one may be frightened and no one overborne, he sends to us poor fishermen from Galilee, ignorant, without money, without personal eloquence, without the authority of the state, without human support. He has willed that they should be thus, deprived of everything, trusting only in God and in themselves. Yet he charges them to make the hardest of all conquests, and what he requires of them is to all appearance impossible, indeed inconceivable. There are but a dozen workers, obscure, timid, knowing nothing of the great world, and he wills that they shall scatter over the world, face powerful forces, triumph over enemies, over hostility to their race, over sarcasm and mockery, that they shall stifle hatred, and win souls and hearts.

Sometimes attempts have been made to explain their victories as the outcome of favourable circumstances, the political unity achieved by Rome, the common language of Greece, ease of communications in the Mediterranean world, the weakness of paganism, the aspirations of the human soul, a certain universal expectation of good. All this is true, but against it we must remember the obstacles they had to surmount; we must realize the difficulty of a single conversion if it was to be, not superficial or merely apparent, but sincere, profound, total and final. No other religion has ever required so complete a change, such a moral effort or heroism of the will. Jesus requires for salvation two things which affect the whole man, *faith and love*; Without these there is no salvation. These two things demand our own consent, whatever the leaders of Protestantism in the sixteenth century may have said. A sovereign respect for the human person lies at the roots of both of them. No one believes without grace; no one loves unless he is drawn by Jesus. But neither faith nor love can be forced, for to speak of a love which is forced is like speaking of a square circle. The religion of Christ is free, and yet it is all-embracing; it demands the whole man. When Jesus wished to sum up his moral teaching he said: "The first commandment of all is . . . thou shalt love the Lord thy God with the love of thy whole heart, and thy whole soul, and thy whole mind, and thy whole strength . . . and the second, its like, is this, Thou shalt love thy neighbour as thyself" (Mark 12. 29–31). Such a religion cannot compel recognition unless it is true, and gives proof of it.

It is here that the particular science dealt with in this short book, the science of apologetics, has its source. If the question is asked, "Why apologetics?", I reply, "Because the Christian religion is supremely divine and supremely human, because it requires the whole man in order to lead him to God, but respects the whole man since God does not want unconscious, irresponsible slaves. What God requires are believers, but enlightened believers, believers who understand what they believe and why they believe it. What God requires are friends, but friends who give their love willingly and who, having given it, in the fullness of their understanding and of their freedom, are ready to suffer all and to die, if necessary, rather than deny the God whom they love.

Plainly, however, the mind and the heart only give themselves to this extent if the proof is clear, palpable and irresistible. When I use these words I do not forget the principle of the freedom of faith and love which I have just stated. Is this contradictory? By no means, for man is a complex being, and is not governed by logic alone. He does not give himself just as he wishes. He is divided and troubled, subject to doubt, uncertainty and change. He wills and he does not will, and it is just this which renders all conversion so admirable, and which makes us understand the need of grace for its accomplishment. Apologetics will thus never be a science like mathematics. Its purpose is to knock at the door of the soul—of the whole of the soul at the same time, understanding, will and heart—and to present what may be called the letters of appointment of Christ the Saviour. This way of acting is quite in conformity with what we may call God's normal way. Having created man free, he will not go back on his word. All constraint, even when analogous to mathematical constraint, is contrary to his eternal design. He is love, and he is love essentially and not accidentally, and it follows that he can create only out of love. He is always consistent in his plan and, while demanding love, leaves wholly free this love without which there is no salvation.

If we look at the whole Gospel, and reflect on the life of Christ, his words, acts and conduct, sufferings and, above all, on his death, we shall see that everything follows a supremely wise law, which is nothing else than the law of supreme love.

A well-managed apologetic must adopt this method of God. It must lay siege without violence, give proof without dazzling the mind, draw conclusions without pretending to triumph over all resistance, try to convince without scorning in advance refusal to be convinced. Apologetics repeats the words of Jesus quoted by St John in the Apocalypse: "See, where I stand at the door, knocking; if any one listens to my voice and opens the door, I will come to visit him, and take my supper with him, and he shall sup with me" (Apoc. 3. 20).

It is then by persuasion, by the power of his proofs, by the beauty of his doctrine, by the charm of his spirit, by the unique character of his whole history, that Jesus wills to conquer minds and hearts. It is right to say minds and hearts, because he does not wish for the heart without the mind, nor the mind without the heart. In the words of Newman, a notional or, rather, a verbal assent is not enough to reach him, but a real assent is needed, that is, an assent which is living and effective.

A complete apologetic cannot then be addressed to the mind alone, but it should declare at once that it looks also to the heart. All its arguments must be bathed in the infinite love of God and of Christ, for without this love these arguments would be only a useless game of clever dialectic. Yet, set in their context, which is the infinite love of a God crucified for us, these arguments possess all their true force.

## *OUR DIVIDED HEARTS*

It will be said: you are giving up, then, the language of the intellect, and you rely on the appeal of emotion, without which you could convince no one. I reply: if the intellect existed by itself, if it did not strike its roots deep into a heart which was divided and too often troubled, if the intellect was not too often the victim of obscure prejudices, it might perhaps be possible to speak to it alone. When the glass of the window is clear the light enters easily, but the glass of the window of our souls is not always so perfectly clear that the sun can enter as it wishes. That is why no apologetic can enlighten the mind unless the heart is prepared.

Glance at the first victories of Christian truth, and see it at grips with Jewish obstinacy and pagan corruption. On the one hand there is the dogmatic firmness of Christianity; we must believe in Jesus Christ, and for this end we must introduce the idea of the Trinity in God, of the Incarnation of God's only-begotten Son, of the redemption through the cross, and all this without the shadow of doubt, submitting the mind, renouncing all scepticism, all vanity, all former beliefs. Neither Jew nor pagan was ready for this. The former clung obstinately to his ancestral traditions and messianic hopes, so different from those Jesus offered him. The latter was sunk in his superstitions; his mind was perverted, for paganism flatters the senses, influences every custom public and private, gathers force from every human frailty, and favours all the lower instincts of fallen nature. In the words of St Paul Christianity is "to the Jews, a discouragement, to the Gentiles, mere folly" (1 Cor. 1. 23).

It must then encounter most formidable opposition. Jesus foresaw this and foretold it; to his apostles, while promising the Holy Spirit, he also promised persecutions. Though they would have God with them, they would almost always have men against them; they would have to go continuously against the spirit of the age. They would always be near the heart of the human problem, so far as this is a problem of immortality and salvation, while they would be only on the edge of the problems with which most men busy themselves.

Right up to our own days it has always been the same. In the next chapter I shall quote a wonderful passage from the Epistle to Diognetus, which shows that from the second century Christians have recognized this strange state in which we live: *both at the heart of the problem and outside problems*. But why should I say "from the second century" when in the Gospels and Epistles this is already fully understood? For us there is only one single problem, which is that of our eternal destiny.

This does not mean, God forbid, that we despise the problems of the present life, but we put them in quite a different category from that of the one thing necessary.

Long before the Epistle to Diognetus, St Paul had said: "If the hope we have learned to repose in Christ belongs to this world only, then we are unhappy beyond all other men . . . if the dead do not rise again? Let us eat and drink, since we must die to-morrow" (1 Cor. 15. 19, 32).

In these last words St Paul is simply quoting a popular

saying of the time. It was a saying of ordinary pagan wisdom, and we find it sometimes engraved on the cups used at the banquets of the wealthy.

It was the tendency shown in this popular wisdom that he sought to trace out, a vast undertaking, and one which, to all appearance, only concerned itself with the mind. The mind was never less "disincarnate" than at that time, unless perhaps in our own.

Undoubtedly Christianity had but few human resources, when it advanced to the conquest of the world. What then was the secret of Christ's confidence when he sent his apostles into the world? He reveals it himself, when he says to them: "the Holy Spirit will come upon you, and you will receive strength from him; you are to be my witnesses in Jerusalem and throughout Judea, in Samaria, yes, and to the ends of the earth" (Acts 1. 8).

Without the help of the Holy Ghost, the conversion of the world would be impossible. Better placed than we are for judging events, the ancient Fathers of the Church, Arnobius, Eusebius and Augustine, believed that the propagation of the faith had been a continuous miracle.

## *NATURE AND LIMITS OF APOLOGETICS*

From all this we can draw conclusions which are important for the subject under discussion. In the first place, we see clearly what is the nature of apologetics. It can be defined as the science which has as its purpose to demonstrate the divine nature of Christianity.

It is a science, and this explains the relative lateness of its birth. It has of course always existed, and in due course I shall give the reason, but it only assumed a scientific form at the time when the need was felt for giving it this form. Particular aspects existed from the beginning, with clear-cut characteristics though summarily expressed; in the course of ages it took on different forms because it had to supply needs which changed with changing epochs and circumstances. Christian preaching could never be without it, because such preaching involved an appeal to the reason, as I have said, as well as to the will and the heart. But then came a day—in the sixteenth century—when theologians realized that all these scattered elements, all these well-known arguments, all these proofs hallowed by time, must be united, and out of them, a systematic whole must be made. On that day apologetics was born.

For greater clarity I must distinguish here between apologies and apologetics. Apologies belong to the history of apologetics, in the sense that they produced it and prepared its whole content. There is indeed no argument of apologetics which cannot be traced to Scripture, patristic tradition or medieval theology. Everything had been said before a systematic demonstration was undertaken.

The need for apologetics is derived from its very nature. As soon as it aimed at proving that belief is reasonable and a duty, it has always been needed. Apologetics opposes fideism in all its forms. The fideism of Luther and Calvin consists in the belief that God gives faith to those whom he saves and refuses it to those whom he damns, without any free cooperation on their part. The fideism of the traditionalists is the theory which defends belief without proof, because God has spoken, and because tradition affirms that God has spoken. But respect for human personality demands that in some sense faith should be sufficiently obscure for the adherence of the human mind to be free, while being also sufficiently clear for this adherence to be reasonable. This clear-obscure character should not surprise us. It is in the nature of things that all that concerns God should lie beyond the scope of our minds, and for this reason be shrouded in obscurity. But it is also in the nature of things that God should be able to furnish proofs accessible to our minds and capable of convincing the reason.

Later on I must explain what these proofs are, but we have only to open the Gospels to realize that they constantly connect the beginning of faith in Jesus Christ with his miracles, or again with the prophecies of the Old Testament accomplished in him. Hence I may now formulate some basic principles, which are the starting point for all scientific apologetics.

## *BASIC PRINCIPLES*

The principles I shall formulate have already been established in several volumes of the present series, and I can refer to these volumes for their proof. No book of apologetics, however, can omit them, for without them there is no religion.

The first of these religious truths is this:

1. There exists a personal God, infinitely just and wise, infinitely good and powerful, who has made all things, and especially the souls of men, which he has created that he may be known and loved by them, and which he destines for eternal happiness with himself.

This first truth leads at once to the second.

2. God can give help to our souls in order to allow them to reach their end, both by assisting the understanding and the will to attain and use the necessary certitude, and also by communicating to them supernatural knowledge by means of revelation.[1]

This second proposition is a logical conclusion from the first. A God who is infinitely wise and good does nothing without due order and love. If he creates beings endowed with understanding and freedom, he wills that they should be able to use these faculties and should find in them their happiness, that is their beatitude. Now our first need is to know; willing follows thought. If we do not know the end we cannot seek it. If man, left to himself, finds it hard to realize his powers, if he is so oppressed by the world outside him that he cannot

[1] See vol. 7 of this series.

evolve the ideals which should direct his life and conduct, God owes it to himself to come to man's aid. For this end God has given him the instinct of prayer. Religion has always existed on earth since man appeared there. From the time that man first had to strive against the elements in order to survive, his chief resource has been religion, trust in God, appeal for divine help through prayers. He has always believed that God listens to his entreaties. This conviction has given him support from the earliest ages.[2]

In the plan of Providence for mankind we can however discern two possibilities, first that God should maintain man in the natural order, and secondly, that God should raise him to the supernatural order. In the latter case God will make his will plainly known, and there will be revelation.

3. Revelation is conceivable in two forms—immediate or mediate. It will be immediate if it is addressed to each soul in particular and without any intermediary, and it will be mediate if God chooses a representative, marking him with his seal and charging him to proclaim to the whole world the favour freely granted him by God.

As is clear from what I have said, it is the second possibility which has been realized. We understand now the action of Christ in sending his apostles to conquer the nations, and the immensity of his action is shown us in all its implications. The Gospel of Christ is a revelation, the charter of salvation for all men without exception. Proof, however, is needed if we are to give it due honour, and it is here that apologetics plays its part. For the purpose I have assigned it is to show the divine nature of Christianity. In fact its purpose goes further still, since it shows the divinity of Christ himself, which *a fortiori* implies that of his doctrine.

Yet plainly God could have offered us for our salvation a religion founded by one who was a great prophet but not united in his humanity to the divine nature. This prophet

[2] See vol. 37 of this series.

might have been rightly called Christ which means God's anointed, or consecrated, and his religion would have been Christianity, but it would not have been *our* Christianity, lacking the dogma essential to ours which is the Incarnation of the Word, the divinity of Christ, and perhaps even the dogma of the Blessed Trinity, which seems only to have been revealed to men in connection with the dogma of the Incarnation which cannot be grasped without that of the Trinity.

4. The means chosen by God to mark with his seal the bearer of his supreme revelation and to attest the divinity of his mission and of his doctrine, have been miracles, a means well adapted for this end since in the nature of the case God alone can give the power to perform miracles.[3]

The four points just formulated are an adequate summary of the volumes which serve as the foundation of the present series.

As to the object of apologetics strictly so-called, this may be clearly stated in the following propositions:

5. In fact there is revelation. God has spoken to the human race. He did this at first by stages, by inspired prophets who followed a primitive revelation and prepared for the coming of the supreme source of revelation, Jesus Christ, the true Son of God, in whom and by whom divine light is shed upon the world. After Jesus Christ there is nothing more to expect, for the revelation is closed. Jesus Christ himself has entrusted this revelation into the hands of an undying and infallible Church, recognizable by four marks, unity, holiness, Catholicity and apostolicity.

Apologetics is not pure speculation; its very purpose prevents this. It is concerned with our supreme destiny. What we want to know is the value of life, if it has a purpose, if it has a meaning, if it realizes our deepest feelings, if it is not out of tune with the general harmony of things. Either apologetics tells us the truth, or the world is irrational. No more fearful

[3] On this see vol. 9 of this series.

dilemma could be formulated. When the Gnostics disputed about the truth of Christianity, Tertullian exclaimed to Marcian who was one of them: *Parce unicae spei totius orbis!* ("Keep your hands from the one hope of the whole world").

It is the aim of apologetics to bring to life faith and love, and this aim has existed from the earliest days. There is no apostolate without the presentation of reasons for belief. Before, however, summarizing the elements of apologetics, I shall give a short account of the history of apologetic literature throughout the centuries up to the appearance of systematic apologetics in modern times. This literature presents two complementary aspects: a negative aspect which consists in rebutting hostile attacks and a positive aspect which emphasizes the proofs of the divinity of Christianity. The following chapters aim at giving an outline of this.

CHAPTER II

# APOLOGISTS OF THE SECOND CENTURY

## *LARGE NUMBER OF THE APOLOGISTS*

From its first appearance Christianity had to contend with many opponents. Jesus Christ foretold this and his own life foreshadowed it. In spite of the beauty of the Gospel, the charm of his character and the persuasive power of his preaching, the Pharisees and Scribes criticized his actions and misinterpreted his miracles, though they could not deny them. They said that he only healed the sick by driving out the devils who caused the sickness, and that he only drove out the devils because he was himself the servant of the Prince of the devils, Beelzebub. Yet Jesus continued to preach and to prove the divinity of his doctrines by his miracles. He had denounced with remarkable vigour what he had called "the sin against the Holy Ghost". Further he had given warning to his apostles in the words: "A disciple is no better than his master, a servant than his lord . . . If they have cried Beelzebub at the master of the house, they will do it much more readily to the men of his household" (Matt. 10. 24). In the same passage he had urged them to preach without fear: "and there is no need to fear those who kill the body, but have no means of killing the soul" (*ibid.* 28).

They had obeyed. The early history of the Christian

apostolate is a history of warfare. The Gospel was propagated in an atmosphere of strife. But on the Christian side the war was essentially defensive and peaceful. Pascal is right in noting the difference in this respect between Mohammed and Jesus Christ: "Mohammed," he says, "does not predict, Jesus Christ predicts. Mohammed killed men, Jesus Christ sent his followers to be killed. . . ."

But even as they went to their death, the Christians protested. Hence, especially in the second century, arose an apologetic literature, which is very instructive to us, and forms a wonderful preface to the immense literature of Christianity. The name *apologists* has been given to the many writers who defended their faith in the course of the second century. The word, apology, taken from the Greek, literally means a speech for the defence, and the apologists were thus the advocates of Christianity. What was urged against Christians for them to be obliged to plead their cause?

## *THE CHARGES AGAINST THE CHRISTIANS*

The charges against the Christians seem to us very strange, but none can be stranger than the accusation made against Christ of driving out devils in the name of Beelzebub. The Christians were said to be atheists because they refused to worship the gods. At the same time they were said to be guilty of the crime of belonging to an unlawful religion and therefore of being enemies of the state, because they undermined institutions based on the worship of the pagan gods. To these accusations, of a more or less legal character, there were added by the populace gross and unheard-of calumnies, and these calumnies were sometimes accepted by educated persons: it was currently reported that the Christians met together to eat the flesh of a child who had first been killed —an allusion to the Eucharist—and further that they indulged in immoral conduct recalling the heinous crime of Oedipus against his mother—an allusion to the Christian kiss of peace.

Moreover, the Christians were often reproached for their indolence, that is, for escaping from the world and its honours, and refusing to carry out public duties, for their contempt of the goods of this life and their pursuit of eternal happiness alone. They were therefore useless persons, bad citizens.

The apologists had, then, to disprove such charges and by showing the superiority of Christianity over paganism to justify their faith. From this twofold task arose a whole literature, of which unfortunately only a part has survived to the present day. In the first place we mention here the works still extant and whose authors are known to us.

## *ST JUSTIN (100–10 to 163–7)*

One of the most ancient and most illustrious apologists is St Justin. He was born at Flavia Neapolis—the ancient Sichem, today Nablus—of pagan parents, about 100–10. He has himself related, not perhaps without exaggeration, how he came to be converted to Christianity. He had a taste for philosophy, and he had passed from one school to another in his search for truth. After having listened successively to a Stoic, then a Peripatetic, then a Pythagorean, for a time he felt himself satisfied with the Platonic teaching. But an old man whom he met by the sea shore near Ephesus, it seems, had made him realize the insufficiency of philosophy and had advised him to study the Scriptures and the preaching of Christ. He followed this advice and received baptism about the year 130.

When he became a Christian he kept the mantle, the sign of the philosopher's calling, and took up the life of a lay missionary, teaching everywhere the doctrine of Christ and presenting it as the most sublime and certain of philosophies. He came later to Rome, and there opened a school the success of which seems to have angered a pagan philosopher, named Crescens, of whom he speaks in his second Apology. It is possible, but by no means certain, that Crescens denounced him as a Christian to the authorities. Undoubtedly he was arrested, appeared before the Prefect of Rome, Junius Rusticus, replied calmly and firmly to the examination of the magistrate, and was condemned, between 163 and 167, to be beheaded, with six other Christians. We still have the authentic acts of his martyrdom, and they form perhaps his finest apology. We admire in them the firmness of his conviction, the nobility of his character, the perfect loyalty he displayed. He was truly an apostle and a saint, one of those witnesses of Christ who "are the cause of their own death". As a writer he lacks elegance and order, often wanders from the point, does not always work out his arguments fully, uses a language which is colourless and sometimes incorrect. He has, however, all the fire derived from deep conviction, and this redeems all his faults. He is precious to us, because he broke new ground. His writings were numerous, but the chief that remain are his two *Apologies*, and his *Dialogue with Tryphon*, which is also an apology but addressed to a Jew.

The first *Apology*, which can be dated between 150 and 155, is addressed to the Emperors Antoninus Pius, Marcus Aurelius, and Lucius Verus, and to the Senate. We cannot say whether in fact it reached these persons, but it was mainly intended for the Roman public in general. The second *Apology*, which was much shorter, completes the first, and must have followed it closely, though the author himself does not connect the two together. It may be dated at the latest at 155.

What is the gist of St Justin's writings? First he rebuts the charges mentioned above which surprise us so greatly. Christians, he says, are not atheists, since they adore the one true God and only reject the vain worship of idols. They do not practise immorality, nor are they murderers, nor enemies of the Roman Empire, but dutiful and peaceful citizens. Christian morality is on the contrary pure and noble. The dogmas and worship of the Christians are worthy of all praise. It is the devils who raise a persecution against them.

In his *Dialogue* with the Jew Tryphon, Justin shows that Jesus Christ was without doubt the Messias foretold in the Scripture and expected by the Jews. He states that the Old Testament has lapsed through the Incarnation of the Word and also through the appeal to the Gentiles which makes of them the "true people of God".

## *OTHER APOLOGISTS*

While Justin is of great importance to us, especially in regard to the confidence we should have in the Gospel story which he rightly calls the "Memoirs of the Apostles", I can deal more shortly with other apologists, either because their writings are to a large extent lost, or because they concern us less directly.

Among the apologists whose writings have not come down to us, I may mention Quadratus, one of the earliest according to Eusebius, who addressed an apology to the Emperor Hadrian (117–38). It has been suggested that it is to be found again in the *Epistle to Diognetus*, mentioned below, which is a precious jewel among the Christian works of that time.

The writings of Aristo of Pella, of Miltiades who lived in the second half of the second century, of Apollinaris, bishop of Hierapolis, and of Melito of Sardis are also lost.

On the other hand we possess the work of Aristides, a Christian philosopher of Ephesus, who praises the purity of the morals and doctrines of Christianity and its striking superiority over the pagan religions, and whose language is inspired by so noble an enthusiasm that his apology has been compared to the beautiful *Epistle to Diognetus*. Might he and not Quadratus have been its author? The critics dispute the question. But the two authors, if they are two, were of remarkable nobility of mind.

Tatian was quite different, an affected writer, and obscure, though impressive. His character seems to have been disagreeable and to have been rather like that of Tertullian. In any case he was inclined to exaggeration, and was unjust to the pagans. He heaps sarcasm on his enemies, and certainly forgets the proverb which says that more flies are caught with honey than with vinegar. For him everything connected with the Greeks is bad: their art is immoral, their literature childish, their philosophy false, even their language is neither pure nor regular. In short Tatian is far more a controversialist than an apologist. He aims rather at rebutting and crushing than at conquering and attracting. His work is full of gall and bitterness. He is the exact opposite of St Justin who sees clearly that the Word inspired both the thinkers of Greece and the prophets of Israel, arguing from the harmony between them. Following Puech, we may date the *Discourse to the Greeks* of Tatian about 171.

Another apologist, contemporary with Tatian, since he addressed his work to the Emperors Marcus Aurelius and Commodus, is Athenagoras, who seems to have lived at Athens, and perhaps also at Alexandria. He was a philosopher, teacher and writer. His work is well arranged, free from useless digressions, and he does not employ false rhetoric, but argues forcibly in a style which is plain and without embellishment, the true style of a philosopher. The title of his apology is *Embassy on behalf of the Christians*. It was undoubtedly written at Athens between the years 176 and 178. The plan of the work could not be clearer or simpler. First he refuted the charges levelled against the Christians, the same as those made fifty years previously, atheism, immorality, cannibalism. Thus the apologies already published had produced no change in this respect; it was only gradually that these absurdities were to be buried in oblivion.

Athenagoras gives the same answers as his predecessors: the Christians are not atheists, they worship one God in three Persons, the Father, Son, and Holy Ghost. It is quite true that they do not offer public sacrifices, and do not venerate the gods of paganism, but God does not require earthly sacrifices, and the pagan gods are not gods but simply deified heroes.

The second charge, that of immorality, has no better foundation than the first. Christians believe in hell and regard even an evil thought wrong. It is the pagans who commit the wicked acts with which they dare to taunt the Christians. As to the cannibalism of which they speak, the Christians are far from committing such a crime. They detest murder and on this account avoid even the games in the arena; they condemn the exposing of children, and believe in the resurrection of the body. Consequently the Christians have a right to justice, and count on the mercy of the Emperors.

This apology is one of the finest of the century. The account which he gives of the purity of the Christians' lives puts Athenagoras on a level with Aristides and with the author of the *Epistle to Diognetus*.

Similar ideas are to be found in the three books *To Autolycus*, by Theophilus, bishop of Antioch, which were written about the year 180. Autolycus was an educated pagan, undoubtedly a magistrate of Antioch. He had asked Theophilus to tell him about his God, and had praised the pagan gods, mocking at the Christian name. Theophilus, boldly obeying St Peter's command to the faithful to give an account of their faith whenever this was asked for, replies to Autolycus by speaking of the true God, of his nature, of his omnipotence, of the certainty that we shall behold him, when we are clothed with immortality. In contrast with this one true God Theophilus refused to admit any divinity in the gods of paganism.

In a second book Theophilus returns to the same theme, and develops it more fully. In his third book he approaches the subject in a way which is most interesting on account of its originality. Autolycus had raised an objection which we meet in our own day. "Your religion is quite new," he said, "your Scriptures are recent. Before this were men without gods?" It is as though someone said at the present day: "Christianity has only existed for 1900 years, while man goes back from 500,000 to 600,000 years. How can it be said that Jesus Christ is the only Saviour of the human race?"

Theophilus of Antioch made substantially the same answer as we make today. Christianity is but the full flowering of the religion of Moses. We add now that the religion of Moses was only the continuation of the patriarchal religion. Even, however, with Moses, as Theophilus thought, we go back a very long way: he supposed it to be 5,695 years from the beginning of the world to the death of Marcus Aurelius. Moses he supposed to have lived 900 or 1000 years before the Trojan war—in his view, more than necessary to show that the true religion preceded paganism.

We cannot leave St Theophilus of Antioch without recalling that he is the first writer to employ the Greek word, *Trias*, in the sense of Trinity. Before him the three divine Persons were named, but the term Trinity was not used.

To conclude this short account of the apologists it will be enough to mention the name of Hermias. He was scarcely an apologist, nor are we at all sure of his date. He considered himself a controversialist rather than an apologist, and he called his book *Scorn for the pagan philosophers*. He describes the philosophers and their schools, but it is in order to convict them of contradiction when they speak of the soul and of the first principle of things. Hermias is a superficial writer, who has left nothing of value.

## *THE EPISTLE TO DIOGNETUS*

It is quite another matter with the *Epistle to Diognetus*, already mentioned here several times, which is one of the finest writings that have come down to us from that distant age.

At the time, however, it seems to have won little celebrity. No ancient author, not even Eusebius or St Jerome, who had read everything, speaks of it. The only manuscript of it which existed perished in 1870. This mentioned St Justin as author of the letter, but surely wrongly. I said above that at the present day opinions vary between Quadratus and Aristides, though possibly neither of them was the author. This short book is a real treasure, which may be taken as a first example of what I may call the apologetic of immanentism. Jesus Christ himself had formulated the principle of this apologetic, when he said: "Be on your guard against false prophets . . . You will know them by the fruit they yield" (Matt. 7. 15–20). This thought was never afterwards absent from the minds of Christians. Neither St Peter, St Paul, St James, St John nor St Jude, in their Epistles, omitted this supreme proof of Christian apologetics formed by the holiness of life to be found in believers.

It can be said, however, that the author of the Epistle to Diognetus has given to this thought the noblest expression. Even now it is much more important for us to appreciate what he has said than to add to it. In any case we have here a most important work of apologetics, and more than that, a whole programme of Christian life.

We can now examine the letter addressed to Diognetus. This letter form is perhaps a mere literary convention and Diognetus may well exist only as the imaginary representative of contemporary paganism. He is supposed to have asked the author of the *Epistle* why the Christians did not worship the gods of the whole world, or at least did not practise the religion of the Jews, and why Christianity had appeared so late.

The author answers these questions in order: the Christians do not worship the gods because they are but wood, stone or metal. They do not share any longer in the religion of the Jews because this religion, though having the true God as its object, is childish and unworthy of him. Having reached this point in the proof, the author describes Christian conduct. He does this in so happy and vigorous a style that the passage devoted to it deserves to have a place in every anthology of Christian authors:

> Christians are not distinguished from the rest of mankind either by country, speech, or customs; the fact is, they nowhere settle in cities of their own; they use no particular language; they cultivate no eccentric mode of life. Certainly, this creed of theirs is no discovery due to some fancy or speculation of inquisitive men, nor do they as some do, champion a doctrine of human origin. Yet while they dwell in both Greek and non-Greek cities, as each one's lot was cast, and conform to the custom of the country in dress, food, and mode of life in general, the whole tenour of their way of living stamps it as worthy of admiration and admittedly extraordinary. They reside in their respective countries, but only as aliens. They take part in everything as citizens, and put up with everything as foreigners. Every foreign land is their home, and every home a foreign land. They marry like all others, and beget children; but they do not expose their offspring. Their board they spread for all, but not their bed. They find themselves in the flesh, but do not live according to the flesh. They spend their days on earth, but hold citizenship in heaven. They love all men, but are persecuted by all. They are unknown, yet are condemned.... They are poor, and enrich many.... Doing good they are penalized as evildoers.... Those who hate them are at a loss to explain their hatred. *In a word: what the soul is in the body, that the Christians are in the world.* The soul is spread through all the members of the body, and the Christians throughout the cities of the world. The Christians dwell in the world, but are not part and parcel of the world.... The flesh hates the soul and makes war on it; the world hates Christians. The soul is locked up in the body, yet is the very thing that holds the body together; so, too, Christians are shut up in the world as in a prison, yet it is precisely they that hold the world together. The soul, when stinting itself in food and drink, fares the better for it; so, too, Christians,

when penalized, show a daily increase in numbers on that account. Such is the important post to which God has assigned them, and they are not at liberty to desert it (*Epistle to Diognetus*, 5–6, abridged).

Whoever he may be, the unknown author who wrote these lines deserves our respect and gratitude. That thought alone, "what the soul is in the body, that the Christians are in the world", is one of the most profound and truest that have ever been uttered on the subject of Christianity. Without Christianity the world has no soul! All apologetics is summed up in this.

## *THE OCTAVIUS OF MINUTIUS FELIX*

When we read the *Octavius* of Minutius Felix we do not leave this same climate of thought. The *Octavius*, too, is one of the finest apologies of Christian antiquity. It is hard to decide whether it preceded or followed the celebrated *Apologeticum* of Tertullian, and critics are divided on the subject. If simplicity is a sign of priority the *Octavius* is earlier. The important point, however, is that the two writings are closely connected, and the one is undoubtedly inspired by the other.

The name of the author of the *Octavius*, who calls himself Marcus, was in full, Marcus Minutius Felix; he was a lawyer and lived at Rome, though he was probably of African origin. He was a convert, and had been a Stoic before becoming a Christian. Octavius was one of his friends, also a convert, and he died at the very time when the book was written. It is in the form of a dialogue: three men are walking by the sea at Ostia. One of them, who is a pagan, blows a kiss to the statue of Serapis. The discussion between Cecilius who is a pagan and Octavius who is a Christian centres round this action. Minutius Felix keeps himself in the background as judge of the discussion. Cecilius speaks first. His language must be that of most educated pagans of the time: What do we know of the gods? he says in substance. Nothing at all. We cannot reach truth. In any case the gods, if they exist, are not concerned with us. Hence the wisest course, in this matter of religion, is to conform to the laws of the country where one lives. Now, that is just what the Christians do not do: they form a secret society, immoral, criminal, the enemy of the human race, and they follow a worship which is utterly absurd, for they worship a crucified man. In Cecilius' eyes it would be better to avoid all novelty in religion and to leave things as they are.

After this opening speech Octavius has his turn, and refutes Cecilius point by point. It is untrue, he says, that we can know nothing of God, for reason by itself proves his existence, and shows that there can be one God only, whose Providence looks after us. Pagan polytheism owes its origin to the devil, and evil spirits still spread against Christians the calumnies mentioned by Cecilius. In fact Christians uphold a pure morality, a reasonable faith and religion, and, in spite of the persecutions they suffer, they find in the witness of their conscience a happiness which no one can take from them. It is therefore false that we should "let things take their course; we must fight superstition, drive out godlessness, and spread the true religion".

The proofs given by Octavius are so fair, plain and convincing that Cecilius recognizes his mistake and is converted to Christianity. The whole dialogue unfolds itself with dignity, honesty and an elegant simplicity. By its simplicity, which I have said may be a sign that it precedes the work of Tertullian, I mean not only the high level of the discussion but in particular the few Christian doctrines put forward. Apologetics is not a complete theory, but, as we say today, an introduction. While Octavius defends the divinity of Christianity, he is careful not to enter on a profound discussion of Christian dogmas. He speaks of God, of his unity, of his Providence, of the Christian life, of the resurrection and of the life to come. As far as possible he keeps to the sphere of human reason, and does not shrink from finding inspiration in the pagan philosophers. He openly makes use of Cicero's *De natura deorum* and *De divinatione*, as well as of Seneca's *De Providentia* and *De Superstitione*. The author of the dialogue is anxious to give to his whole work a Latin classical stamp, both in its matter and its form. If he speaks neither of Jesus Christ, nor the Trinity, the Gospel, sin, redemption, the sacraments, that is because his purpose is first to draw men to Christianity as teaching a lofty morality. Once converted Cecilius will be instructed in all the rest. Thus we have here already an apologetic the true aim of which is thoroughly grasped and which is carried out most effectively.

## *THE APOLOGETICS OF TERTULLIAN*

If, as we may suppose, Tertullian, following Minutius Felix, wished to carry his proof still further, he has not failed to acknowledge either its vigour or its truth. His own work is dated in the year 197, and this enables us to place that of Minutius Felix either a little earlier or a little later.

Tertullian, too, was a lawyer. He was born at Carthage, the son of a Roman officer stationed there. His youth was not virtuous, but was inspired by an inclination for hard work. He had a thorough understanding of Roman law, and of the practice of his profession. He had read widely. He was over thirty years old when he was converted to Christianity about the years 193–5. We know nothing of the circumstances of his conversion. About the year 200 he received the priesthood, though he was married. He wrote much against paganism and heresy until the day when he himself fell into the Montanist heresy about the year 213, and broke away from the Catholic Church. His mind was vigorous, assertive, and independent, but with a tendency to run to extremes, to reason rashly, to be impatient, and to indulge in paradox. He himself declares impatience to be his chief fault, and it seems that he meant by this an inability to endure contradiction, to submit problems brought before his mind to a calm and sober examination.

As a writer he may be put in the first rank. Bossuet, who often quotes him, shows very plainly his admiration. Without doubt he has great faults; he is sometimes affected, slovenly, and mannered. He aims at being concise, and, if he succeeds, this is sometimes at the cost of clearness. He always has something of the orator about him, seeking for effect and not always quite careful about the accuracy of his language. But he has life and energy, arranges his matter with care and without useless digression; his style is individual, vigorous and colourful, carrying the reason along without a moment's rest. He is rightly regarded as the chief creator of theological language. If there is a Christian Latin, distinct from pagan Latin, it is largely to him that we owe it. St Cyprian, paying no attention to the errors of Tertullian's old age, showed the esteem in which he held him by saying to his secretary, when he wanted one of his works: *Da mihi magistrum* ("Give me the master").

The apologetic works of Tertullian are five in number: *Ad nationes* (to the pagans—a lively criticism of pagan manners and beliefs, as described by Varro), *Apologeticum* (his work of apologetics which continues the same subject, treating it more fully, and belongs to the year 197), *De Testimonio animae* (the witness of the soul, which may be regarded as completing the *Apologeticum*), *Ad Scapulam* (to Scapula, written about 212, in which the author threatens the cruel governor Scapula with God's punishment, an idea repeated by Lactantius), *Adversus Judaeos* (against the Jews, a book which proves the truth of Christianity by the prophecies of the Old Testament).

Of these works I shall refer here in particular to the *Apologeticum*. Before Tertullian, as we have seen, the apologists were concerned to declare the innocence of the Christians, and as a contrast to criticize paganism. Tertullian adopts the same plan, but he applies it in his own way, taking his stand firmly on the basis of law, the Romans being open to legal arguments. Tertullian did not, therefore, keep to generalities, but he knew how to compose a true counsel's speech in favour of the Christians to whom he belonged. His whole treatise may be summed up in the four following propositions:

1. The procedure used against the Christians is irregular and absurd. 2. The laws made against them contradict the common and the natural law. 3. The crimes of godlessness and treason imputed to them are non-existent. 4. The Christian society is lawful, their doctrine true, their conduct, both private and public, beyond reproach.

From our point of view at the present day it is especially this last part which belongs to apologetics properly so-called. Truth of doctrine, holiness of conduct, are the subject matter essential to all apologetic.

History, however, cannot forget what Tertullian says about the hatred of the pagans. "They prefer to be ignorant about what they hate", says the author, speaking of the pagans. "Because they already dislike, they want to know no more. But thus they prejudge that of which they are ignorant to be such, that, if they came to know it, it could no longer be the object of their aversion."

Yet, what strange criminals were these persecuted Christians:

> You find that criminals are eager to conceal themselves, avoid appearing in public, are in trepidation when they are caught, deny their guilt when they are accused; even when they are put to the rack, they do not easily or always confess; when there is no doubt about their condemnation they grieve for what they have done. In their self-communing, they admit their being impelled by sinful dispositions, but they lay the blame either on fate or on the stars. They are unwilling to acknowledge that the thing is theirs, because they own that it

is wicked. But what is there like this in the Christian's case? The only shame or regret he feels is at not having been a Christian earlier. If he is pointed at, he glories in it; if he is accused, he offers no defence; interrogated, he makes voluntary confession; condemned, he renders thanks. What sort of evil thing is this, which wants all the ordinary peculiarities of crime—fear, shame, subterfuge, penitence, lamenting? What! is that a crime in which the criminal rejoices? to be accused of which is his ardent wish, to be punished for which is his felicity? You cannot call it madness, you who stand convicted of knowing nothing of the matter.

But it is when he speaks of the decree of Trajan, who was nevertheless a good Emperor, that Tertullian is supreme. Trajan, answering Pliny the Younger, had decided: "These men need not be sought out, but, if they are accused, those should be pardoned who repent, and the obstinate punished." At that the lawyer Tertullian cries out:

O miserable deliverance—under the necessities of the case a self-contradiction! It forbids them to be sought after as innocent, and it commands them to be punished as guilty. It is at once merciful and cruel; it passes by, and it punishes. Why dost thou play a game of evasion upon thyself, O judgment? If thou dost not inquire, why dost thou not also absolve? Military stations are distributed through all the provinces for tracking robbers. Against traitors and public foes every man is a soldier; search is made even for their confederates and accessories. The Christian alone must not be sought, though he may be brought and accused before the judge; as if a search had any end but that in view! And so you condemn the man for whom nobody wished a search to be made when he is presented to you, and who even now does not deserve punishment, I suppose, because of his guilt, but because, though forbidden to be sought, he was found.

The law so interpreted itself bears witness that the accusations against the Christians are not believed. Tertullian nonetheless examines the list of charges: infanticide, cannibalism, incest (an allusion to the Eucharist and to the kiss of peace). But have you any proof? Have you witnesses? Can you mention any place where these crimes have been committed? Do you not see that these crimes are improbable and impossible? Would you yourselves commit them? If they horrify you, why do you impute them to the Christians who are men like you? Indeed, not content with being men, the Christians desire to be the most religious, the most virtuous, of men. They are said to worship a god with the head of an ass! How absurd: "The object of our worship is the One God, he who by his commanding word, his arranging wisdom, his mighty power, brought forth from nothing this entire mass of our world . . . for the glory of his majesty. The eye cannot see him, though he is (spiritually) visible. He is incomprehensible, though in grace he is manifested. He is beyond our utmost thought, though our human faculties conceive of him."

This God has not left men to themselves. He has willed to make himself known; he has spoken to men by revelation. This revelation is in the Scriptures, the antiquity and majesty of which impress themselves on the mind. The whole revelation is accomplished in Christ, whom we may define as *Homo Deo mixtus*, a man mingled with God.

Tertullian provides a lengthy discussion of Christian morality, and this part of his apologetic is the most eloquent and most beautiful. His conclusion is famous:

> But go zealously on, good presidents, you will stand higher with the people if you sacrifice the Christians at their will, kill us, torture us, condemn us, grind us to dust; your injustice is the proof that we are innocent. Therefore it is of God's permitting [not of your own will] that we suffer. For but very lately in condemning a Christian woman to the pimp rather than to the lion, you made confession that a taint on our purity is considered something more terrible than any punishment and any death. Nor does your cruelty, however exquisite, avail you; it is rather a temptation to us. The oftener we are mown

down by you, the more in number we grow; the blood of Christians is seed.[1]

This last phrase is one that has echoed through the ages. It has for ever a part in Christian apologetics. And the work of Tertullian from which these words are taken is one of the few masterpieces of the literature of the world.

[1] Translation from *Ante-Nicene Christian Library.*

## CHAPTER III

# THE APOLOGETIC OF THE CHRISTIAN CENTURIES

### *CHANGE IN FORM*

It is natural to Christian apologetic to assume different forms according to the needs of the time. In the last chapter I considered the principal works of the Christian apologists in the era of persecution. After the victory which the legislation of Constantine gave it Christianity changed its mode of speech without changing its teaching. Only the principal works can be mentioned here, with lengthier consideration of those of the first rank.

It is enough to mention the *Praeparatio Evangelica* and *Demonstratio* of the scholar Eusebius. In them we have a learned summary of all the Christian scholarship which confronted Hellenism.

The short popular treatise of St John Chrysostom on the divinity of Christ should also be noticed, and again the *Graecarum affectionum curatio* of Theodoret of Cyrus, writers of the fourth and fifth centuries.

We must not, however, be content with a mere passing glance at the great work of St Augustine, *De Civitate Dei* (The City of God).

### *ST AUGUSTINE'S CITY OF GOD*

Perhaps the strongest apologetic argument that can be put forward in support of a doctrine is its power to enlighten us in face of human problems, both small and great, the breadth of vision it gives to those who profess it, the height it attains in the philosophy of history, the care with which, thanks to such a doctrine, the divine is united to the human, in order to reveal the meaning not only of each individual destiny but also of the whole succession of events which fill the troubled annals of the race of Adam.

St Paul said—though only incidentally and without insisting on it—"It is all for you, and you for Christ, and Christ for God" (1 Cor. 3. 23), that is, that the whole of creation has its meeting point in Christianity. This is the point that the *Epistle to Diognetus* had expressed, in its own way, by saying that "Christianity is to the world what the soul is to the body". We shall find the same thought in all the great Christian thinkers, in Pascal as well as in Bossuet or Teilhard de Chardin, though in different forms.

In St Augustine we have for the first time a writer great enough to cover all human knowledge of his time. His work, the *City of God*, is a kind of fifth-century encyclopedia.

We find references to every past age; St Augustine examines every problem of philosophy in order to give an appropriate solution. The ancients said of Varro and Pliny that they had read everything, and the same may be said of St Augustine; his work, for his period, covered an immense field. Not only is it an apology for Christianity but also a philosophy of history, a treatise on ethics, on physical science, on metaphysics, and even on political science. It may be truly said that Charlemagne wished to carry out in practice St Augustine's political theory.

Here I shall only mention the apologetic side of his work.

### *ANALYSIS OF THE CITY OF GOD*

The circumstances which led to the book show that it answered to the needs of the time. Every great work of apologetics has this character, and that is why, in every such work, parts become out-dated, when the apologist meets the crisis or objections of his time. Alaric had just taken Rome, in the year 410. A cry of distress and horror had risen throughout the Empire. The most terrible calamities harassed the Roman world. "It is the gods who are avenging themselves because we have abandoned them," cried the last pagans, "it is the fault of Christianity, that we are afflicted in this way". This was the accusation which Augustine wished to refute. He worked for thirteen years—from 413 to 426—at this book, the most important he wrote, which he called *De civitate Dei*, the *City of God*. Amid all the cares with which he was continually beset, it is not surprising that he had often to interrupt work upon his book. Hence there is a certain lack of connection between the parts. Digressions are numerous, and it is sometimes difficult to see how certain details are relevant to the main subject. Yet the aim of the author is quite clear. Augustine wished definitely to arraign the whole past, and by means of his pen Christianity examines the pagan gods and philosophers. He wishes to prove that the former could not govern the destiny of the peoples who worshipped them, while the latter could not, by their own efforts, attain full knowledge of the truth.

The work contains twenty-two books. The first ten are mainly apologetic in character, the remaining twelve historical and theological.

It is in the first part that Augustine refutes the objection of the pagans. You draw your argument, he says in substance, from the calamities which oppress us. But calamities are either physical or moral. The former occur in every age. Many other empires have been overwhelmed, and pagan Rome has not been spared more than others. It is not because it has become Christian that it has been struck yet again. As to moral calamities, far worse than physical, they may be attributed directly to the pagan religion, because its gods have given an example of wicked conduct, and because that religion tolerated the worst excesses. If boast is made of the conquests of Rome, she owes them rather to natural virtue rather than to gods who are weak and divided. It is worthy of a just God, the God of the Christians, the only true God, to give a natural reward to the natural virtues.

In Augustine's eyes, however, we must rise to a higher level. Man's history as a whole is comprised in the struggle between two cities, the City of God and the earthly city. But as the name should come from that which is the chief, the whole book is called the City of God, and not the two cities.

This human race, writes Augustine, is divided into two classes—*duo genera*—one made up of men who live according to man, the other made up of men who live according to God, and we call them mystically the two cities (15. 1.).

Today we should say: there are two religions, one of this world and the other of the next, one of earth and the other of heaven, one of man and the other of God. These two religions, like the two cities of Augustine, are, as he says, entangled and mingled in this life—*perplexae in hoc saeculo invicemque permixtae*. They seem confused and God alone can distinguish them. They will not be completely separated until the last judgement.

Augustine devotes all the second part of his work to a comparison of the two cities, and for this purpose he goes back to the beginning of the world, indeed he goes beyond our world, and penetrates to the mystery of the creation of the angels. For the two cities begin in heaven with the creation of the angels and the revolt of Lucifer. From heaven they come to earth with the creation, temptation, and fall of the first man. Their history continues from one century to the next. Good and evil ever oppose one another: Cain and Abel, Sem and Japhet against Cham, Esau against Jacob and so on. At length, however, the cities will be separated. The city of God will vanish into heaven, the city of evil will be punished in hell.

Throughout his work Augustine is careful to set the City of God round the one Mediator, Jesus Christ, and around his Church which is the *communio electorum*, and which is "on pilgrimage" in this world, struggling against its enemies until the triumph comes which awaits it.

But when Augustine speaks of a struggle, he means only a moral struggle; the heavenly city desires but one thing which is to live on good terms with the earthly city. On the other hand it would be wrong to say that St Augustine concerns himself only with matters of religion and morality, and the next world, and has no interest in this world and in human happiness. On the contrary he is convinced that to preach Christian virtue is to work for the happiness of mankind. Christianity represents the *divine order*. Now, tranquillity of order is the very definition of peace: "an arrangement of similar and dissimilar parts which gives to each its proper place" (19. 13). But peace in its true meaning, peace of the soul, peace at home, peace in the state, social peace, finds its condition and security in the peace of the heavenly city. Augustine here reaches the ideal which seems to him the supreme good of mankind: "perfect order, perfect union in the enjoyment of God and in the mutual enjoyment of all in God."

If, as I have said above, many parts of this great work are out-of-date, we should realize that it marks an epoch. For the first time a man mastered the ages and traced out what we call at the present day "the meaning of history". And as, according to him, everything depends upon Christ and his Church, if only we are to come to God, the whole work constitutes the most magnificent apologetic. The book had an immense influence throughout the Middle Ages. More than five hundred manuscripts of it exist in the libraries of Europe, the oldest dating back to at least the sixth century and perhaps the fifth.

Between 1467 and 1495, that is just after the invention of

printing, twenty-four editions were published. An earlier translation, that of Raoul de Presles, in 1375, had made the work so popular that artists sought in it for subjects to give them inspiration. In a fine book which appeared in 1909 Count Alexandre de Laborde published a study of the illuminated MSS of the *City of God*. He discovered sixty-two, four of which are earlier than the translation of Raoul de Presles. I may add that the central theme of the Two Cities inspired the celebrated meditation of the Two Standards by St Ignatius Loyola, and the *Discours sur l'histoire universelle* by Bossuet.

I must not leave St Augustine without explaining that it would be inaccurate to say that all his apologetic work lies in the *City of God*. On the contrary it may be said that all his work is apologetic, and that many passages in the *City of God* must be interpreted in the light of what he says in his *Sermons*, his *Letters*, and other works. Manifestly a book like his immortal *Confessions*, more read even than the *City of God*, is a book of living apologetics. There we see, ineffaceably expressed, the power of persuasion, penetration, transformation, found in the doctrine of Christ, when acting upon a tortured nature, which has experienced all the troubles, temptations and weaknesses of mankind. Is not the best apologetic, that is, the best proof of the divine character of Christianity, the power it has to do good in a heart such as that of Augustine, which we feel is very near to our own hearts, in spite of the difference in time? Was not Teresa of Avila overcome by reading the *Confessions*? And is it not in the first lines of that book that we find the phrase so often repeated and which lies at the base of the so-called apologetics of immanence: "For thyself hast thou made us, O Lord, and our hearts are restless until they rest in thee?"

These words unintentionally echo what Tertullian says about "the witness of the human soul which is naturally

Christian". Christianity would not be "true" for us, if it were not as "profoundly human as it is divine."

### *THE APOLOGETIC OF THE MIDDLE AGES*

During the long period which we call the Middle Ages apologetics had no longer to combat paganism. The complete victory of Christianity made an apology for Christianity unnecessary among the community of the faithful. The enemies of the faith were of two kinds: within, the Jews, who were mingled with the Christians but obstinate in their ancestral traditions and, after the Crusades, the Arabs and Mohammedan Turks outside.

Against the Jews the Christian apologists prove the messianic character of Christ by means of the prophecies of the Old Testament, and of the miracles of the New Testament. They establish also the abrogation of the law of Moses, replaced by the law of the Gospel, and the divinity of Christianity, shown especially by its miraculous victory over paganism, on the one hand, and over Judaism on the other. Many of these apologies, however, are disfigured either by ignorance of the real doctrines of the Jews, or by the scorn they show for the pagans. It is only when we reach the thirteenth century and St Thomas—the great thirteenth century—that apologetics regain their true spirit, a fitting loftiness of doctrine, and an indisputable solidity of reasoning.

Yet before his time certain works should be mentioned, if only to show the permanence of the apologetic spirit.

In the seventh century, Isidore of Seville (†636) wrote his *De Fide catholica ex Vetere et Novo Testamento contra Judaeos* (the Catholic faith against the Jews, taken from the Old and New Testaments).

In the eleventh century St Fulbert, bishop of Chartres (†1028) published his *Tractatus contra Judaeos* (a treatise against the Jews) in which he shows that the prophecy of Jacob, "Juda shall not want a branch from his stem, a prince drawn from his stock, until the day when he comes who is to be sent to us, he, the hope of the nations" (Gen. 49. 10), has been fulfilled in Jesus Christ.

A little later St Peter Damian (†1072) produced his *Antilocus contra Judaeos* (refutation of the Jews), and his *Dialogus inter Judaeum requirentem et christianum a contrario respondentem* (dialogue between a Jew who questions and a Christian who answers).

Sometimes, even in the title of a work, an attack is made on the opponent, as in the work of Peter the Venerable (†1156), called *Tractatus adversus Judoeorum inveteratam duritiem* (treatise against the inveterate obstinacy of the Jews).

Peter the Venerable treats the Saracens, too, no better, in the two works he directs against them. The first is called *Summula quaedam brevis contra haereses et sectam diabolicae fraudis Saracenorum sive Ismaelitarum* (Summary of the case against heresies and the sect of the Saracens and Ismaelites with their diabolical trickery); and the second: *Adversus nefariam sectam Saracenorum* (against the wicked sect of the Saracens).

St John Damascene (†749), four centuries earlier, had shown himself less aggressive in his treatise called "Discussion between a Saracen and a Christian".

In fact it was necessary for convert Jews or Saracens to explain their position more exactly in order that a really effective proof of Christianity and refutation of their errors should be given.

The most successful work, for this very reason, was the *Pugio fidei adversus Mauros et Judaeos* (the dagger of the faith against Moors and Jews), which was published at Paris, simultaneously in Latin and Hebrew, in 1270, by a convert rabbi, Raymond Martini, a disciple of Raymond of Peñafort, who had become a Dominican.

The work has two parts. In the first the author refutes the errors of the philosophers who deny both the possibility and the fact of divine revelation. In the second he writes a very learned criticism of Judaism, quoting against it not only Scripture but also the talmudic tradition and rabbinic theology, and he proves from the prophecies of the Old Testament that Christ is the Messias. Finally, in the third part he defends the chief doctrines of Christianity against the attacks of unbelievers. On account of the content and the deep learning which distinguishes it this work marks an epoch.

Shortly before its publication the greatest theologian of the time—and perhaps of any time—St Thomas Aquinas, had written, for the use of missionaries who wished to work at the conversion of the Mohammedans, a book of first importance which may be regarded as the most systematic of medieval works of apologetics: the *Summa contra Gentiles*. This really deals more with the philosophy of religion than with apologetics. Yet all the elements of what we should call classical apologetics are to be found here. St Thomas has especially in view the errors of Arabian philosophers, but he does not attack them directly. He confines himself to refuting them indirectly by showing that the Christian doctrines which belong to the philosophical order are proved by reason, and that those which go beyond the realm of philosophy and are of the dogmatic order, are also in accordance with reason and in no way contradict it. Hence the *Summa contra Gentiles* has two parts. The first, which occupies books 1–3, treats of natural theology, proved by reason alone. From our point of view this part is introductory. Only the second part composes the apologetic properly so called. It explains the mysteries of the faith, shows how they rest on divine revelation, and how their credibility is founded on the prophecies of the Old Testament, on the miracles of Christ recounted in the Gospels, and on the subsequent miracle of the conversion of the world to Christianity, a miracle which includes and continues all the earlier miracles.

As we shall see later, all classical apologetic is already to be found in this second part of the *Summa contra Gentiles*, and St Thomas has given here, as in all theology, in his sober, bare, and precise style, a model of explanation which cannot be surpassed.

## *APOLOGISTS OF THE RENAISSANCE*

Among the apologists of the Renaissance there are two who deserve to be mentioned specially. First, there is the famous Florentine preacher Girolamo Savonarola, who published in 1497, shortly before his tragic death, a work called *Triumphus crucis, sive de Veritate fidei libri IV* (the triumph of the Cross or of the truth of the faith in four books). In the first book he treats of the existence of God and of the immortality of the soul. The second book shows the divinity of Christianity, but refers above all to the fruits of holiness in the world. In the third book the author applies human reason to the great mysteries of the faith, and in the last he replies to the objections of philosophers, astrologers, idolators, Jews and Mohammedans against Christianity.

Here we have already the full scheme of our modern apologetics. Savonarola insisted rightly on the point that the divinity of Christianity is shown more clearly in the moral virtues of Christians than in the miracles themselves. Every true saint is himself an apologetic.

The second work of this age of transition which I should like to mention is that of the Spanish humanist, Juan Luis Vivès, printed at Basle in 1543: *De Veritate fidei christianae libri V* (the truth of the Christian faith in five books). It is a proof of Christian doctrine in the traditional style of apologetics, that is, accompanied by a refutation of Judaism and Mohammedanism. It is interesting to notice that at the time when his book appeared the author did not attack Protestantism, and did not enter into the fierce debate which embroiled Catholics and Lutherans and Calvinists. Vivès quotes many of the Fathers of whom he had a profound knowledge, and shows himself in particular a follower of St Augustine. He also follows in the steps of St Thomas, whom he praises as "the best of the scholastics and the most balanced of all the writers of the schools". He had also profited from the works of Marsilio Ficino and Savonarola, but, in his last book, he has an original contribution to make by emphasizing the moral and social benefits of Christianity. Thus he opened up a path along which, after him, modern apologetics and in particular the authors of the seventeenth century have followed. The work, which was the fruit of his maturity, was published three years after the death of Vivès by his friend Graneveld.

## *THE APOLOGETIC OF PASCAL*

With the coming of modern times Christian apologies have multiplied. A new fact emerges; unbelief creeps in among the Christian churches, divided and violently hostile to one another since the Protestant revolution. Apologists have no longer to combat Jews or Mohammedans, but hedonists, sceptics, and free-thinkers.

Among the many writers whom we may count in the ranks of apologists, I shall mention two, on account of their celebrity, Pascal and Bossuet.

Pascal's fame alone, it may almost be said, makes an argument for Christianity. That a thinker of genius, and a writer such as he, should have formed the plan of composing a work of apologetics, modelling it upon Montaigne's famous *Apologie de Raymond Sebond*, proves by itself that in his eyes Christianity contains the whole of truth needed by man and all that we can hope to know of it in order to accomplish our destiny.

We know for certain that he dreamt of leaving to the Church and to posterity, as a witness of his inward faith, an apology for the Christian religion against atheists, unbelievers, hedonists of his time and of every time. This important scheme was suggested to him by his sister Jacqueline, and, as the illness of which he was to die on the 19th August 1662, at the age of thirty-nine, prevented him from doing any continuous work, he had to be content with writing on some loose sheets the flashes of thought concerning the plan which crossed his mind. Immediately after his death these sheets were at once collected. They were found all put together in bundles but not in any order, and it was very difficult to decipher these scraps. Only some of them were chosen, and these were published in 1670. Our present editions are complete, and very different from the first. Even now, however, it is disputed what was the plan of Pascal. Without going into details, which do not concern us here, Pascal's plan for apologetics may be summed up in the following ideas.

1. There is much both of greatness and weakness in man, greatness because of his desires, ambitions, and destiny, weakness because of his mind and the knowledge he has of the means to carry out the task assigned him by his nature. What then must he do? It is impossible for him to remain indifferent: "We should have to lose all feeling in order to be indifferent to what a man is. Between us and hell or heaven, there is nothing but life, the most fragile thing in the world." Can you rely on yourselves? "I am in dreadful ignorance of everything." Shall we take a wager? It is a terrible risk: "There is a chance of gain against a chance of infinite loss and what you hazard is finite." So take the risk without fear. Trust in the only light which shines on your horizon, that of the Christian religion. It is not contrary to reason; it is venerable because it has such a knowledge of men. The doctrine of the fall from which it starts alone explains the nobility and the baseness we find in ourselves. We can love this religion because it alone offers us true good. It gives us God. "This is what faith is: God perceived by the heart." Only one obstacle holds you back: your taste for passing pleasures: "you would soon have faith if you had left pleasure..."

2. Would you try to find the secret of life from the philosophers? They have spread so many lies among men, have fallen into so many contradictions, that we cannot trust in any purely human teaching.

3. Other religions are full only of vanity and error, and can give us no help.

4. The Jewish religion is "the most ancient in the world, the most perfect and the only one that has always been maintained in a nation without a break". From it we have received the Bible, and the Bible is the only book which explain's man's misery, and offers the remedy. This book alone can speak of the sovereign Being, it alone contains prophecies which have been fulfilled, and miracles which are fully proved, it alone has opened the way for the Messias.

5. Finally, it is on the Messias that we must fix our eyes. The divinity of the Messias is proved by his very person, by his teaching, and by his miracles. To reach us across the ages he has sent us his apostles. Such men were neither deceivers nor deceived. The whole history of the Church is in harmony with its beginning. Martyrs, saints, miracles, which have marked every century, all prove that God alone "could control the outcome of so many different purposes".

I hasten to say that this cold analysis gives a very imperfect idea of the mighty monument which Pascal wished to raise. His *Pensées*, though it has only been possible to collect them in such a disconnected state, is one of the supreme books of Christian literature. Its beauties of detail are striking and countless, for Pascal has the gift of moving our hearts. What especially he has put in a light that can never be extinguished are the degrees of being, that is, the place of man in the general whole. He says:

> The infinite distance between body and soul represents the distance, infinitely greater, between souls and charity, for that is supernatural... All bodies, the firmament, the stars, the earth with its kingdom, are not equal to the least of souls, for

the soul knows all this and itself and the body knows nothing. All bodies together and all souls together and all they produce are not equal to the least movements of charity. This is of an order infinitely higher. Out of all material things and souls no movement of true charity can be drawn; it is impossible, for this latter is of a different order, supernatural.

That is why, according to Pascal—and according to all Christians—Jesus Christ is above everything: "Jesus Christ, with no riches, with no outward display of knowledge, exists in his order of holiness. He has invented nothing, and has not ruled, but he has been humble, patient, holy, sacred to God, terrible to the devils, without sin. Yet has he come with great pomp and wonderful splendour to the eyes of the heart which sees his wisdom."

These are words never heard outside the Christian religion, and here is the best proof of the heights to which this religion has raised mankind.

### *THE APOLOGETIC OF BOSSUET*

With Bossuet we are still within the circle of great men who, through their Christianity, have done honour to the human race, and who, by their adherence to the Christian faith, have proved the power it possesses to conquer and rule.

To give a complete account of Bossuet's apologetic it would be necessary, as with St Augustine, to review all his works, which are immense. I shall pause only shortly at the second part of the *Discours sur l'Histoire universelle*. Like St Augustine, who always inspires him, Bossuet rises above the centuries. He shows how all human history, the chief features of which he has summarized in his first part, is given its crown and explanation by the true religion, in its successive stages: the religion of the patriarchs, the religion of Moses, the Christian religion. With the coming of Jesus Christ, however, a new day has dawned for everything. In him alone all the ages have found their fulfilment.

> Everything is sustained by his personality [writes Bossuet], his life, his teaching, his miracles. The truth of this is shown everywhere; everything conspires to make us see in him the master of the human race and the model of perfection. He alone, living among men, and in sight of the whole world, has been able to say without fear of contradiction: "Which of you shall convince me of sin?", and again, "I am the light of the world; my meat is to do the will of my Father; he that sent me is with me, and he hath not left me alone. For I do always the things that please him." His miracles are of a special order and a new character ... He does nearly all of them upon men themselves and to heal their infirmities. All his miracles display goodness rather than power and do not so much surprise those who behold them as touch their hearts deeply. [In Jesus Christ all becomes clear, and human history has a meaning. In this is shown plainly the greatest proof of the truth of Christianity.] By this teaching of Jesus Christ God's secret is opened to us; the law is wholly spiritual, its promises introduce us to those of the Gospel and form their foundation. Everywhere we see the same light: it rises under the patriarchs; it grows brighter under Moses and the prophets; Jesus Christ, greater than the patriarchs, with more authority than Moses, more enlightened than the prophets, gives it to us in its fullness.
>
> [He concludes:] It is thus that God reigns over all peoples. Let us speak no more of chance or fortune, or let us speak of them only as words with which to cover our ignorance. That which is chance in relation to our uncertain judgement is a fixed purpose to a higher judgement, that is, to the eternal judgement which gathers all causes and all effects in a single order. In this way all things tend to a single end, and it is because of our failure to understand the whole, that we see chance or irregularity in particular events.

We ought to understand Bossuet's outlook, for the whole problem of apologetics—and of all philosophy—is contained in it: Is there order in things? Is the evolution of things designed or is it left to itself, that is, to blind forces without purpose? We find this dramatic dilemma in Teilhard de Chardin who, in quite a new way, but following St Augustine, Pascal, and Bossuet, has asked the question we have just been discussing: is there purpose, that is, Providence and wisdom, or the unknowable processes of material activity?

Apologetics should make us choose between the two.

## CHAPTER IV

# CLASSICAL APOLOGETICS

### *THE DETERMINING FACT*

"In old days, God spoke to our fathers in many ways and by many means, through the prophets; now at last in these times he has spoken to us with a Son to speak for him; a Son, whom he has appointed to inherit all things, just as it was through him that he created this world of time; a Son, who is the radiance of his Father's splendour, and the full expression of his being; all creation depends, for its support, on his enabling word. Now making atonement for our sins, he has taken his place on high, at the right hand of God's majesty" (Heb. 1. 1–3).

The Epistle to the Hebrews, one of the treasures of the New Testament, opens with these solemn lines. The second author—whether St Paul himself, or one of his intimate disciples and assistants—asserts most emphatically this fact which dominates all the events of our human history, that *God has spoken.* But, if he has spoken, it is certainly not in order to say nothing of importance, on the contrary it is in order to say everything, to teach men all they must know and believe, if they wish to be saved.

The fact of divine revelation gives at once a plain answer to the question put in the last chapter. The question is whether things are governed by Providence or Chance—this latter word meaning here activity of the forces of nature without definite purpose and certainly without any meaning to us.

In answer to this question eternal wisdom has spoken, and its infallible mouthpiece is Jesus Christ. The whole revelation is called the Gospel.[1]

The primary duty of apologetics is to show the historical reality of revelation. Without searching for early, imperfect forms in which this revelation appeared, these being only outlines and signs of the future, apologetics may be content with proving that Christ was sent from God. The sending of him, indeed, includes implicitly the sending of the prophets who preceded him. The revelations of the Old Testament are confirmed by those of the New Testament.

## *THE KEY-POINTS*

What, then, are the key-points of apologetics? They may be summed up shortly as follows:

1. Jesus Christ declared that he was sent by God, and was therefore the Messias foretold by the prophets.

2. This assertion of Christ is firmly assured (a) by the intellectual and moral excellence of Christ himself; (b) by the miracles which proved that the mission he received from God is genuine; (c) by the prophecies which foretold it.

In strict logic apologetics has not to prove the sincerity of Christ, but only that he was sent from God. He might have been only the greatest of the prophets. The expectation of a Messias did not necessarily imply the mystery "hidden from ages and generations" in the words of St Paul, that is, the mystery of a God made man,[2] for a revelation was possible without the Word becoming incarnate. This revelation also, coming from God, would have been a law binding us, and have given us the grace of eternal salvation.

Apologetics is concerned in the first place with Christ himself who deigns to give his own proofs. It asks of him

[1] On this subject reference may be made to vols. 66–70 in the present series.

[2] See vol. 24 of this series.

above all who he is, what he says of himself, and if he speaks in his own name or in the name of God.

### *JESUS CHRIST, GOD'S REPRESENTATIVE*

When we open the Gospel we are surprised at first to see that Jesus usually refers to himself by the modest, but suggestive, name of the Son of Man. To us there is something of the unknown about this name, and the Jews themselves were astonished at it. On the lips of Jesus, however, it had a messianic meaning, which he explained when he was before the high priest Caiphas, saying: "A time is coming when the Son of Man will be seated in power at God's right hand" (Luke 22. 69). To anyone who knows the prophecies of Israel these words explain everything. Daniel had written: "Then I saw in my dream, how one came riding on the clouds of heaven [of the future], that was yet a son of man; came to where the Judge [the Eternal] sat, crowned with age, and was ushered into his presence. With that, power was given him, and glory and sovereignty; obey him all must, men of every race and tribe and tongue" (Dan. 7. 13–14).

Undoubtedly then Jesus claimed before Caiphas the title of Messias of Israel, of God's representative, who is sitting "in power at God's right hand."

The title, however, which Jesus Christ assumed before the whole Sanhedrin, the title under which he had decided to suffer the condemnation to death by which he should carry out his mission of redemption,[3] he had already taken solemnly before the disciples.

"Then Jesus," St Matthew tells us, "came into the neighbourhood of Caesarea Philippi; and there he asked his disciples, What do men say of the Son of Man? Who do they think he is? Some say John the Baptist, they told him, and others Elias, others again, Jeremy or one of the prophets. Jesus said to them, And what of you? Who do you say that

[3] See vol. 25.

I am? Then Simon Peter answered, Thou art the Christ, the Son of the living God" (Matt. 16. 13–16).

Christ's answer to this "confession" of St Peter's shows his clear approval, and leaves no room for doubt about it: "Blessed art thou, Simon son of Jona," he says: "it is not flesh and blood, it is my Father in heaven that has revealed this to thee." And, using at once the powers he held from God, Jesus promises Peter that he will build his church on the rock which is himself, and that he will give him the power of the keys.

If any doubt can remain about the implications of this passage, it is removed by the conclusion given in the Gospel: "Then," it is recorded, "he strictly forbade them to tell any man that he, Jesus, was the Christ" (Matt. 16. 20).

Nothing could be easier than to multiply proofs of the messianic character of Christ, or, to be more precise, of the clearness of his assertions about this character.

These proofs are to be found on almost every page of the Gospels. I shall quote only two more:

"Now John had heard in his prison of Christ's doings," St Matthew writes, "and he sent two of his disciples to him; Is it thy coming that was foretold, he asked, or are we yet waiting for some other?"

The question was clear to every Jew at that time. He that was coming in the language of the time was one of the commonest expressions to refer to the Messias. Thus John the Baptist wished to give Christ an opportunity to declare himself. Jesus accepts the respectful request made to him, and answers:

"Go and tell John what your own ears and eyes have witnessed; how the blind see, and the lame walk, how the lepers are made clean, and the deaf hear, how the dead are raised to life, and how the poor have the gospel preached to them. Blessed is the man who does not lose confidence in me" (Matt. 11. 1–6).

Here certainly is an answer which is not within the comprehension of everyone. We shall meet it again in the course of our proof. For the moment I need only observe that it is a plain assertion that he is the Messias, that it appeals to the miracles on the one hand and to the prophecies on the other, by a very clear allusion to Isaias. All classical apologetics is thus summed up in this one passage.

At this point we may recall the text placed at the beginning of this book: "All authority in heaven and earth has been given to me." Either there is no question of a Messias or else these words imply an assumption of the character of the Messias, that is, of God's envoy, of the consecrated or anointed one of God, which is precisely the meaning of the word Messias or Christ.

But it would be a betrayal of the Gospel truth, and absurd restriction of it, if we reduced to these few texts, despite their strength, all the assertions of Christ on the subject of his messianic character. In fact in every line of the Gospels he presents himself as the Messias. It is not only his words which reveal to us his divine authority and his title of God's representative, or in the language of tradition, of "mediator between God and men". It is all his acts, his whole attitude and everything he says. From the time when he first shows himself to the world and begins to speak, all are struck by one thing, that he speaks "with authority and not as the scribes and pharisees". He is not content to claim superhuman powers; he exercises them before the eyes of all; he reforms and perfects the law, saying: "You have heard that it was said to the men of old.... *But I tell you.*" He forgives the sins of the paralytic, he proclaims himself master of the Sabbath, he commands the devils and they obey, he shows himself master of the elements, for the tempest is calmed by his word, he wills that he should be loved more than father or mother or children. He claims titles of supreme significance; he is the door, the good shepherd, the vine of which we are the branches. He demands faith in himself as we have faith in God:

"Do not let your heart be distressed," he says; "as you have faith in God, have faith in me. . . . I am the way: I am truth and life; nobody can come to the Father, except through me. . . . Whoever has seen me has seen the Father. . . . The words I speak to you are not my own words; and the Father, who dwells continually in me, achieves in me his own acts of power" (John 14. 1–10).

We must gather together all these features, compare them with one another, meditate on them as a whole, to form an idea—even the least idea—of the personality of Christ. He is to be worshipped as the Son of God, as the Word made flesh. It is enough for our present purpose that he puts himself forward as the mouthpiece of God himself. Our first point, then, is indisputable: Jesus Christ declared that he was sent by God, and that he was thus the Messias foretold by the prophets.

When he was on the cross undoubtedly his enemies mocked at his claims: "Come down from that cross," they cried to him, "if thou art the Son of God." And they repeated to one another: "He trusted in God: let God, if he favour him, succour him now; he told us, *I am the Son of God*."

But their mocking words only prove what I have said, namely, that Jesus made himself out to be the Messias, the envoy of God, and that it was for this that he was condemned to death. The whole Gospel turns simply upon this title of Messias which we acknowledge as belonging to Jesus. So true is this that throughout the centuries he is referred to by this name, Christ, which means, Messias, and that he is rarely called simply Jesus, but rather Jesus Christ.

What then is implied by this claim of Jesus, during the whole of his life and even in death?

### *SIGNIFICATION OF JESUS' CLAIM*

The words of Jesus should at once, and of themselves, suffice to convince us. For there are moral impossibilities which are as clear as physical impossibilities. The theory of an error, and *a fortiori*, of a lie, on the part of such a man in reference to his personality is a moral impossibility: it is impossible that he should be deceived, or should deceive us.

Buffon's remark is often quoted: "the style is the very man." Now Christ has a "style" which always expresses the depths of his being. A word is not a dead thing. A leaf, fallen from the branch and covered with mud, unshapen and withered, can retain nothing and reveal nothing of its origin. But the living leaf lets us know the tree to which it belongs and, when we know one leaf, we know all those of the same tree. They are of the same kind, have the same life within them, possess the same specific essence.

So too with the words of the Gospel. We know the character of Jesus, through all his words and all his acts. Each separate feature makes the whole clear, and the whole throws light on each detail. The Sermon on the Mount witnesses to the divinity of Christ's mission.

The lips which said: "Blessed are the poor in spirit; . . . blessed are the patient; . . . blessed are the merciful; . . . blessed are the peacemakers; . . . blessed are those who mourn, blessed are those who hunger and thirst for holiness, blessed are the clean of heart" are the same lips which answered the messengers of John, or the confession of Peter, or the challenge of Caiphas. He who blessed the sick to heal them, he who preached the Gospel to the poor, and "went about doing good" as was said of him, is the same who was put to death because he said that he was "the Son of God". The whole Gospel declares the truth of this claim, because the whole Gospel witnesses to the utter sincerity, complete straightforwardness, supreme uprightness of the character of Christ. He could neither be deceived nor deceive us. He was not the man to let himself be influenced by his surroundings, or to become the sport of a people's ambitions or of the prejudices of a race. On the contrary, everything shows that he saw into the hearts of his fellow countrymen and found there aspirations which he refused to encourage. Amid a narrow, gross, and fanatical society his glance pierced through to a vision of the future which baffled everyone but alone was to prove itself worthy of God. From the beginning he could have assumed one of the titles which the prophets had lavished upon him. There was a striking text of Isaias on this subject: "For our sakes a child is born, to our race a son is given, whose shoulder will bear the sceptre of princely power. What name shall be given him? Peerless among counsellors, the mighty God, Father of the world to come, the Prince of peace (Isaias 9. 6). Later on, the disciples of Christ had no scruple in giving him these honours. He himself keeps to this mysterious title, Son of Man, which is found in Daniel, but the glory of which was grasped by no one. In the Gospel we always find him anxious to curb enthusiasm, to discourage nationalist sentiment, to keep to the sphere of the spiritual and divine. Far from being moulded by his times, inflamed by the feelings around him, swept away by his followers, he gradually instilled into men's minds the true idea of the Messias, as willed by God, and as we must believe.

He preaches of a spiritual coming. He sows the seed of love. He utters terrible words such as "I am come to cast fire on the earth". And one day the best loved and most inspired of his disciples was to utter the phrase which enlightens everything: "God is love", and again, "God so loved the world, that he gave up his only-begotten Son so that those who believe in him may not perish, but have eternal life" (John 3. 16).

In all Christ's actions, in all his teaching, throughout his wonderful and tragic history, there is, then, such a balance, unity and consistency, that the claim to be the Messias and even the Son of God comes naturally from him, without startling us or seeming strange or improbable. His supreme wisdom, gentle kindliness, appealing humility and miraculous power, are precisely the characteristics fitting to God's envoy and representative, the mediator between God and man, God's own Son. This is what the *Vicaire savoyard* of Rousseau, whom I certainly do not count as a Father of the Church, felt so strongly and expressed in the well-known passage:

> The highest wisdom made itself heard from the midst of the most furious fanaticism, and the simplicity of the most heroic virtues gave honour to the most wretched of all peoples. The death of Socrates, quietly discussing philosophy with his friends, is the pleasantest that could be desired; that of Jesus, dying in agony, assaulted, mocked, cursed by a whole people, is the most horrible that could be dreaded. Socrates, taking the cup of poison, blessed the man who offered it to him and who wept! Jesus, in the midst of frightful torture, prayed for his cruel executioners. Yes, if the life and death of Socrates are those of a wise man, the life and death of Jesus are those of a God.

Throughout the Gospel there is, then, a living harmony which confirms in advance, explains, and gives authority to, the assertion of Jesus about himself.

## *THE MIRACLES*

Hence Christ's word is good enough for us. But was it enough for the general run of men, for the humble and ignorant, for the mind of an age when the divine was traditionally shown by miracles? Even at our own time would the Gospel without miracles have sufficient authority to make us accept it, with all the lofty demands it imposes? A beautiful code of morals, a beautiful dream, a beautiful plan: "Glory to God, peace to men . . . Love one another . . ." Undoubtedly no one refuses to reverence profoundly such a magnificent idea. But for us it is no question of a polite gesture. Jesus demands an absolute service of faith and love. Without this nothing in the world will be changed, and heaven will remain closed to souls.

The most obstinate rationalists are ready to admit the unique beauty of the Gospel. The *Vicaire savoyard* has just proved this. But it is not in order to receive the homage just quoted that Jesus Christ spoke, taught, died on the cross and gave the Holy Ghost to his apostles before sending them to conquer the world. In fact history shows that *faith* arose, grew, was strengthened, and spread, owing to the *miracles* of Christ.[4]

The enemies of our faith are sometimes scandalized by miracles. They try to make distinctions. They accuse our apologetic proofs of "extrinsicism", an ugly word which means that we prove from appearances, from what is irrelevant, from dubious facts added and superimposed on the doctrine we desire to substantiate. Hence they wish to regard the stories of miracles in the Gospel as additions, legendary compositions, spontaneous productions of the popular spirit. They accept the sayings of Christ, for no one could have invented them, no one could make them up. But they reject the marvellous as they call it, on the ground that the marvellous has always flourished in every age, whenever there have been prophets or founders of religions, so that there is no more proof for one than for another.

There are answers to these objections. You say: there are miracles everywhere, hence there are none. I answer: there are miracles and miracles, there is evidence and evidence. It is the business of the critics to distinguish true miracles from false, honest, well-informed witnesses from vague, uncertain, legends.

You say again: the accounts of the miracles were added later. But you know quite well that this is false, that the Gospel accounts are not composite, that they all have the same source and our manuscripts agree. You know quite well that the stuff of the Gospel narrative is so continuous and connected that no thread can be taken out without tearing the stuff itself. If you remove the miracles you make the faith

[4] I refer again to vol. 9 of this series.

unintelligible. St Augustine pointed this out fifteen hundred years ago: it would be a greater miracle that the world should be converted without miracles.

But look at the facts. Two things are certain: that Jesus, whom they wish to turn into a wise man so as not to worship him as God, believed in his own miracles, constantly appealed to them, and based his authority on them, and also that his first disciples only followed him on account of the miracles.

In particular we can look at the first of these two facts.

### *JESUS AND THE MIRACLES*

I claim that Jesus himself appealed to his miracles in order to make men believe in his mission, and here are some references. One day a paralytic was presented to him. He forgave him his sins, and, when murmurs arose, he replied: "Why do you cherish wicked thoughts in your hearts? Tell me, which command is more lightly given, to say to a man, Thy sins are forgiven or to say, Rise up, and walk? *And now, to convince you that the Son of Man hath authority to forgive sins* while he is on earth (here he spoke to the palsied man), Rise up, take thy bed with thee and go home" (Matt. 9. 4–6).

This is a striking miracle, but what is important is the connection established by Christ between this miracle and his power, which the Jews themselves consider to be reserved to God. The miracle is performed expressly to guarantee the superhuman power of forgiving sins.

Another example, and one which I have already mentioned in reference to the disciples sent by John. Jesus wishes to prove that he is really "he that is to come". To prove it he appeals to the miracles: the blind see, the lame walk, the lepers are cleansed, and so on. But why should anyone speak here of "extrinsicism"? Do you think it extrinsic to the doctrine of salvation that the author of that doctrine should show himself to be good to sufferers? When honour was to be paid to revelation, was it not fitting that honour should be paid to

God's goodness? If the Son of God came upon earth, nothing can seem more reasonable and right than such a profusion of good deeds. He himself said: "Can you expect the men of the bridegroom's company to go mourning, when the bridegroom is still with them?" The bridegroom was there. Was it not fitting in the highest sense that this divine marriage with our poor humanity should be celebrated by such wonders of his goodness; did not the doctrine harmonize perfectly with the miracles? There might perhaps have been talk of "extrinsicism" if Jesus had caused signs in the heavens to appear, as his enemies urged him to do. When the devil set him upon the pinnacle of the temple, and tempted him to throw himself down, in order to make men recognize him as Messias, this was "extrinsicism". We should say today that he proposed a miracle which would have been spectacular but unnecessary, doing good to no one, and only producing a wondering astonishment. That was not the way in which Jesus performed his miracles. When we are told he raised the daughter of Jairus, or the son of the widow of Naim or Lazarus, the brother of Martha and Mary, there are two things we must not say: first, that the witnesses of these facts were ignorant of the laws of nature, and spoke of a miracle when there was a normal working of these laws, and, secondly, that it was not in closest harmony with the doctrine of goodness and mercy which is the soul of the whole Gospel.

## *THE PURPOSE OF THE MIRACLES*

What endows the miracles with their character of supreme goodness is not so much that they cure illness, suffering or infirmity, nor even that they save men from death, but that they give rise to faith, that they render it at once reasonable and a duty. I cannot insist too strongly on this point in apologetics. Miracles belong to an order higher than the natural, and it would be the gravest of errors to see in them a kind of disorder, on the ground that they are contrary to the laws of nature. This objection, so often repeated, is without any foundation. It is untrue that a miracle breaks the laws of nature, or that it does them any injury. The dead have not risen again in violation of the laws of nature, even after Jesus raised Lazarus or the son of the widow of Naim. The dead whom he raised did not escape death later on. Neither Lazarus nor the daughter of Jairus were made immortal by the miracle performed upon them. In point of fact not only does a miracle not break the laws of nature, or do them any injury, but a miracle presupposes and requires the laws of nature. If there were not fixed laws in nature, established by God himself, and which he alone can suspend, there could not be any question of a miracle. In order that there shall be a miracle there must be an event, which is visible, verifiable, proved by unquestionable evidence, clearly produced outside of, and above, the laws of nature.

The argument which men have always spontaneously framed with regard to miracles may be formulated thus: such an event is beyond the power of nature, as, for example, the causing of a body to come forth from the tomb, when it had been shut in there for four days and was already in a state of decomposition—"Lord, the air is foul by now; he has been four days dead," said the sister of Lazarus—and the giving life to this body. Now, since no human power can break the laws of nature or withdraw itself from the action of these laws, this must be the work of God. The intermediary he has chosen—in this case, Jesus—is thus equipped with the power of God, consecrated by God, through miracles, as his representative. And if he performed the miracle to guarantee a doctrine, this doctrine must be regarded as coming from God.

Consequently, it is both reasonable and a duty to believe, because God is the supreme truth, and the supreme wisdom, and because everything he says has no other aim than our good and our happiness. This is a duty because, as St Paul says, "You cannot cheat God" (Gal. 6. 7).

To show that this reasoning is sound, it is enough to question Jesus himself, and to know, from his own lips, what he expected from his miracles, and the importance he attached to them.

Now, in view of what I have said, his miracles were his letters of appointment to men, his direct appeal to faith. Without the miracles his work would have lacked necessary official consecration. Jesus himself declares: "If I had not done what no one else ever did in their midst they would not have been in fault" (John 15. 24). What makes the Jews inexcusable is the abundance of signs granted to them. This very word, sign, which is constantly given to the miracles in our Gospels, proves it. When Jesus said that "they would not have been in fault" without the "signs", this means that, with the "signs", they are not free from sin. Jesus uttered terrible curses against the unbelieving cities. This is because miracles make faith a duty.

> Woe to thee, Corozain, woe to thee, Bethsaida: Tyre and Sidon would have repented in sackcloth and ashes long ago, if the miracles done in you had been done there instead. And I say this, that it shall go less hard with Tyre and Sidon at the day of judgement than with you. And thou, Capharnaum, dost thou hope to be lifted up high as heaven? Thou shalt fall low as hell. Sodom itself, if the miracles done in thee had been done there, might have stood to this day. And I say this, that it shall go less hard with the country of Sodom at the day of judgement than with thee (Matt. 11. 21–4).

Jesus Christ speaks here, as he does everywhere, as master of events, as supreme judge, as representative of God's justice. But he connects the responsibility of men directly with his own miracles.

## *THE WITNESS OF HISTORY*

History bears witness that the language of Jesus was understood as I have just said; it connects faith directly with miracles.

The first time St Peter spoke to the people of Jerusalem, on the day of Pentecost, it was his miracles that he directly appealed to as proof of the divine mission of Christ: "Men of Israel, listen to this, Jesus of Nazareth was a man duly accredited to you from God; such were the miracles and wonders and signs which God did through him in your midst, as you yourselves well know. . . . you, through the hands of sinful men, have cruelly murdered him. But God raised him up again, releasing him from the pangs of death . . . We are all witnesses of it" (Acts 2. 22–33).

The classical apologetic was now fixed for ever. To convert the world the great argument of the apostles was the miracles of Christ, and above all the miracle of the resurrection, which they never ceased to preach and which, in their eyes as in ours, is in no way an unnecessary miracle, in the sense I explained above, but a pledge to us of our own resurrection, a proof of our immortality and hence of the value of life. "If Christ is not risen again," says St Paul, "neither shall we rise, and we are of all men most miserable" (1 Cor. 15; Douay version).

The authors of the Gospels constantly attribute the origin of faith to Christ's miracles. After the wonder worked at Cana for two poor people newly married, St John's account concludes: "So, . . . Jesus began his miracles, and made known the glory that was his, so that his disciples learned to believe in him" (John 2. 11). A few lines further on he says again: "At this paschal season, while he was in Jerusalem for the feast, there were many who came to believe in his name seeing the miracles which he did."

St John also, when recounting the visit of Nicodemus to Jesus, puts into his mouth the following words: "No one, unless God were with him, could do the miracles which thou doest" (John 3. 2). But this language is not peculiar to St John. Before him Mark was already saying the same. Thus in Mark Jesus casts out an evil spirit and "all were full of astonishment", says the evangelist, "What can this be? they asked one another. What is this new teaching? See how he has authority to lay his commands even on the unclean spirits, and they obey him! And the story of his doings at once spread through the whole region of Galilee" (Mark 1. 27–8).

Another time he healed a leper. "But he," says St Mark, "as soon as he had gone away, began to talk publicly and spread the story round: so that Jesus could no longer go into any of the cities openly, but dwelt in lonely places apart; and still from every side they came to him" (Mark 1. 45).

After healing the paralytic, in reference to whom Jesus claimed the divine power of forgiving sins, the evangelist remarks: "all were astonished and gave praise to God; they said: We never saw the like".

It is, therefore, historically true that the fame of Jesus was that of a wonder worker. That is what I meant when I argued that the miracles are part of the stuff of the Gospel, that if we suppress them we give up any attempt to understand the life of Christ, that they are intimately connected with his words, his teaching and his whole life. Men came to him from all sides, at first not so much in order to hear him, as because he healed the sick. The crowds pressed around him, and he had to make use of a boat, in order that he might be able to get free from their over-enthusiastic attention. We know, from the account of the multiplication of the loaves, that thousands followed him right into the desert. Wherever he appeared crowds gathered and surrounded him, the possessed and the sick were brought to him, and he took advantage of the concourse to deliver his message. If more listened to his words it was not so much on account of the sublimity of his teaching, as it is with us, as on account of the divine fascination which his miracles gave to all he said.

The connection between his doctrine and his miracles is plain to everyone; they are inseparable. And it is his miracles which render his doctrine effective, just as, to us, it is his doctrine which makes us understand his miracles, and puts them in a higher order willed by God himself.

The esteem in which Jesus was held is an undeniable fact and we must either give up trying to explain it, or admit the reality of the miracles which were its chief cause. Thus we reach the conclusion of St Augustine, already quoted: those who deny the supernatural are committed to a miracle which is greater than any other, namely, that in a country where precise traditions included the history of so many prophets, all wonder workers, though Jesus himself had performed no miracle, he deceived his disciples and made them believe in his divine mission.

The reference just made to the sacred traditions of the Jews leads to a second argument of capital importance in classical apologetics. The first was that of miracles, the second, which must now be considered, is the argument from prophecy.

### *THE ARGUMENT FROM PROPHECY*

Jesus appealed not only to his miracles, but also, in order to convince men's minds, to a still greater fact, if that is possible, that of the prophecies. This means that he connected himself and all his teaching with an immense past, that he took over all that was living in the Mosaic law, all that had come from God in early ages. He gave to his own religion—to our religion—an antiquity greater than any other, he carried it right back, through the Scriptures to the beginning of things, to the origin of man. And he asserted boldly that the Scriptures led up to him alone, that they prepared the way for him, and that he only fulfilled them.

"You pore over the scriptures," he said to the unbelieving Jews, "thinking to find eternal life in them (and indeed it is of these I speak as bearing witness to me)" (John 5. 39).

Before this, one Sabbath day, he read in the synagogue at Nazareth the passage of Isaias in which the sending of the Messias as comforter is splendidly foretold and, when all eyes were fixed on him, spoke these simple words which proclaimed him as Messias: "This scripture which I have read in your hearing is today fulfilled" (Luke 4. 21).

Later on, after his resurrection, appearing on the way to Emmaus to two disciples, whose hopes had been dashed as a result of his death, he revived their courage, and made their hearts burn by explaining the messianic oracles: "Too slow of wit, too dull of heart to believe all those sayings of the prophets! Was it not to be expected that Christ should undergo these sufferings and enter so into his glory? Then, going back to Moses and the whole line of the prophets, he began to interpret the words used of himself by all the scriptures" (Luke 24. 25–7; cf. 45–9).

This lesson was not lost, and the prophetic argument became the object of constant study and meditation, and the chosen means for preachers and apologists who wished to prove the divinity of Christ. This argument may have lost its force for us. What nowadays we find valuable in it is, as I mentioned above, the antiquity of the religion of Christ. It did not start from nothing, which would be a strong objection against it. It completed, fulfilled and restated a mighty whole. The argument from prophecy is thus concerned with this whole body of the scriptures in the Old Testament, which are no less sacred to us than they were to the Jews. And the argument from prophecy derives all its richness for us from the fact that it is an answer to the only question which matters: *is the world planned* or *does it act by mere chance*? The argument from prophecy proves that, from the earliest ages, human evolution led towards Jesus and his Church.

### *STRENGTH OF THE ARGUMENT IN HISTORY*

What we ought to appreciate clearly is the strength of this argument in reality, that is, in history, and in the practical circumstances in which it was employed. To understand the full force of this argument from history we must picture to ourselves the wonderful vision which opened before the mind of a Jew, brought up on the Bible, when he suddenly saw all the messianic passages become clear, receive life and meaning, like dry bones scattered and then gathered together to live again, and all this, hitherto misunderstood, explained quite naturally, by the life, passion and death of Jesus. It was like the sudden raising of a curtain to reveal a fairy-like vision. The prophets had foretold everything. All was known—yet was not known! Isaias had seen the mysterious virgin who brought forth Emmanuel. Micheas had pointed to Bethlehem as his birthplace. The voice of the Precursor, "crying in the wilderness, Prepare the way of the Lord, straighten out his paths", had been heard also by Isaias. The miracles of Jesus, the nature of his preaching, the features of his character, even his name, Son of Man, but especially his rejection by his own people, his sufferings and death, then his resurrection and victory, his spiritual kingdom, unfailing and glorious, the pure sacrifice instituted by him—all this was foreseen and foretold in its entirety. From the earthly paradise, from age to age, the divine characteristics of the future Redeemer had been drawn in full detail. Every seer had added, confirmed and completed it. To the prophecies properly so-called were added signs. And now, until the end of time, it was startling to see such a clear conclusion, so long and sure a preparation, so undeniable a purpose, and to recognize in the gentle and mysterious Jesus all that, for so many centuries, the Patriarchs had desired and the Jews awaited.

The secret of the unshakable conviction which inspired the apostles, and which they were able to spread over the world was derived, in large measure, from the certainty that flowed from this divine harmony between a whole past age of saintly hope, and a present which lit up every shadow and satisfied every desire.

We need only glance again at the apologetics of the apostles to grasp the supreme importance of the argument from prophecy. When St Peter first began to preach on the day of Pentecost, he quoted a prophecy of Joel about the descent of the Holy Ghost and another of David about the glorious resurrection of Jesus (Acts 2. 17–36). After him the evangelists, and especially St Matthew, who preached in Palestine, never wearied of pointing out at each event in our Saviour's life how the sacred oracles were fulfilled.

Like St Peter and the other apostles, St Paul had but two arguments to convert the peoples—the resurrection of Christ, the miracle of miracles, and the prophecies. At Thessalonica he reasoned for three Sabbath days with the Jews, as the Acts say, "out of the scriptures, expounding these and bringing proofs from them that the sufferings of Christ and his rising from the dead were fore-ordained". At Berea he did the same, and the Jews "welcomed the word with all eagerness, and examined the scriptures, day after day, to find out whether all this was true; so that many of them learned to believe" (Acts 17. 2, 11). When he reached Rome it was again the argument from prophecy to which he turned. "So they [the Jews] made an appointment with him, and met him at his lodging in great numbers. And he bore his testimony and told them of the kingdom of God, trying to convince them from Moses and the prophets of what Jesus was, from dawn till dusk." And, when some believed while others remained unbelieving, Paul showed them that this very incredulity of some was foretold by Isaias (Acts 28. 23–31).

## *CONCLUSION*

Classical apologetics, whose main features I have just summarized, thus deals with two contrary perils. On the one hand it rebuts the theological rationalism of adventurous thinkers such as Hermes, in the nineteenth century, who held that the truths of faith could be proved by reason alone, and on the other hand, it disowns the traditionalist fideism, which held that reason has only to yield to faith, asking for no proofs.

Apologetics professes to offer neither an apodictic proof nor an appeal for blind submission. There are arguments, very forceful and very sound, but they leave faith its freedom. Faith is made reasonable by arguments, it is claimed as a duty, but it compels none, for then it would involve no merit. A preparation for faith is necessary, if the truths of faith are to be accepted. But it is not right for any Catholic to reject, as out of date and not suitable to modern times, the arguments which have converted the world. On this point the Vatican Council is precise. In the Constitution *Dei Filius*, published on April 24th, 1870, the Council first explains the preliminaries to faith: the existence and attributes of God, the meaning and possibility of revelation, and the sources of this revelation. When it reaches the point at which faith arises, it speaks as follows: "Yet in order that the service of our faith should be reasonable God has willed that to the inward help of the Holy Ghost there should be joined outward arguments for his revelation, namely, works of God, principally miracles and prophecies which show clearly the omnipotence and infinite knowledge of God, and are sure signs of revelation, fitted to the understanding of all."

A little further on the Council mentions as a summary of all the signs, *the fact of the Church*.

It is this fact that I propose to examine in the following chapter.

## CHAPTER V

# THE CHURCH IN CLASSICAL APOLOGETICS

### *THE CHURCH AND JESUS*

There exists between the Church and Jesus an undoubted parallelism which apologetics should explain. The personality of Jesus is at once an argument in support of his claims: all that we know of him witnesses to his divine character. The same is true, *mutatis mutandis*, of his Church. Of course the Church, in its members who are men, is not impeccable, and can never say, what Christ said, "Can any of you convict me of sin?" But it has features which raise it above mere human institutions.

That is what the Vatican Council declared emphatically, immediately after speaking of the proofs of faith:

> In order that we may be able to carry out our duty of embracing the true faith and of persevering always in it God has instituted his Church through his only-begotten Son, and has impressed upon it clear signs of his institution of it, so that it may be able to be recognized by all as guardian and mistress of the revealed word. For to the Catholic Church alone belong all those many and remarkable signs which God has granted to make evident the credibility of the Christian faith. Moreover, the Church, through its wonderful diffusion, its eminent sanctity and inexhaustible richness in every good, its catholic unity and its unconquerable stability, is itself an important and lasting

motive of credibility, and undeniable witness to its divine mission. Thus it is like a standard set up to the nations, and draws to itself those who do not yet believe, while it assures for its children a firm base on which to rest their faith.

The study of the Church, of its institution, and of the marks which it has received from its divine founder, thus forms an essential part of classical apologetics.

## *INSTITUTION OF THE CHURCH*

"All authority in heaven and on earth has been given to me." These words of Christ are proved true by the past, the present, and the future, looked at from the time when they were said. By the argument from prophecy it is shown that all the past had worked for Christ and worked towards him, that he dominated the most distant ages, since the fall of Adam. At the same time when he spoke, after many other miracles he had just manifested by his resurrection a power over the present, wholly divine. And by instituting his Church he was about to influence the future, the whole future, founding it not for a time only, but for all the ages to come. By this alone the rule of Christ over all ages was to be asserted. Between the institution of the Church and the revelation of the Gospels, there was the same relation as between the creation of the world and divine Providence. Providence is creation as it continues to exist. The world in one sense is a daily creation. It is the same with the revelation of Christ. He did not come to bring to men the doctrine of salvation and the sacraments of life which they needed, and then to leave these indispensable treasures uncared for. He owed it to himself and to us to provide for their care for ever. He said himself: "I will not leave you friendless: I am coming to you." Once he has taken possession of mankind Jesus unites himself with it. Mankind becomes the completion of himself. He is its head; we are its members. He is the vine; we are the branches. The Church and Jesus Christ are as husband

and wife. "What therefore God hath joined together, let not man put asunder." For all these reasons Bossuet could write: "You ask me what the Church is: the Church is Jesus Christ spread abroad and communicated, it is Jesus Christ wholly, it is Jesus Christ as perfect man, Jesus Christ in his fullness."

## *ORIGIN OF THE CHURCH*

The Church draws its origin, as does Jesus Christ himself, from the depth of God. It is a continuance of the mystery of the Incarnation, which is a mystery of love. It has an essential part in the divine plan, which we shall have to consider in the last part of this book, following the steps of Fr Teilhard de Chardin. If there is any meaning in creation and in the history of created things, that is, in what we call evolution, it is because history tends towards Christ and is prolonged in the Church. The "meaning of history"—so often referred to, and rightly so because it is our business to work at it—lies in this and nothing else. It consists in giving to creation an ultimate meaning worthy of it, which implies tracing it back to the Infinite from which it came. To do this we have to give to it not only a ruler, Jesus Christ, but also to this ruler a people, to this king a kingdom, to this shepherd a flock.

So true is this that the Church, in a sense, existed before the Church. Jesus Christ, when speaking of the Church, called it "my Church", but this does not mean that it was not outlined and foretold before him. There had been a Church, that is to say a "Kingdom of God", a "reign of God", a "family of God", a "people of God", in the Old Testament. The first Christians, while worshipping the new gift made to them, did not hesitate to seek in the past the beginning of their Church. The Church is the ark of salvation. All those who have gained salvation could only do so through Jesus Christ, and all, for that very reason, have entered the one ark. Fr de Lubac writes:

> Do not suppose that the Spouse or the Church only existed from the time that the Saviour came in the flesh; it existed from the beginning of the human race, and even from the creation of the world; and even—and I take St Paul as my authority—before creation of the world. For the Apostle says: "He has chosen us out in Christ before the foundation of the world, to be saints, to be blameless in his sight, for love of him; marking us out beforehand (so his will decreed) to be his adopted children through Jesus Christ." And it is written in the psalms: "Bethink thee of the company thou hast gathered long ago." Thus the first foundation of the Church was laid at the beginning. That is why the Apostle says again that the Church was founded not only upon the apostles, but also upon the prophets, and Adam himself is counted among the prophets.
>
> It is supremely important [Fr de Lubac adds] that all should be aware of the extension of the Church. Our consciousness will become more vivid, and our own existence will be enlarged, and thus we shall realize fully what is meant by the name, Catholic, which we bear.[1]

Catholic means universal. We must not restrict our idea of Christ's work. We should understand nothing of the majesty of Christ and of his work, if we had a narrow idea of the Church which he has taken in his hands and made his own.

## *THE ULTIMATE PROOF OF THE CHURCH*

While the Church has existed from the beginning, it remains no less true that it received from Jesus Christ a new and henceforth unalterable constitution, and that he thereby made it his own. God could do no greater work than the Incarnation. Hence he could not give to the totality of beings—including the angels—a more perfect crown. But this crown was not something superimposed like a statue upon its pedestal. Jesus Christ must have a close link with all other human beings. That is what we mean when we say that Jesus Christ is the

[1] H. de Lubac, *Splendour of the Church*, London and New York, Sheed and Ward, 1956, *passim*.

head, and we are the members. We live his life as he has deigned to live ours. The Church comes from Jesus Christ, as surely as the harmony of the body results from the function of the directing organ which is the brain. That is what our "separated brethren", the Protestants, do not seem to see, and it is especially in reference to them that our apologetic takes its shape. To us it is almost incomprehensible that they do not see that the Church, as we have it and live it, is derived from the Incarnation itself. Their position is like that of the deists, who deny Providence, while admitting creation. They want the whole work of our salvation to be entrusted to a book, and this book to be left for free discussion, or, as they say, free criticism. Now this very book, which they appeal to, witnesses against their theory. It is nowhere recorded in it that Jesus Christ wrote, or commanded his apostles to write, a book, or that men should be guided by a book alone, however sacred. Jesus Christ knew very well that in the past scripture had not succeeded in maintaining the unity of faith of the people of God. The Sadducees did not interpret scripture as did the Pharisees. Between the two parties there existed differences as grave, as essential, as those which exist between Protestants and Catholics. Jesus Christ would thus have been very blind if he had entrusted the future of his teaching to a book, especially if he did not write that book himself, and did not entrust the teaching to an unquestionable authority. Moreover, it was not only the teaching which he had to pass on, but also the perpetual sacrifice and the sacraments. Christ's religion was not only a truth to believe, but also a worship to practise and a life to receive and to foster in the heart.

## *CHRIST'S PLAN*

Now leaving aside generalities, let us, as I have intended throughout, face the facts themselves as certified by the sources.

Everything shows that Jesus wished from the first moment

of his active career to establish his Church. It was not a sudden improvisation on his part, but was openly foretold from the beginning, then prepared, organized, consolidated, and finally given life from himself, and set to work.

When Jesus began his public life, that is when he broke his silence at the hour determined by his Father, in order to fulfil his mission, what did he do? He sought out John the Baptist on the banks of the Jordan and received baptism from his hands. By this he meant to link the Church of the New Testament firmly with that of the Old. John the Baptist summed up the whole past. He was the last of the prophets, the last of the "types". By his baptism in a sense he gives Jesus his commission. He shows this by that remarkable name, or rather definition, "Look, this is the Lamb of God." Two disciples of John the Baptist who were there and heard these words, Andrew and John, hastened to inform Simon, Andrew's brother and John's friend: "We have discovered the Messias." This was an amazing act of faith for pious Jews. Peter came next, and then Jesus began to show his plan: "Jesus looked at him closely, and said, Thou art Simon, the son of Jona; thou shalt be called Cephas" (which means the same as Peter) (John 1. 42).

We cannot reflect too often on this episode. It proves by itself that Jesus knew where he was going and what he wished for, from that moment. He did not know Peter beforehand. There had been no need to introduce him to Jesus. Jesus spoke to him at once as to one who was expected, whom he wished to receive, and to associate with himself and for whom he had a settled plan. "Thou shalt be called Cephas." This name is for him a definition, a programme, a plan for the future. But why did Jesus wish to have a "rock", why did he need a rock, a *Cephas*? For the moment he said no more; he did nothing out of season. The hour was to come when Simon would understand why he had become Cephas, and we too shall understand. Of the words "Thou art Peter, and it is upon this rock that I will build my church", Luther said that Jesus only meant to speak about himself, for he alone was the rock. We agree that Jesus alone is the rock, but this does not imply that Simon did not also become the rock. Jesus was the rock essentially, while Simon became the rock, as "Vicar of Jesus Christ", and by the will of Jesus Christ. To deny that Simon is Cephas is plainly to give a false interpretation to Christ's words, since Jesus himself gave him this name which he did not have before. Manifestly Jesus is the rock, and St Paul repeats "And the rock . . . was Christ", and again: "You are no longer exiles, then, or aliens; the saints are your fellow citizens, you belong to God's household. Apostles and prophets are the foundation on which you were built, and the chief corner-stone of it is Jesus Christ himself. In him the whole fabric is bound together, as it grows into a temple, dedicated to the Lord" (Ephes. 2. 19–21).

This is a general view of the subject, not merely a view worked out by the human mind, but the vision authorized by an apostle inspired by God. He speaks of the prophets as well as of the apostle because he is teaching, as I am about to do, that the Church goes back to the beginning of the human race. This, however, does not contradict the function of "corner-stone", assumed by Jesus. Jesus certainly is, and will remain to eternity, the "corner-stone" of his Church, but he has communicated to Peter his function, his authority, and his power. From the first moment of his meeting with him on the banks of the Jordan far in advance he wished to foretell the plan he had already formed and which existed in the eternal decrees even before the creation of things, if it is admitted that the creation of things has a meaning. "Thou shalt be called Cephas." Those words have a deep significance. St Leo the Great has a magnificent commentary upon this:

> He joins him to himself with an inseparable bond, and wills that he shall have the same name as himself. "Thou art Peter", he says, and this is how we must understand him: being myself

the inviolable rock, the corner-stone, the foundation apart from which none can be laid, I tell you that you are also the rock because you are joined to me in the strength of a single force, and that the prerogatives which belong and will belong to me you have in common with me, by the communication I make of them to you.

## *FULFILMENT OF THE PLAN*

Thus Jesus had his plan settled from the beginning. When he speaks of the Kingdom of God or of the Kingdom of heaven it is of his Church that he is thinking. Now he continually speaks in this way in his first discourses. He went further when he chose the Twelve. He had chosen his principal "rock", but he wished to have others which should form a part of the "foundation", though remaining subordinate to the principal "rock". Hence his Church was to have a hierarchy; all were not to be equal. In a kingdom there is need of a supreme authority, because there is need of harmony and unity. So the Twelve were to have a chief. So long as he himself was present he would be chief, but later on he prepared for a successor. When he wished to take his first disciples from their former life, which was that of humble fishermen on Lake Tiberias, he performed a great miracle for them, wonderfully adapted to their capacity, a miracle which spoke, as it were, their own language. He brought about the miraculous draught of fishes, and said to Peter: "Henceforth thou shalt be a fisher of men", and then to his companions: "Come and follow me, and I will make you into fishers of men."

For all the rest of his public life he was to be surrounded by his apostles. They were trained or, as we should say today, they spent their novitiate at his side. To them alone he explained everything, that they might repeat it later on; to them alone he explained the hidden meaning of the parables. He prepared them even more directly for their future mission, by sending them in pairs to preach, before his own arrival, and for this purpose he gave them instructions which have remained the rules for every apostolate.

The plan which he followed was shown more clearly when he said to Peter: "Thou art Peter, and it is upon this rock that I will build my church; and the gates of hell shall not prevail against it; and I will give to thee the keys of the kingdom of heaven; and whatever thou shalt bind on earth shall be bound in heaven; and whatever thou shalt loose on earth, shall be loosed in heaven" (Matt. 16. 18–19).[2]

Jesus Christ, however, was not content with a single promise made in favour of St Peter. On two other occasions he made it clear that his plan was continuing, that no change was made, and that Peter remained at the centre of his future organization.

The first occasion occurred at a most solemn moment. The Master had just instituted the Eucharist and announced the betrayal by Judas. The apostles were well aware that the hour was now approaching when the "Kingdom" was to begin. Being very human they disputed about precedence. Jesus gently rebuked them. He reminded them that to reign is to serve. "I am here among you as your servant," he said. Yet he promised to bring them all to his Kingdom, and to make them eat and drink at his table: "you shall sit upon thrones, judging the twelve tribes of Israel." He said this to explain why he had chosen twelve. But he added at once this surprising reflection, which gives us a glimpse of the invisible world, of which our very destiny makes us a part: "Simon, Simon, behold, Satan has claimed power over you all that he can sift you like wheat." So Satan has requests to make, demands to bring forward, claims to enforce! There are laws which are beyond our understanding, as man's history unfolds, and especially without doubt the following: "I, Satan, have undergone a trial

[2] On the Church and her mystery, see vol. 48 of this series. Here I keep to what is required by the present subject.

and have failed; in the name of eternal justice I demand that all others, all the 'elect', should also undergo a trial in proportion to their nature." It was in virtue of this law that Satan had been permitted to tempt Job, and the same will happen until the end of time. This explains the light and shade in the history of the Church. To whom will the victory fall? Jesus, after the dreadful revelation he has just made, adds simply here with assurance: "But I have prayed for thee, that thy faith may not fail; when, after a while, thou hast come back to me, it is for thee to be the support of thy brethren" (Luke 22. 27–32).

How much that is new these words contain! "When after a while thou hast come back to me": Peter, then, was to fall. Jesus does not hide this from him: "I tell thee, Peter, by cock-crow this morning thou wilt thrice have denied knowledge of me."

The denial, however, was only to be momentary. Peter was "come back" to our Lord, an undying example for all sinners. Repentance covers all! The last words of Christ to Peter show this.

Jesus was denied by Peter; he was abandoned by all his apostles. The faith his miracles had caused disappeared before the shameful death of Christ on the cross. But Jesus did not change his plans. All was to begin again as he had foretold, by means of the supreme miracle of the resurrection. Faith came back as the appearances of the risen Christ increased in number. Peter was among the first to be won back, and a special appearance was granted him. Yet a threefold wound remained in his heart, that of the threefold denial. Then, as though Jesus wished to recall the triumphant dawn of his public life, he repeated the miracle of the draught of fishes. It was then that he definitely gave Peter his commission. The terms he used are clear in the Gospel account. Jesus did not give powers to him without the gift of an inward state, authority in the Church was to be inseparable from love:

Jesus said to Simon Peter, Simon, son of John, dost thou care for me more than these others? Yes, Lord, he told him, thou knowest well that I love thee. And he said to him, Feed my lambs. And again, a second time, he asked him, Simon, son of John, dost thou care for me? Yes, Lord, he told him, thou knowest well that I love thee. He said to him, Tend my shearlings. Then he asked him a third question, Simon, son of John, dost thou love me? Peter was deeply moved when he was asked a third time, Dost thou love me? and said to him, Lord, thou knowest all things; thou canst tell that I love thee. Jesus said to him, Feed my sheep (John 21. 15–17).

This time Jesus spoke no more of the future. The hour had come when Peter must assume his functions and exercise them.

## *THE COMING OF THE HOLY GHOST*

Here, however, an objection will be made. Is this possible? Can Jesus Christ contradict himself by giving such power to men? Does not the Gospel say: "Jesus would not give them his confidence . . . because he could read men's hearts." Such is the plea we find put forward by the dissenting churches, especially the Protestants.

We must reply: Would it not have been a far greater contradiction to entrust the future of his teaching and his worship to a book, left open to man's free discussion, when he himself had written no book and had commissioned no one to write in his place? On the other hand was it beyond the power of one who said: "All authority in heaven and on earth . . . has been given to me" to confer on men, not as men but as his representatives, infallibility in teaching?

Whatever answer is made to this question, it is historically certain that this is the way chosen by Christ. Either we must dethrone him, take from him his title of mediator, representative of God, Son of God, or we must believe his word. In the very first line of this book I quote the words which set the Church on its foundation of infallibility: "All authority in heaven and on earth, he said, has been given to me; you, therefore, must go out, making disciples of all nations, and baptizing them in the name of the Father, and of the Son, and of the Holy Ghost, teaching them to observe all the commandments which I have given you. And behold I am with you all through the days that are coming, until the consummation of the world" (Matt. 28. 18–20).

Let us understand these last words clearly: they are a direct answer to the objection mentioned above. Jesus means: "You are only men; without me, you could do nothing. But I am with you, to support you and inspire you, not merely for a day, but for all days until the end of the world."

To speak of representatives of Christ in the Church, as if it were a question only of fallible, changing men, is to deny Christ, since it is to forget the promise he has made. What we must see in the Church is not men but the body of Christ, given life by Christ, dwelt in by Christ, rendered godlike by Christ. He himself has taken care to give striking expression to his thought and to his plans for he promised the Holy Ghost to his disciples and to his Church.

At the present day this is so familiar to us who believe that we do not realize what a great thing it is. Moreover, this gift of the Spirit has always been beyond the grasp of our minds. But whoever thinks of Christ's Church or speaks of it, without taking into account the Holy Ghost, whoever speaks of the indefectibility, the infallibility, of the Church, the indelible marks by which it will always be possible to recognize the Church among the dissident Churches, without reference to the Holy Ghost, misinterprets Christ's thought and forgets the most important aspect of his institution of the Church.

We saw above that it was said that "Satan has claimed power . . . so that he can sift [the disciples] like wheat". We may suppose that the permission given to Satan will last as long as the Church lasts. But Jesus added: "I have prayed for thee." And what was the result of the prayer? We find it in some other words of Christ: "If you have any love for me, you must keep the commandments which I give you; and then I will ask the Father, and he will give you another to befriend you, one who is to dwell continually with you for ever . . the Holy Spirit, whom the Father will send on my account, will in his turn make everything plain, and recall to your minds everything I have said to you" (John 14. 15–26).

This, then, was to be the fruit of Christ's prayer that faith fail not, and this promise is so important in Christ's view, it will affect so profoundly the whole future of the Church, that he insists on it in the following words: "I have still much to say to you, but it is beyond your reach as yet. It will be for him, the truth-giving Spirit, when he comes, to guide you into all truth" (John 16. 12).

Nevertheless, we must notice very carefully that the truth-giving Spirit will not say anything different from Christ. Jesus cuts short all future illuminism by the following words: "He will not utter a message of his own; he will utter the message that has been given to him; and he will make plain to you what is still to come. And he will bring honour to me, because it is from me that he will derive what he makes plain to you. I say that he will derive from me what he makes plain to you, because all that belongs to the Father belongs to me" (John 16. 13–15).

### *PENTECOST, THE BIRTH OF THE CHURCH*

All this could have been brought about without any external sign, since the Holy Ghost cannot be perceived by the senses. His coming affects us closely, but is invisible. Yet Jesus, adapting himself to human nature, willed that the first descent of the Holy Ghost upon his Church should be manifested by a number of signs. Once again a miracle occurred, but it remained such as I have explained, it was a sign, a language, or, if you like, a parable in action.

Jesus, then, rose, and showed himself to his disciples. He

caused faith to rise again in their hearts. The elements of the Church were joined together again. The hierarchy existed and could act when the right time came. Jesus was to leave the earth. By his ascension, says the Epistle to the Hebrews, he obtained "a ransom" that "lasts for ever", in the sense that he entered into the sanctuary not made with hands, and entered with the Blood he had shed. There his sacrifice was accomplished, and he entered into the glory of the Father. The Christian religion received from him all its impulsive strength. But he promised that this strength is to be given by the Holy Ghost. A last time, before leaving his disciples, he said to them: "The Holy Spirit will come upon you, and you will receive strength from him; you are to be my witness in Jerusalem and throughout Judea, in Samaria, yes, and to the ends of the earth" (Acts 1. 8). Profoundly impressed with this last promise the apostles returned to the upper room. They devoted themselves to prayer, and awaited the fulfilment of Christ's words. Faith filled their souls to their depths.

What a difference between their dispositions now and those which filled their souls on the morrow of the Passion. Then there was a nameless desolation, hopeless disillusion. In the upper room they grieved, but expected nothing more. Now they prayed, believed, hoped, and awaited what was to come, and the miracle was performed on the day determined by Christ. The wonderful event burst upon them: "When the day of Pentecost came round," it is recorded in the Acts of the Apostles, "while they were all gathered together in unity of purpose, all at once a sound came from heaven like that of a strong wind blowing, and filled the whole house where they were sitting. Then appeared to them what seemed to be tongues of fire, which parted and came to rest on each of them; and they were all filled with the Holy Spirit, and began to speak in strange languages, as the Spirit gave utterance to each" (Acts 2. 1–4).

At this moment the Church, so long foretold and prepared, was born. A new age began which shall only end with the world itself. Without doubt we must agree that human history now took a new direction: something had changed. To prove this it is sufficient to look at those men in whom the Holy Ghost had just come to dwell. They were no longer the same men, and they were no longer merely men. When we think of the Church, we must never forget this.

How can we verify this presence of the Holy Ghost? By the whole history of the Church.

## *A NEW SOCIETY*

When the Holy Ghost came upon the apostles they knew what they did not know the moment before, and they acted at once, without faltering or hesitation. A new society appeared, open to all men. A concentration of the spiritual powers of mankind began to take place; a universal brotherhood was started. Time works on its side, and the ages, through a thousand choices, will work for it. Let us examine the powers which are exercised in this society, and see how they are exercised: they are nothing else than the powers of Christ. They are different from human powers, because his "Kingdom is not of this world" but they are far higher than human powers because they bind or loose on earth and in heaven. They bind minds by doctrine, consciences by Church discipline, souls in their depths by the life of grace. The powers given to his Church by Christ are thus three in number: power to teach, power to govern, all this culminating in power to sanctify. The first of these powers enables her to tell us what we should believe, the second what we should do, while the third enables her to communicate supernatural life through the sacrifice and sacraments.[3]

[3] For the further development of this outline I refer to the volumes in the fifth part of this series ("The Life of Faith") nos. 48–59.

## *THE CHURCH AS VISIBLE*

In order to complete its task apologetics must next explain the way in which the true Church of Christ may be recognized. To appreciate the importance of the question we must glance back at the proof as a whole.

*God has spoken to men.* This is the starting point for apologetics. I have shown that God, who spoke formerly through the prophets, Adam *himself being included in their number*, spoke finally through Jesus Christ. In Jesus Christ all divine revelation had its completion. He presented himself as a messenger of God. He claimed all power in the spiritual order. There is no salvation except in him, with him, and through him. Even those who do not know him, either because they lived before him or because they lived where his preaching had not reached, can only be saved—though they themselves do not know it—through him. And to accomplish on earth the mission of redemption which had been given him, he instituted a Church to which must belong, in one way or another, all those who are to be saved. But when I say, "in one way or another", does this mean that membership of the Church is left to chance, or that it is only optional, or that she does not show herself externally at all? In other words has Christ instituted a *visible* Church, or has he willed that she should be *invisible*?

Certain heretics have adopted this second theory and if we are to believe them, the Church is the society of the "just", or the "predestined", who are only known to God.

All I have said proves the opposite. At no time has the Church been entirely invisible. By the will of Christ from the beginning she possessed an order, a hierarchy, an organization. The theory of the invisible Church is opposed to the whole Gospel, the whole New Testament, the whole history of the Church. Jesus declared plainly that his Church would not be a society which was secret, obscure, and unknowable. On the contrary he said: "You are the light of the world; a city cannot be hidden if it is built on a mountain-top. A lamp is not lighted to be put away under a bushel measure; it is put on the lampstand, to give light to all the people of the house; and your light must shine so brightly before men that they can see your good works, and glorify your Father who is in heaven" (Matt. 5. 14–16).

Far from being invisible the Church is the *sign* set up before men that they may approach the one Saviour who is Jesus Christ. This visible character of the Church follows as a necessary conclusion from the fact of revelation. It would be useless for God to show us the way to salvation through his Son, if we did not know where to find this Son, and how to be united to him. It is in the Church that he is found, through the Church that we meet him and are united to him. Nor is the Church difficult to find, and this is one of the most striking facts of the history of every age. From her first years it has been possible to know the Church, but as time has gone on this has become easier. In our days the Christian Church—including under this name all the religious bodies which acknowledge Christ—literally fills the world. No educated man can be ignorant of her existence. But among the Churches which profess the doctrine of Jesus Christ there is one, and one alone, which bears the visible marks by which we can recognize Christ's true Church, and that is the Church which is Catholic, apostolic, and Roman. This Church is clearer to see than any other, and she will never become less visible.

### *THE MARKS OF THE TRUE CHURCH*

To prove to himself that the Catholic, Roman Church was indeed the true Church, the future Cardinal Newman, in about 1843, two years before his conversion, when still an Anglican, asked what communion the Fathers of the Church would choose if they were to return to this earth. And he had no doubt whatever of the answer to his question. But a still bolder hypothesis may be suggested. Let us call back in thought upon the earth the immediate disciples of Christ, and ask them to choose between the three chief branches of Christianity, the Catholic, Roman Church, the separated Greek Church, and the Protestant Church. Where will they first turn? Will they admit for a moment that Christ's promise could have deceived men's hope, and that the true Church has disappeared never to return? Surely not. "Though heaven and earth should pass away," Christ said, "my words shall stand." Jesus Christ promised his apostles that he would be with them until the end of the world, and therefore his Church cannot fail. But where is she? By what distinctive features would Peter and Paul, John and Matthew, and all the rest, recognize her? The Nicene Creed, which is really that of Constantinople (381), answers: "I believe in one, holy, catholic, and apostolic Church." Jesus Christ willed that his Church should be one, holy, catholic and apostolic.

What are these sure, visible, unquestionable marks of the one true Church? To put the question is already to give the answer, Peter would go straight to the Church where sits the "successor of Peter", the "Vicar of Jesus Christ". The apostles, joined with Peter, would recognize in the bishops their own successors. They would see at a glance what is lacking in the other Churches which acknowledge Christ. The Greek Church, in which we agree that the apostolic succession exists, lacks Peter. Thus it is a true Church but *separated*, or, as we say, schismatic.

This Church also lacks unity, for it is in fact only a federation of Churches, put together but not coordinated, some of them being dangerously exposed to the encroachment of the civil power. Finally this Church lacks catholicity, for it is really confined to certain peoples and does not exist elsewhere.

The Protestant Churches, which we can only refer to in the plural, differing as they do so much from one another, are further still from the true Church than the separated Greek Church. We call the Protestants our "separated brethren", but, if we hold certain points in common with them, we condemn in them both their reliance on the Bible alone which, instead of being a principle of unity, has shown itself from the beginning as a principle of disruption and division and, never ceasing to be thus, has led to numberless separate parties, and also their lack of apostolic succession, and their particularism, which contradicts catholicity.

Let us see, then, in face of those notorious defects, how the Catholic, Roman Church possess the four marks of the true Church.

1. In the first place, *unity*, an essential, inevitable mark, the absence of which is enough to disqualify a Church. Religion is one, because God is one, because Jesus Christ has willed unity. "One fold and one shepherd" is what he says. But he has gone further still, and has put forward the ideal of a unity as close, as intimate, as perfect, as indestructible as that which exists between himself and the Father. "Holy Father," he said, "keep them true to thy name, thy gift to me, that they may be one, as we are one.... It is not only for them I pray; I pray for those who are to find faith in me through their word; that they may all be one; that they too may be one in us, as thou, Father, art in me, and I in thee; so that the world may come to believe that it is thou who hast sent me" (John 17. 11, 20–1).

These last words are especially to be noticed. We see from them that the unity of the Church is a ground for belief. It is undeniable that the breaking of unity, whether by the eastern schism or the Protestant revolt, by the violation of the unity of Christianity has lessened its power to shine forth before men, and that is what has been felt very strongly by the promoters of the vigorous movement, called the ecumenical movement. It is clear, however, that the power of Christianity to shine forth before men is only preserved by the wonderful unity of the Catholic, Roman Church: unity of government, unity of doctrine, unity of worship, a unity in which is realized the noble words of the Acts of the Apostles: "There was one heart and soul in all the company of believers." Only in this Church can we say quite truly that there is one fold and one shepherd, and only in this can the strong ecumenical movement just mentioned find the ideal it seeks. It is precisely in order that this ideal may be upheld that the Catholic Church stands aside from this movement, while praying the Lord that it may achieve its end. But if the Roman Church alone possesses the unity willed by Christ, it is clear, and need not be emphasized, that she alone possesses perfectly the two other marks of catholicity and apostolic succession.

There remains that mark which is more inward, more profound, and less visible to the eye, the mark of holiness. If we speak of the holiness of her principles, doctrine, sacraments, worship, plainly this cannot be denied to her. But if we speak of the holiness of souls, I shall only point out this, that the Catholic Roman Church alone has the courage to beatify and canonize those of her children who practise virtue to a heroic degree. There is no canonization of saints outside her, and this shows a difference which cannot fail to impress an honest mind. It should be noticed carefully that I do not say there are no true believers who are real servants of God and of his Christ, outside our body. I do not even say that, among these good servants of Jesus Christ, there are not many who, if they had lived in the bosom of the true Church, and had benefited from all the means of sanctification to be found in her, would not have deserved the honour of canonization. I simply assert the fact that their Churches have never dared to decree these honours to them, even among the Christian bodies which approve of honouring the saints. The Catholic Church alone continues without fear to present saints as models to her children, to recognize in them virtue practised to a heroic degree. And she goes still further, for before beatification and canonization she demands the seal of a miracle, which she regards as confirmation by God himself of her judgements.

Just as the apostles, gathered at Jerusalem, could say, "it is the Holy Spirit's pleasure and ours . . .", so the pope, when he canonizes, could say the same, and in doing so follows the most ancient tradition of the Church of Jesus Christ.

Such, then, in outline is what I have called classical apologetics. Jesus Christ is the envoy and representative of God; his doctrine, sublime in itself and confirmed by miracles and prophecies, comes from God, and this means that it is reasonable and ought to be accepted.[4] This doctrine has been entrusted to a Church which is deathless and guaranteed against all error by the help of the Holy Spirit. Finally, this Church is visible, which means that she can be recognized among all the rest by the marks which result from her very essence. These marks are unity, holiness, catholicity, and apostolic succession, and I say that they result from the very essence of the Church, because the truth is one, has no aim but to make us holy, is for the benefit of all men, and is rooted in the apostolic succession. Hence there is no question here of *extrinsic* characteristics but of those which are strictly *intrinsic*, and this entirely refutes the charge of "extrinsicism", which has been made, though very wrongly, against this form of apologetics. It remains for me to consider whether any other apologetic may not be able, not indeed to suppress or to supplement this, but at least to add to it and to give it valuable support.

[4] By the word reasonable, the meaning of which is made clear throughout these pages, it is implied that nothing is more reasonable for men than to trust God's word, even though that word teaches him mysteries impenetrable to reason. It is supremely reasonable to acknowledge that there are truths which are beyond the scope of reason.

CHAPTER VI

# MODERN APOLOGETICS

## *LAWFULNESS OF OTHER FORMS OF APOLOGETICS*

Before starting to examine modern forms of apologetics, I must deal, at least shortly, with the preliminary question: Are such forms permitted; are they lawful? I answer without hesitation, Yes, to this question, but with a few conditions: first, that they do not contradict classical apologetics and, secondly, that they are in some way connected with it. No one may reject classical apologetics, for, as we have seen, it has been sanctioned by the Vatican Council, and the principles then laid down have been repeated by St Pius X in his Encyclical *Pascendi*. These two documents, which we must not reject, indicate the proper end for Catholic apologetics, and the essential means for gaining this end.

In fact, however, the very words of the Vatican Council leave the door open to other arguments than those which it puts in the first rank. For, when it mentions the arguments which it calls *facta divina*—works of God—it is careful to say that the miracles and prophecies are only the first of these arguments, thus leading us to conclude that there are others. The Church does not indeed reject any light, whatever its source, or any proof, provided it shows itself to be effective. It might be said that there are as many kinds of apologetics as graces of conversion. Everything that serves to touch a heart, to give rise to faith in a soul, belongs to apologetics. The classical arguments are only those which history shows to have been the most effective, to have had the greatest influence, in short, those which are best adapted to human nature. Miracles and prophecies, the greatness of the Church, are the most effective signs. But it is not impossible to find others and to include them in apologetics. When Bergson, for example, tells us that he was inclined towards Christianity because it was the religion of the "open city", and that he was later brought to the gates of Catholicism because the great Catholic mystics, such as St Teresa, or St John of the Cross, alone have had a direct experience of God in the higher states of prayer, he shows us a form of apologetic adapted to the mind of a great thinker, but not perhaps useful to others. If we look at it more closely we see that the argument of the "open city" is really the same as that of catholicity, and that the argument from mystical experience of God is an aspect of the argument from the holiness of the Church.

However, we shall find some new forms of apologetic if we consider recent attempts in our time to demonstrate Christian truth. Of these attempts, I will mention only the three following: the *method of transcendence* of Abbé de Broglie, the *method of immanence* of Maurice Blondel, and the *method of evolutionary convergence* of Fr Teilhard de Chardin.

## *METHOD OF TRANSCENDENCE*

This method was proposed by Abbé Paul de Broglie, in a work entitled, *Problèmes et Conclusions de l'Histoire des religions* (Paris, 1885). Abbé de Broglie was the son of the *duc* Victor de Broglie, minister of Louis-Philippe, and brother of the historian and politician, Victor-Albert de Broglie. An orphan at the age of four he was brought up by a Protestant grandmother but in the most genuine Catholicism. After studying at the Lycée Bourbon (Condorcet) he entered the Polytechnique, and became a lieutenant in the French navy. In 1867, when he was thirty-three, he entered Saint-Sulpice to become a priest, and was ordained in October, 1870. His education was thoroughly scientific, and thus better than anyone else he was prepared to meet the grave objections of scientific materialism against every kind of religion and especially the Christian religion. He was appointed by Mgr d'Hulst, professor of apologetics at the Institut catholique in Paris. With his penetrating mind he saw that he must place himself on the same ground as the thinkers of the age, in order to prove that Christianity came from God. He had to deal with two chief movements, Positivism and Naturalism. The first denied even the possibilty of metaphysics, in the name of science which only knew, and only wished to know, what was "positive", that is, observable and measurable facts. The second claimed absolute autonomy for human reason and rejected all revelation, all supernatural religion, and the very possibility of miracle and prophecy, by means of which Christian apologists held that they proved the divine origin of Christianity.

Abbé de Broglie himself started from facts. He spoke as a man of science who knew what the scentific approach meant. In his view there are facts which upset the postulate of the naturalist criticism as the fundamental dogma of positivism.

He reasons as follows. It is a fact that religion has existed throughout the world as known to history. There has been not only a religion but many religions. The scientific method consists first in knowing them, separating the common features by which they are alike, comparing them together to find out if any one of them surpasses its fellows and merits our adherence. Hence it is by a detailed examination of the known religions that he shows the *absolute transcendence*, first of the Jewish religion, and then of the Christian religion which is but its final completion. The study of the history of Israel, in spite of violence done to the texts by supporters of naturalism, sets before us an immense and unique fact, of which the opponents of the supernatural can give no plausible explanation: the monotheism of the Hebrews. How could this small nation, without political power, without a special civilization, without any philosophy to speak of, prove an exception to the universal polytheism? We cannot account for this in any satisfactory manner. But this is not all, and is not perhaps the chief point: there is in the history of the Jewish people a second transcendent feature which distinguishes it from every other religion, the fact of messianic prophecy. This prophecy is written in the texts. It precedes the events foretold and it is undoubtedly fulfilled. Christ came to fill in the outline sketched by the prophecies, and did it in opposition to the ideas of his time. He did it by his life and by his death. The formation of Christian teaching is in other ways also inexplicable by natural means. It was at the same time original, unique, and inclusive of all that went before. In it we find a synthesis "of all that is good in the different religions", but a synthesis not made deliberately, and not resulting from an unnatural combination of former doctrines. It far surpasses not only all previous religions, not excepting Buddhism, but even Judaism, which itself already surpassed every other form of religion. We can draw but one conclusion, namely, that this religion is due to a more than human cause. That is what its author, Jesus Christ, has always asserted, and what his disciples have ever maintained. The truth of this is shown if we examine the content of this religion.

What especially deserves to be remembered in Abbé de Broglie's work is the authoritative refutation of a famous article by Taine in the *Revue des Deux-Mondes*. In this article Taine put forward the positivist theory that the inorganic world is fully explained by the hypothesis of Laplace, which accounts for every condition of matter by the play of mechanical forces. The organic world is explained by the hypothesis of evolution. Evolution is at the root of everything, and evolution itself is only a particular example of the universal mechanism.

In answer to this system which seemed at that time to have the support of all the scientists, Abbé de Broglie did not hesitate to point out a glaring error in the writer's statement. A transition is made from the less known to the better known, which is contrary to any sound method. Very different spheres are confused when human reason is derived from animal consciousness, animal consciousness from the evolution of life, and life itself from the play of the mechanical laws of matter. But on what ground is this asserted? From experience? By no means, for we cannot experience reason as derived from sensation, sensation from life, and life from inorganic matter. There are many other things which cannot be explained by this very unscientific method—the soul, reason, the validity of the principles on which this rests, moral obligation, free will, the fact of religion. These are the things we know directly, and it is from them that we must start. Unless we mix an unsound metaphysic with our science without noticing it, it is impossible to prove the least contradiction between science and faith, either in the study of the inorganic world, or of the organic world. The place which Christianity assigns to man in nature in no way contradicts science. A genuine science will say, on the contrary, that religion must be necessary for man in his evolution, because in fact it has always existed. There is no useless organ, and religion has been an indispensable organ in the progress of civilization. Even though we agree that science has eliminated from religion certain superfluous beliefs, such as that the earth is motionless in the centre of the universe, the existence of the empyrean, a comparatively recent date for the appearance of man, and so on, what does this prove? That science can and should help religion by freeing it from outdated prejudices. These prejudices, however, are not religion itself, but a false idea of religion, or rather, a sort of mythology attached to religion, which conflicts with modern discoveries. But once these necessary corrections have been made religion itself remains and Abbé de

Broglie could conclude that "Christianity gives to the idea of God and to that of the supernatural a form acceptable to the scientific spirit. It is thus its function to produce harmony in human nature, and to satisfy at the same time all its instincts."

Such was the synthesis so ably worked out by the bold and judicious mind of Abbé de Broglie. The ideas he developed have succeeded. Very few scholars at the present day will be found to maintain that science is opposed to religion. To know is one thing and to believe is another; both are necessary. To know is needed for the present life, faith is needed for the life to come.

Taine himself seems to have appreciated his opponent's ideas, when he recognized the undoubted value of Christianity in the history of civilization. He too wished to base himself on facts. Speaking of religion in general he wrote these lines which seem to me a true apologetic, and which have the advantage of introducing us to the thought of Blondel:

> Manifestly here we see in the soul a new agent and controller, a strong organ of increase, well adapted, effective, acquired by internal change and repair, like the wings with which an insect is provided by moulting. In every living organism, the need, by groping and selection, produces the organ which is possible and necessary. In India for centuries before our era there was Buddhism, in Arabia six centuries after our era there was Mohammedanism; in our western society it is Christianity. To-day, after eighteen centuries, on two continents, from the Urals to the Rocky mountains, among the Russian peasants and the American settlers, it has the effect, as formerly among the workmen of Galilee and in the same way, of substituting love of others for love of self. It has not changed either in itself or in its effects. In its Greek, Catholic or Protestant forms it is still, for 400 million human beings,[1] the spiritual organ, the great wings needed to raise man above himself, above his own miserable life, and his narrow outlook, to lead him, through patience, resignation and hope, to tranquillity, to bring him, by

[1] Today we should have to say 750 millions.

way of temperance, purity and goodness, to devotion and sacrifice. At all times and in all places, for eighteen centuries, as soon as these wings fail or are damaged public and private conduct is lowered. In Italy during the Renaissance, in England at the Restoration, in France under the Convention and the Directory, we have seen man becoming pagan as in the first century; at once he finds himself as he was in the time of Augustus and Tiberius, that is pleasure-seeking and hard; he abuses others and himself, brutal or calculating selfishness has gained the ascendant, cruelty and sensuality are displayed; society becomes a disreputable mass of cut-throats. When we see this, we can appreciate the contribution of Christianity to our modern society, giving it modesty, gentleness and kindness, upholding honesty, good faith and justice. Neither philosophic reasoning, nor artistic and literary culture, nor even feudal, military and knightly honour, no code, no administration, no government can take its place for this purpose. It alone holds us back on the dangerous slope, puts on the brake when without knowing it, our race is continually on the point of slipping down towards the abyss. The old Gospel, whatever its modern dress, still today gives most help to the social instinct."[2]

Even though Catholic theology may make some reservations as to certain expressions of the historian, it is clear that such an avowal can be called Taine's apologetic.

When this passage was published after Taine's death, a year had passed since a young philosopher had presented at the Sorbonne a doctoral thesis which had attracted general attention and some surprise. It was the work of Maurice Blondel.

## *BLONDEL'S METHOD OF IMMANENCE*

I must explain at once that Blondel's thesis was by no means offered as an apologetic. It kept firmly to the ground of philosophy, and only appealed to human reason in a strictly dialectic form. It may be said indeed to represent the

[2] *Les Origines de la France contemporaine*, vol. 2, pp. 118–19, Paris 1894. Taine died in 1893.

triumph of pure dialectic, unlike the philosophy of Bergson, which represents the triumph of intuition. In any case it is certain that Maurice Blondel introduced a new and wonderfully fruitful method.

Nevertheless, as there is nothing absolutely new under the sun, as Scripture says, ancestors have been sought and found for Blondel, and certainly those suggested are not among the least: St Augustine, Pascal, on the one hand, Maine de Biran, Newman, Cardinal Deschamps, Gratry, on the other hand, but more directly still Boutroux and especially Ollé-Leprune of whom Blondel was the favourite pupil.

Maurice Blondel was born at Dijon on November 2nd, 1861. He studied at the *Ecole normale*, and on June 7th, 1893, presented a thesis with the title: *L'Action, essai d'une critique de la vie et d'une science de la pratique*. It has often been said that a man becomes the slave of his thesis, that it affects his whole life, and extends its influence over his whole career. Seldom has this been more true than in the case of Blondel. He never ceased to return to the ideas of his thesis until his death on June 5th, 1949 at the age of 88 at Aix-en-Provence, where he had lived since his appointment to the University of that town in 1897.

Maurice Blondel is not an easy author. He makes no sacrifice for clarity, and seeks only forcefulness and accuracy. It was only with difficulty that he got his thesis accepted, and it needed all the influence of Boutroux to bring this about. When it was submitted the philosopher, Paul Janet, told him with a smile, "I spent an hour reading one of your pages, and then I could not understand it . . . I calculate I should need forty-five days to read your thesis." The candidate quickly replied: "I offer no excuse for defects of which I am guilty . . . clarity is a virtue of the French school, but there is a certain clarity which is often deceptive and dangerous, because those who do not understand it are left with the impression that they do. We shall try in vain, and shall never render meditations simple and easy which demand a training like that of higher mathematics."

To quote these words is important because I must offer an explanation for the clarity with which I shall try to present the thought of Blondel. In a book like the present clarity is indispensable, but manifestly there is a danger of giving a false notion of the philosophy of the master of Aix-en-Provence which is truly profound.

I think the starting point of the Blondelian reasoning can be stated as follows. We find ourselves faced with man, and with reason which thinks it is sure of itself, which claims to be self-sufficient, rejecting all external and higher help in the name of its immanence, its autonomy, its indisputable supremacy. Apologists have failed until now to tackle resolutely the problem of the relationship between the supernatural and the natural, or, when they have attempted it, they have not looked at it squarely in its full length and breadth. For several centuries the forces of unbelief have tried to prove an essential contradiction between the two orders, a kind of incompatibility between Christianity which imposes its dogmas from outside, by means of authority, and mankind which, in its thought and in its conduct, wishes to rely only on itself, on its reason and sense of right. Hence we must decide whether the Christian religion is a slavery, an oppression of mankind, or an illumination, a liberation.

Maurice Blondel did not of course seek to express in his thesis the problem just outlined. He came at once to the heart of the subject, and started from man himself. But he began by showing that in man thought is not necessarily the principal thing, but rather action. It is action which furnishes the finest and most perfect expression of human personality. The words of Christ "you will know them by the fruits they yield" remain ever true. It is by his acts that a man is judged and not by his words or even by his knowledge. Thus action is ultimately of greater value than pure thought. Of course thought guides action, but in its turn action affects thought. We must live as we think, or else, sooner or later, we shall think as we live. Action is thus that in which the whole man is committed, and it is by analysing action as seen in every man that we shall find the laws of human perfection, of human destiny. A philosopher like Blondel does not, however, study human conduct, as Taine did at that time, from the point of view of an historian of civilization. To the eyes of Taine history witnesses that, without Christianity, man tends towards the brute while, with Christianity, man becomes human again, and tends towards the very ideal of reason and of right. Blondel reaches the same conclusion, but by the method of dialectic without appealing strictly to history.

The philosopher, then, starts from the heart of man. He finds in it a contradiction, a confession of weakness. At first sight when we look at man, at every man, we are forced to observe that there is a baffling disagreement between what is willed and what is done, between thought and action. Thought gives light to the "willing will", traces out its path, and gives it its rule. Action reveals the "willed will", and is quite different from the "willing will". "It is not the good my will prefers, but the evil my will disapproves," says St Paul, "that I find myself doing." And the pagan poet says the same: *video meliora proboque, deteriora sequor* ("I see what is better and approve it, but I do that which is worse"). This confusion in action reacts on thought itself: we are the prisoners of our acts. How are we to be reasonable, consistent in ourselves? "It is difficult," writes Seneca, "to be one." Yet man needs to be himself.

"Man's need," says Blondel in his thesis, "is to integrate himself, in such a way that nothing that he is remains foreign or opposed to his will, and nothing that he wills remains inaccessible or denied to his being."

If he is not consistent or if what he finds in the deep aspirations of his being is not granted him, he is a complete failure. Thus arises the problem of human destiny, which is the problem of the whole man, a problem we cannot avoid, and which lies at the very heart of life. Either life is absurd, and then we cannot speak of reason and understanding, since we are, as Pascal says, incomprehensible to ourselves, or life has meaning, and then we must have recourse to something other than the powers we possess, we must appeal to some power that can help us, infinitely greater than ourselves, which alone can realize that capacity for infinite perfection which lies within us. Only the firm conviction of our insufficiency could perhaps make us stretch out our arms towards this "unknown God" of whom Paul spoke before the Areopagus.

However, to reach this point we must carry on the inquiry with sincerity and thoroughness.

> We must welcome all the negations which are mutually destructive, as if it were possible to adopt them all; we must enter into every prejudice as though it were justified, into every error as though it were sincere, into every passion as though it were as generous as it boasts, into every system of philosophy as though each one contained the infinite truth it believed itself alone to possess. We must ourselves reflect everyone's consciousness of right, and make ourselves the fellow workers of everyone, in order to see if they can be justified or must be condemned, so that they may be their own judges, may see where their will leads them, however free and however much their own, that they may learn what they do without knowing it, and what they already know without willing it or doing it (Introduction to *Action.*)

The whole of the thesis is devoted, then, to this immense inquiry. Blondel examines one after another the attitudes men adopt in face of action and destiny, and the doctrines they have proposed to settle this tragic problem. He shows us everywhere insufficiency, lying or error.

We find the solutions of the aesthete and the pessimist in-adequate, a lack of coherence and sincerity in both. Inadequate, too, is the satisfaction promised us by science, with all its discoveries, however valuable they may be. Inadequate also is that completion of life provided by association with other human beings, through friendship or marriage or a common country or a common humanity. Morality and metaphysics are inadequate, which can bring us to an intermediate end, but not to that final end which corresponds to the thirst for the infinite we experience. Very clearly too modern superstitions are inadequate which profess to replace religion and are called universal brotherhood or agnosticism or natural religion, and which strive to get rid of the infinite object of our will. We cannot, then, withdraw without surrendering, or advance by our own resources. We cannot, by ourselves alone, do what we will and will what we should. Out of this sad conflict, which is the great human drama, there bursts forth the admission of a single necessary being. The thought of God appears as the only way of salvation, and with the thought of God the inevitable transcendence of human action.

But it is not enough to think God, to think of God. With the idea of God two possibilities arise, and we must make a choice. The idea of God is inevitable to every man, in our own age as in all ages. But in face of this idea man remains free. The dilemma in its full force is this—either to reject God and to claim that we are sufficient for ourselves and to will infinitely without loving the infinite, but by loving ourselves—or else to efface ourselves in order to establish God in ourselves, and to live fully in him and by him. It is thus either to love ourselves so that we despise God, or to love God so that we despise ourselves: "two loves have made two Cities," says St Augustine. Blondel returns to the same thought. "Either to be god without God, or to be god with God and through God." But we must be careful. If we choose to be without Being we do so at our cost; if we only will to be through Being and with Being we find salvation. What then is needed in order that we may be able to adopt this second course, which alone leads to the fullness of human destiny? To find God and what he wills for us, and the way that he has chosen to come to our help is an impossibility for us. But he has come to us; he has spoken to men; the initiative has been taken by him. The fundamental aspiration which the study of action makes us realize can only be satisfied by revelation.

Such was the thought of Blondel in its first stage. On the Catholic side he was at once accused of inaccuracy. He seemed to make the supernatural a complement to the natural, and to abolish the distance between the two orders which Pascal had so forcefully distinguished. Blondel might have thought that the following passage in Pius X's encyclical *Pascendi* against modernism was aimed at himself: "We cannot help deploring . . . that Catholics are met with who, while repudiating immanence as a doctrine, nevertheless make use of it as a method of apologetics, who do so, we say, with so little caution that they seem to admit in human nature, in respect to the supernatural order, not merely a capacity, a fittingness—as Catholic apologists have sought to emphasize—but a true and strict need of it."

It is not so much human action which is transcendent as divine revelation, but it remains true that nature awaits, hopes for, desires, without knowing what, and that this awaiting, this unconscious desire corresponds to, because it needs, divine revelation. Man has in a high degree a close fitness for Christianity, but, when Christianity presents itself to man, it must nevertheless show its proofs, and it does this through classical apologists as explained above, and nothing can wholly replace this apologetic. Blondel, as I have said, spent the rest of his life in revising his thesis and perfecting it.

I need not analyse in detail here Blondel's thought in its final form. It did not change essentially in the matter that concerns us here, that is, the apologetic which is derived from it. It should be noticed, however, that he was able to apply to his original thesis all necessary corrections; so that the *En-*

*ciclopedia cattolica* in the article on the philosophy of action, by Professor Sciacca of the University of Genoa, concludes with these words: "It is essentially a concrete philosophy, a philosophy of 'real knowledge' (and not of 'notional knowledge'), open to revelation and dogma, but remaining always a philosophy which recognizes the validity of reason and understanding, in a logic of action which completes and controls them. Hence it is a philosophy of the whole man, and it seems unjust to accuse it of fideism or agnosticism or pragmatism or even of immanentism in the true and the strict meaning of the word."

In short Maurice Blondel's whole philosophy can be summed up in that profound sentence of St John of the Cross: "The health of the soul consists in the love of God."

## *TEILHARD DE CHARDIN'S METHOD OF EVOLUTIONARY CONVERGENCE*

Fr Teilhard de Chardin reached the same conclusions, but by a very different path. With him we are not dealing with a philosopher; nor is he a very trustworthy theologian.[3] He was a learned man, a very great specialist in palaeontology, who did much for the science at which he worked, but, like Maurice Blondel, he had no intention at all of writing apologetics. Nevertheless, he reached conclusions drawn from his special subject, palaeontology, astonishingly like those of Blondel. The resemblance indeed goes further, much further, and Blondel's work in its final form contains a dialectic akin to the speculation of Fr Teilhard de Chardin, on the evolutionary process.

Blondel also draws up a table of the stages of evolution analogous to that which we find in Teilhard de Chardin, in virtue of a dialectic inherent in creation as such. "Matter offers the antinomy of exteriority and unity, which is at once resolved by the organic unity of the smallest living thing, but

[3] Very grave criticisms have been made against him, from the point of view of theology, especially as regards original sin.

for this there appears another antinomy immanent in biological life and formed by the spontaneity of the living thing and the possibility of its destiny. Hence there is a connection between the world of life and the world of the mind capable of freedom, but this freedom, incapable of freeing itself completely, creates a new, more cruel and more insoluble antinomy."[4]

Fr Teilhard de Chardin was born at Orcine, Puy-de-Dôme, of an ancient family of Auvergne in 1881. He quickly made himself known by his work on palaeontology, then by sensational discoveries, especially that of *sinanthropus*. When quite young he entered the Society of Jesus, and became Professor at the Aurora University at Pekin, and was later Professor at the *Institut catholique* at Paris and director of the laboratory of geology concerned with the origins of man at the *Ecole pratique des Hautes Etudes*. Among his best-known works I may mention: *Comment je crois; Le Milieu divin*; *L'Esprit de la Terre*; *Le Phénomène chrètien*[5]; *Comment je vois*. To these works must be added a number of important articles in reviews.

Fr Teilhard de Chardin died on the 10th April 1955 at the age of 74. Three days later Pope Pius XII in a speech to the Pontifical Academy of Science spoke of those who wished to be "discoverers of the intentions of God". Teilhard de Chardin surely deserved this title.

His starting point is evolution, which is taken for granted. Evolution," he says, "is neither a theory nor an hypothesis; nor a system, but a general condition to which henceforth all theories, all hypotheses, and all systems, if they are to be conceivable and true, must be adjusted and with which they must agree".[6]

[4] This summary is by Etienne Borne, in *Recherches et Débats*, March 1955, p. 159.

[5] To be published in English in the near future.

[6] Here too certain critics have observed that evolution remains a working hypothesis, a suitable framework, not a certainty.

The whole problem lies in knowing whether this evolution is *planned or not*. It is only on this point that science has not yet decided. To Fr Teilhard de Chardin there is no doubt that science must recognize sooner or later that it is planned. We have only to look at it in geology and palaeontology to be convinced. All the evidence points to a development in evolution, and this means that it has a tendency and is not due to mere chance. From the beginning matter tends towards increasingly complex states—from the atom to the molecule, from the molecule to the living cell. By complexity Fr Teilhard de Chardin means: (1) the formation of groups of elements ever becoming more numerous; (2) the organization of these elements ever becoming closer; but with time—a time which is duration (*durée* in the Bergsonian sense) and which acts upon beings—matter does not evolve only towards complexity and to the point at which life appears, but it continues its course towards consciousness. It becomes continually richer, and gains in depth what it loses in extent. Among the immense galaxies a planet like the earth is but a grain of sand. But it is then that *consciousness* becomes *mind* by becoming reflective. The cosmic growth ends in man, the cosmic development is carried on by the development of man. From life we pass to mind. And, as a definite end was then attained, from the appearance of man evolution of species suddenly stops. Henceforth evolution only takes place in the sphere of mind. It is man himself, the fruit of evolution, who henceforth takes in hand his own evolution. "After the era of lower forms of evolution, comes the era of *autoevolution*." But, as evolution is irreversible, personal centres of consciousness are in lasting possession of the stage they have reached, for in it evolution reaches its culmination. Either this evolution, so strongly and visibly designed, is absurd, or those personal centres of consciousness which we call *souls*, have a destiny worthy of them, worthy of the aspirations which move them, that is to say, are immortal.

"If it is not to suppress itself," says Fr Teilhard de Chardin, "evolution, when it becomes reflective, cannot be conceived as continuing in a cyclic or closed universe; it is incompatible with the hypothesis of a universal death."

Thus all goes to show that evolution has willed mind, and that it is irreversible. It would lead to a meaningless result, if mind were only a passing vapour. The immortality of the soul is, in Fr Teilhard de Chardin's view, plainly written in the nature of mind, and is derived from physical, and not only metaphysical, laws.

Hence we must know *what becomes of mind*. Here, too, there should be, and there is, a point of convergence, a point of cosmic attraction. He calls it provisionally the Omega point, which means, the final point. Now we are dealing with persons, possessing intelligence and will. Evolution can only go on towards further development. Here is seen the wonder of wonders in this evolutionary development. Evolution must be able to focus itself upon an end which is known and loved, and this end cannot be a mere abstraction. It must be a person, for only a person is capable of attracting persons.

"Without an Omega which is both lovable and loving, reflective consciousness can certainly not produce its fullest and highest effort. Now is not this highest effort a necessary condition for the success of the evolutionary process in which we find ourselves engaged?"

After describing the majestic movement of evolution up to man, to Christ and his Church, which is nothing else than the fullness of Christ, Fr Teilhard does not claim to *prove* from this fact either the Incarnation or the Redemption. But, like Maurice Blondel, he finds a remarkable convergence. While the early champions of the theory of the evolution of species often tried to direct this theory against religious faith, Fr Teilhard suggests that evolution postulates and implies not only faith in God, but also faith in Jesus Christ. "What reality demands in order to be coherent," he writes, "is granted by

God's gift." Reality is preadapted to the supernatural gift of the Incarnation and Adoption. Reality is not constructed to reach its perfection, to realize itself without this supernatural gift which consists in man becoming godlike, being called to be the coheir of Christ. He is prepared for God's work in bringing him to his supernatural end, shown in the Incarnation. In other words, God's plan, without which no creation is possible, may be seen as a continuous line running from matter to life, from life to mind, from mind to Christ, the Church being Christ's mystical body.

"Christ," he concludes, "*hic et nunc*, occupies for us, in position and function, the place of the Omega point."

Christ occupies a cosmic position and function; all has been made by him and all for him. "The Incarnation", a critic has said, "is the keynote of Teilhard de Chardin's whole vision of reality."

In May 1953 Fr Teilhard published, in *Recherches et Débats*, an article entitled, *En regardant un cyclotron*. This consisted of reflections on human energy falling back on itself. In it he discussed the most recent forms of human evolution. He had been invited to inspect the great cyclotrons of the University of Berkeley in California. But in this concentration of material energy he beheld "another and invisible cyclotron", that is, a "local concentration of human energy". How much knowledge, labour and capital has been used in these enormous enterprises for nuclear physics, which are now being multiplied in the world! What does it mean? In Fr Teilhard's eyes this is undoubtedly in the direct line of evolution, of the continuous passage from the simple to the complex and of the dispersed to the concentrated. Just as men passed in former days from tribes to empires, in our days and before our eyes they bring about concentrations of free, intellectual, energy, in the sphere of scientific research, that is, of a greater and greater control of matter and of all nature. Fr Teilhard tells us that we have at the present day an astounding sight before our eyes, "that of human efforts, bursting from the four quarters of the universe". On every side new machines are appearing:

> Electronic miscroscopes and huge telescopes, inter-planetary rockets, calculating machines.... We are plunged in a whirlwind of research ... a real maelstrom, which sucks all that surrounds it into its depths. So let us recognize this once for all. Life in us men is not at its ebb; not only has it ceased to divide into different parts, but further, gathered into itself through the need for knowledge, it has just reached, by a converging action, a paroxysm of the power which characterizes it, and has caused to develop in the universe, simultaneously and one by means of the other, Organization and Consciousness, that is to say, has forced matter inwards by dint of making it more complex.

But in what direction does this development itself tend? Must it not follow the double law of all evolution—irreversibility and need of total unity? Evolution will not turn backwards, but in order to go forwards it must group men together and direct them towards a "super-life". This "super-life" awaits us and summons us in Christ and his mystical body. Fr Teilhard de Chardin concludes:

> Thus the more I tried to stretch out into the future and foretell the progress of the immense physico-psychic spiral in which I found myself engaged by history, the more to my eyes what we still call too simply "research" was charged, coloured, and warmed by certain powers (Faith, Adoration) hitherto regarded as strangers to science....
>
> For the more carefully I looked at it the more I saw this research compelled by inner necessity to concentrate its effort and its hope ultimately about a divine focus.[7]

This profound theory of Fr Teilhard de Chardin's is not, I think, spoiled if we say that in view of "the tornado of scien-

[7] *Recherches et Débats*, May 1953, p. 130.

tific research", it is the duty of Christians, whether by the powerful unity of Catholicism or by the great ecumenical movement, to effect a "tornado of faith and love."[8]

[8] It should always be remembered that Fr Teilhard de Chardin was above all a visionary, a man of bold theories, which have neither the precision of science, nor the prudence and sureness of the highest theology. Yet nonetheless classical apologetics are in some sense confirmed, in so far as the objection made against it of the existence of evolution is interpreted by a supporter of evolution of the stature of Fr Teilhard de Chardin, as the best proof of the divine origin of Christianity.

CHAPTER VII

# A FULL, LIVING APOLOGETIC

## *CONTINUITY*

The first conclusion we can draw from this necessarily brief examination of modern apologetics is that it does not in any way contradict classical apologetics. In fact it is in the direct line from classical apologetics. It prepares the modern mind for it, speaking the language which men nowadays more easily understand. A philosophy of action, like that of Maurice Blondel, suits a generation increasingly involved in activity and anxious to know the meaning of that activity which makes up its whole life. A vision of universal evolution like that proposed by Fr Teilhard de Chardin is well adapted to attract the attention of palaeontologists and biologists, historians and even modern philosophers. But neither of these apologetics, not being sought for itself and hence being the more effective, takes the place of the apologetics used by Christ himself and after him by his apostles. It is therefore natural and necessary to unite these two lines of reasoning, which join at the centre. The first line starts from above, that is from revelation itself, and reaches man by the "signs" which guarantee the divine origin of this revelation. The second line starts from below, that is, from man himself, and rises until it reaches this revelation, without which both individual life and universal evolution have no meaning.

Hence I call it a *full* apologetic if it takes all points of view into account, if it includes the thinker's meditation and the scholar's vision, if it appeals to the depth of man's soul, speaks to his reason, to his conscience, his need for understanding, his sense of the infinite, his thirst for love, his desire for a boundless beatitude for which he feels himself to be made, and again if, starting from the preaching of Christ, from his words and actions, his light and his love, his life and his death, his further life in the bosom of the Church, the apologetic is found to correspond exactly with what man requires.

The Christian apologist must, however, be sure to remember that no light must be excluded when the problem is so vast as is that of the conquest of souls. A Christian proof cannot neglect any available element, or else it will never do its work. Hence it must aim at combining as far as possible the whole material for an apologetic, and must be capable of explaining every fact, subjective and objective, which affects the problem of faith. In the very nature of the case these facts are so many that it is impossible in practice to hope to put them all together so as to give a definite answer which will cover every point. On the one hand, a religion like Christianity which claims to be the only true religion, the only one willed by God, and revealed by God, must include, as it were, all creation, must crown the totality of things, must perfect the whole structure of universal being, and must exclude nothing concerned with mankind. On the other hand this same religion must satisfy every need, every individual taste, and show itself capable of leading every individual to his immortal destiny.

This theoretical demand has been answered, as we have seen, by the more modern forms of apologetics. For example, Blondel has shown clearly that Christianity satisfies the whole man, and that without it man cannot look for his perfection. And Teilhard de Chardin has drawn up a scheme to show how the whole of creation rises to an Omega point, which can only be Christ and his Church, which is inseparable from him and forms one body with him, through whom all creation passes from the finite to the infinite.

## *APOLOGETICS AND FAITH*

Throughout this book I have argued that the purpose of apologetics is to bring faith to birth in souls. I have tried to sum up the grounds for faith, but I have said, or at least implied, again and again, that faith cannot be caused automatically by apologetics. It is of the essence of faith to be free, which means that the act of faith can only be brought about by use of the will. Undoubtedly, it is an act of the reason, but not of the reason moved from within. The mysteries of faith are not seen in their compelling clarity within us. We cannot look at the Trinity in such a way as to be forced to confess the existence of the Trinity in the same way that we are forced to say at midday on a cloudless day: The sun is shining. The Trinity is "revealed" to us by Jesus Christ, and it is reasonable for us to believe Christ's word, once we have grasped that Jesus Christ, foretold by the prophets for so many centuries, pointed out by John the Baptist, the last of the prophets, and endowed by God himself with the power to work miracles, has really the right to tell us: "I am the way, the truth, and the life." It would indeed be unreasonable *not* to believe, when we have examined the proofs of the divine mission of Christ. Moreover, not only is the act of faith reasonable in the sense explained, but it is a duty, because God does not speak without purpose, and because *we owe it to ourselves* not to reject the one means that can exist for our salvation. Thus we have an obligation to believe not only towards God who loves us and wills the salvation of all, but, still more so if possible, towards ourselves, in the sense that, if we are lost, God's infinity is in no way lessened, while we lose all and miss our human destiny.

When, however, apologetics has proved these two points,

that it is reasonable and a duty to believe, then it has accomplished its task. It remains for each of us to do our duty and to make, with God's grace, the act of faith, which will continue as love.

The freedom of the act of faith is derived not only from that character of the truth of faith which I have just explained but also from the very nature of faith, which cannot be what Newman calls a purely *notional* assent, but a *real* assent, that is, one which affects the whole being. It is here that the will has to intervene. An honourable man does not make a promise lightly. He does not make a total submission, as he does in the Christian religion, without weighing the pros and cons, and without assenting by his will to God's will which is presented to him.

However, the limits of apologetics are shown by its very object. We do not prove Christianity, but we prove its right to our adherence through faith and love. We do not prove it because to do so would be to bring it down to the natural order, to dethrone it, and deprive it of its transcendent character. But we prove that it deserves and demands our confidence. It is this characteristic of being fit to be believed that we call its credibility. The way in which apologetics treats revealed truth should not deprive it of any of its supreme importance, as would be the case if we professed to "prove" the truths of faith, as Hermes wished to do, and as he thought he could do. A proof of credibility is not only possible and useful but it is necessary in order that the act of faith may be a deeply human act, that is, one that can be called neither arbitrary, nor rash, nor done out of habit. That is why apologetics is not merely addressed to unbelievers in order to gain their faith, but also, perhaps especially, towards believers in order to give their faith that gravity, depth and solidity which it ought to have. Only by a thorough understanding of the reason for belief can Christians carry out the duty which St

Peter urged upon those of his own days, when he wrote to them: "Be ready at all times to answer for it, but courteously and with due reverence" (1 Peter 3. 16).

Yet we must not expect the same level of apologetic knowledge in everyone. For some it should be truly scientific, but for many others a general understanding is enough. The simple faithful can and should appeal to the authority of the Church, whose direct representative for them is their parish priest, while the educated man should know the grounds for his adherence to the faith in a much more detailed and personal way. But there again we find a whole range of different apologetics. The reasons of a man like Bergson for belief are not the same as Blondel's and Teilhard de Chardin's, though they are of the same order. And those of a man like Alexis Carrel, converted suddenly by a miracle at Lourdes, are again different. Faith can enter by many ways, but the essential thing is that it should penetrate and take root in the depths of the soul.

## *LIVING APOLOGETICS*

If we try to decide from the facts of history the most usual ways by which faith has entered souls, we shall have to say that it has entered in spite of the fact that apologetics can be called abstract and dead. At first faith was a kind of divine contagion, the result of contact between one person and another. If we analyse the growth of faith in the first apostles we shall reach roughly the following result. John the Baptist set himself to preach in the desert. His evident holiness drew disciples to him from all sides. His speech, his appearance, his way of life opened the hearts of the simple to him. That is what I call living apologetics. It is the soul which sets souls on fire. He pointed out Jesus, calling him the Lamb of God. He brought him his first disciples. But as soon as they saw and heard Jesus, they were vanquished. There again is living apologetics, a contact of soul with soul. Yet to Jesus this contact was not enough. From the first he showed his will that the presence of divine authority should be recognized in him. His words to the disciples, and especially to Bartholomew (Nathanael), "I saw thee when thou wast under the fig-tree," were for those to whom he spoke personal, intimate, and decisive arguments. All through the Gospel we see him continue his work of penetration: the miracle at Cana, the miraculous draught of fish, the many miracles which are scattered throughout the Gospel preaching, then the resurrection, and, to crown all, Pentecost and the descent of the Holy Spirit, all this gives to the faith of the apostles an indestructible foundation. Thus at the beginning we have something complete and wonderful, which will influence the world. Again, the apostles, St Peter, St Paul, St John, those we know best, acted like their Master not only by their words but by their treatment of others, by their personality and their miracles. Through them a living apologetics has continued, and this stream of life has gone on from age to age. When Jesus said, "You will know them by the fruit they yield", he explained the secret of living apologetics. When Tertullian wrote, "The blood of the martyrs is a seed", it was apologetics of the same kind, which he set beside that which he proposed throughout his work. It is by the contact of one person with another that Christianity is spread, perpetuated and multiplied. In the foreign missions the personality and holiness of the missionary signify and achieve as much as, and more than, his words. Such a man as the Curé d'Ars perhaps converted more people than Lacordaire or Ravignan, his contemporaries. The crowds that go to Lourdes or Fatima, or other places of Catholic pilgrimage, find there grounds for belief which they cannot always put in syllogistic form. It is true that reasons for belief are of the highest importance, but undoubtedly they are not the means used most often by God to give rise to faith in men's hearts. Even when these reasons are recognized, they do not necessarily give the final impulse which moves the will to produce the act of faith in cooperation with divine grace. It is entirely in the Christian tradition to believe and to assert that the prayers of Christians for the conversion of unbelievers are more effective than arguments. Cardinal Newman specially loved those words of St Ambrose which he put at the beginning of his great book, *The Grammar of Assent: Non in dialectica complacuit Deo salvum facere populum suum*—"It is not by argument that God has been pleased to save his people". This does not mean that we should get rid of argument. The apologists of Christianity have all made use of it, each one trying to use it better, and nothing is more striking than to see the most formidable difficulties, as for example at first was the theory of the evolution of species, turn out after examination to favour Christianity, as we have seen in the case of Blondel or of Teilhard de Chardin. But argument does not do everything. The Church has not been wrong in proclaiming Teresa of Lisieux patroness of the missions. Within her cloister, not alone but with her companions and followers, she has perhaps done more for the conversion of unbelievers than the missionaries over the whole world. I might quote some episodes in the conversion of the Eskimos given by Mgr Turquetil at the beginning of this century, which furnish clear proof of this. So, too, a historian has been able to say that Teresa of Avila did more to stem the advance of Protestantism than the Society of Jesus itself. Of course all I have been saying about this is only conjecture, for God alone knows how faith grows in souls.

## *CONCLUSION*

In view of all that I have said my conclusion shall be brief. Christianity has been presented throughout this book from the widest standpoint. Jesus Christ did not wait for the events and discoveries which have in our own days brought together all peoples, and anticipated that concentration of all humanity which Fr Teilhard de Chardin considers as the "Omega point" of universal evolution. I have stated throughout that Christ has taken all nations under his care. A religion which is proud to assert its divine origin owes it to itself to pass beyond human horizons and to include all the peoples of the world. What it did at a time when such a view might seem impossible, is a proof of the supernatural origin of our religion. Christianity wishes to work more than ever for the final unity of the human race. "One fold and one shepherd": this ideal of Christ, who is the one Good Shepherd, more than ever attracts mankind.

Christianity alone can give to the whole of creation its full meaning, and the philosophy of history will reach a conclusion of which our faith makes us certain, and which may be put in the words of St Paul, already quoted: "Everything is for you, whether it be Paul, or Apollo, or Cephas, or the world, or life, or death, or the present, or the future; it is all for you, and you for Christ, and Christ for God" (1 Cor. 3. 22–3).

# SELECT BIBLIOGRAPHY

COVENTRY, John, S. J.: *Faith seeks Understanding: an Essay on Faith and Reason*, London and New York, Sheed and Ward, 1951.

GLENN, P. J.: *Apologetics*, London and St Louis, Herder, 1931.

LEBRETON, Jules, S. J.: *Life and Teaching of Jesus Christ our Lord*, London, Burns Oates, and New York, Macmillan, 1958.

NEWSHOLME, Henry P.: *Matter, Man and Miracle*, London, Burns Oates, 1954.

PIEPER, Josef, and RASKOP, Heinz: *What Catholics Believe*, London, Burns Oates, and New York, Pantheon, 1951.

SHEED, F. J.: *Theology and Sanity*, London and New York, Sheed and Ward, 1947.

THE SPIRIT OF WORSHIP

IS VOLUME

108

OF THE

Twentieth Century Encyclopedia of Catholicism

UNDER SECTION

X

*THE WORSHIP OF THE CHURCH*

IT IS ALSO THE

30TH

VOLUME IN ORDER OF PUBLICATION

*Edited by HENRI DANIEL-ROPS of the Académie Française*

# THE SPIRIT OF WORSHIP

*By GASPAR LEFEBVRE, O.S.B.*

*Translated from the French by* LANCELOT C. SHEPPARD

HAWTHORN BOOKS · PUBLISHERS · *New York*

 This book was manufactured in the United States of America and published simultaneously in Canada by McClelland & Stewart, Ltd., 25 Hollinger Road, Toronto 16. It was originally published in France under the title, *L'Esprit de Dieu dans la sainte Liturgie*. © Librairie Arthème Fayard, 1958. The Library of Congress has catalogued The Twentieth Century Encyclopedia of Catholicism under card number 58-14327. Library of Congress Catalogue card number for this volume: 59-14520. The Catholic University of America Library has catalogued this volume based on the Lynn-Peterson Alternative Classification for Catholic Books: BQT184.T9.v.108/BQT4143. Suggested decimal classification 264.02.

*First Edition,* November, 1959
*Second Printing,* March, 1962

NIHIL OBSTAT

Andreas Moore, L.C.L.

*Censor Deputatus*

IMPRIMATUR

E. Morrogh Bernard

*Vicarius Generalis*

Westmonasterii, die II JULII MCMLIX

# CONTENTS


INTRODUCTION 9

I. DEFINITION OF THE LITURGY 11
Liturgy 11
Public Worship 14
The Official Worship of the Church 18
The Priesthood of Christ and His Mystery of Redemption 21
Formulas, Rites and Other External Signs 24

II. THE LITURGICAL YEAR AND THE HOLY SPIRIT 29
The Different Phases of the Drama of Redemption 29
Liturgical Use of Scripture and Tradition 33
Christmas Cycle: Advent, Christmas, Epiphany 36
Advent and Christmas Seasons 36
Our Saviour's First Coming 37
The Annunciation to Mary and Joseph 37
The Visitation: of Mary to Elizabeth and of Christ to John the Baptist 38
Presentation of Jesus in the Temple 39
Prophecies Inspired by the Spirit of God 40
Prophecies Concerning the Messiah 40
Prophecies Concerning the Precursor 42
The Second Coming of Our Lord in the Christmas and Advent Liturgy 42
The Holy Spirit Prepares Us for This Second Coming 43
The Epiphany: the Coming of the Wise Men 45

The Manifestation of Jesus at the Jordan 45
The Manifestation of Jesus at Cana 48
Easter Cycle: Septuagesima, Lent and Passiontide 49
Septuagesima 50
Season of Lent: Ash Wednesday 51
Sundays of Lent 52
Passiontide 55
The Paschal Triduum: Maundy Thursday, Good Friday, Holy Saturday 58
The Commemoration of the Lord's Supper 58
The Arrest and Condemnation of Jesus 60
Death of Jesus on the Cross 62
Our Sharing in the Passion of Jesus 64
Easter Cycle: Easter, Ascension and Pentecost 64
Eastertide 64
Jesus' Victory on the Cross 65
The Negative Side of the Mystery of Redemption 65
The Positive Side of the Mystery of Salvation 66
Third Phase of the Drama of Redemption 67
Role of the Holy Spirit in the Church 69
The Ascension 71
Jesus in Heaven and the Church on Earth Ask for the Sending of the Holy Spirit 73
Pentecost 73
The Coming of the Holy Spirit on the New-Born Church 73
The Action of the Holy Spirit in the Primitive Church 76
The Election of Matthias 77
The Lame Man at the Beautiful Gate 77
Ananias and Sapphira 78
St Stephen, Deacon and Martyr 79
Peter and John in Samaria: Simon Magus 80
Philip and the Queen of Ethiopia's Steward 80
Saul's Conversion 81

Peter's Preaching 82
Saul and Barnabas in Cyprus 82
The Council of Jerusalem 83
Paul at Ephesus 84
Paul Leaves Again for Jerusalem 84
Paul on His Way to Rome 84
St Peter's Epistles 85
St John's Epistles 86

III. THE SACRAMENTAL LITURGY AND THE HOLY SPIRIT 88
Baptism 89
Baptismal Water 90
Ceremonies of Baptism 91
Confirmation 92
Penance 92
The Eucharist 93
The Sacrament of the Sick 94
Orders 95
Exorcists 95
The Subdiaconate 96
The Diaconate 96
The Priesthood 96
The Episcopate 97
Consecration of the Holy Oils on Maundy Thursday 99
Blessing of the Oil of the Sick (Before the Paternoster) 99
Blessing of the Chrism (After the Communion) 99
Blessing of the Oil of Catechumens (After the Communion 100

IV. THE SEASON AFTER PENTECOST 102
The Holy Spirit Ever Active in the Church 103
The Mystery of Christ and the Church 105
The Blessing Promised to Abraham 107
Fraternal Charity 111
Holiness in the Church 112
The Final Apotheosis 115

V. Devotion to the Holy Spirit in the Liturgy 117
In the Unity of the Holy Spirit 117
Prayers Addressed to the Holy Spirit 119
Graces Asked of the Holy Spirit or Granted by Him 121

Conclusion 124

Select Bibliography 127

# INTRODUCTION

As is indicated by its title the purpose of this book is to show how the Church, under the inspiration of the Spirit of God, the Spirit of truth and love, who came down upon her on the day of Pentecost, ensures the spiritual life of all her members by making them take part in her official worship, the sacred liturgy, "the primary and indispensable source of the true Christian spirit" as Pius X and Pius XI pointed out.

The descent of the Holy Spirit on the apostles opens an entirely new phase in the history of salvation in which God the Father in his mercy took the initiative not only by sending us his Son as mediator for our reconciliation but also by making us the gift of him who was divinely to vivify the Church and through her complete our Saviour's work. "Jesus Christ", declared Leo XIII, "entrusted the Holy Spirit with the task of completing the work which was laid upon him by his Father."

Our risen Lord, the victor over the Prince of this world and over death, having fulfilled his mission of setting us free, returned to his Father. As the one High Priest of the New Law gloriously he exercises his priesthood in heaven. "Jesus continues for ever," writes St Paul, "and his priestly office is unchanging; that is why he can give eternal salvation to those who through him make their way to God; he lives on still to make intercession on our behalf" (Heb. 7. 23–4).

Consequently, it was at his request that the promise of St John the Baptist concerning him "who will baptize in the Holy Spirit", and confirmed by Jesus himself, received its solemn fulfilment when the apostolic community, gathered together in the Cenacle, was endued with the Spirit of God.

This visible Pentecost never ceases to take place invisibly in souls, for at every moment "Jesus Christ, who died, nay, has risen again, and sits at the right hand of God, is pleading for us" (Rom. 8. 34). Thus the whole Church is under the dominion of the Spirit of God, and especially the members of the hierarchy for it is of them that the Apostle is speaking when he says to the "presbyters" of Ephesus: "Keep watch, then, over yourselves, and over God's Church, in which the Holy Spirit has made you bishops; you are to be the shepherds of that flock which he won for himself at the price of his own blood" (Acts 20. 28).

Under the guidance of this Spirit of God, who proceeds from both the Father and the Son, the Church must continue our Lord's work, establishing God's kingdom in souls by associating them with the mysteries of Christ and especially with his risen life. In this context the liturgy plays a rôle of capital importance and it is therefore essential to know in what it consists.

Here we begin, then, by giving a definition of liturgy and proceed to analyse each of its elements in order to substantiate its validity. Next, we show how our definition, by its very nature, justifies the title of this book, and go on to explain in greater detail how through the agency of the Church every year the Holy Spirit in the liturgical cycle implements the mystery of the redemption as it is revealed to us by the holy Scriptures and tradition. In this way we can see how the action of the Spirit of God in the liturgy contributes to the glory of God and to the sanctification of souls.

CHAPTER I

# DEFINITION OF THE LITURGY

Among all the descriptive and explanatory definitions of the liturgy the following appears the best summary of what it is in its essential features: the liturgy is the public and official worship by which the Church avails herself of the priesthood of Christ and his mystery of redemption by means of formulas, rites and other external signs through which the Christian community is mercifully sanctified by God and renders filially to God the Father, through his divine Son and under the impulsion of the Holy Spirit, all honour and glory. Each of these terms requires explanation.

## *LITURGY*

The word liturgy is derived from the Greek *λειτουργία* (from *λεῖτος*, public, and *ἔργον*, action or function). At Athens it denoted a public service and was used both in civilian and religious contexts. The term means, then, an action or function of general interest of an official character and beneficial to all.

From the point of view of worship, which here concerns us, the word is used in the Septuagint to denote the ministry performed by the priests in the sanctuary or tabernacle of the old Covenant[1] and in the court of the Temple of Yahweh.[2] The same word occurs in the New Testament. St Luke speaks of the priest's "turn of office" and "ministry" performed by Zachary in the "sanctuary of the Lord".[3] In the Acts of the Apostles the worship offered by the Christians of Antioch is also termed "liturgical".[4]

St Paul says of Jesus, the High Priest of the New Law who exercises his priesthood in the heavenly tabernacles, that he is the *ἁγίων λειτουργὸς*, that is, "the minister of holy things".[5] And often, using the term in a wider sense, the Apostle applies the word liturgy to the offering that he himself made to God in a spirit of sacrifice by his missionary activity or that the faithful accomplished by practising charity in the form of alms and so on.

For example, he reminds the Romans: "So much I owe to the grace which God has given me, in making me a priest of Jesus Christ for the Gentiles, with God's Gospel for my priestly charge, to make the Gentiles an offering worthy of acceptance, consecrated by the Holy Spirit" (Rom. 15. 16; cf. 2 Cor. 9. 12). By following in the first place the etymological meaning of the word liturgy we can say that the liturgy is the public and official worship of the Church.

This worship is performed by the Church, publicly and officially, for the good of all Christendom, and even for the good of the whole world. Thus at the offertory of the Mass the priest, acting in the name of the Church, prays for "all the faithful" (offering of the host, *Suscipe sancte Pater*), for "the welfare of all holy Church" (*Orate fratres*) and for "the whole world's salvation" (offering of the chalice, *Offerimus*).

[1] Exod. 28. 35; Numbers 4. 33.
[2] 1 Paral. 23. 28.
[3] Luke 1. 9 and 23.
[4] Acts 13. 2.
[5] Hebrews 8. 2.

By taking this definition as our starting point we give full emphasis to the following provisions of canon law concerning divine worship: "If worship is celebrated in the name of the Church by persons legitimately deputed to this end and by acts ordained by the Church it is called *public*; otherwise it is private" (can. 1256). And the following canon adds: "It is the prerogative of the Holy See to regulate the sacred liturgy and to approve liturgical books" (can. 1257).

In his book *Liturgy, the Life of the Church*, originally published in French in 1914 but still apposite to the present time, Dom Lambert Beauduin states:

> Liturgical piety derives its transcendent character above all from what we can call its hierarchical character.... Catholic prayer has its laws, which the Church applies with constant fidelity in her worship (p. 19). All the liturgical books that day for day regulate our sacrifices, our adorations and our prayers draw all their powers of praise, of intercession, and of sanctity from the fact that they are given to us by the supreme head of the hierarchy. That they have come down to us from St Leo, St Gelasius, St Gregory, is of little importance for the moment. Their transcendent and incomparable title in the eyes of the Father who is in heaven, and in the eyes of the faithful, is that they form the great prayer presided over by the Vicar of Christ, the reigning Pontiff. Every time that the faithful in the Catholic world associate themselves with holy Mass, the divine Office, the solemnities of the liturgical cycle, with any liturgical act, they share in the adoration and the prayer of the supreme Pontiff, and through him of the entire Church; they are the children that nourish themselves at the table of our common parent, the Holy Father.... As a school of respect for and attachment to the supreme head of the visible hierarchy, the liturgy also greatly strengthens the bonds of every diocesan Church. The bishop there appears as the father and pontiff of his Church, whether he personally performs the liturgy in his cathedral, his mother-church, or whether he does so

through his cooperators in the parishes, his daughter churches (p. 21).[6]

To say that the sacred liturgy is authentically the prayer of the Church and her official and public worship is an assertion of its transcendence. Thus in his encyclical *Mediator Dei et hominum* Pius XII states formally that "unquestionably liturgical prayer, being the public supplication of the illustrious Spouse of Jesus Christ, is superior in excellence to private prayers".

## *PUBLIC WORSHIP*

In his conversation with the Samaritan woman our Lord said of worship rendered to God that the time "is coming, nay, has already come, when true worshippers will worship the Father in spirit and in truth; such men as these the Father claims for his worshippers. God is a spirit, and those who worship him must worship him in spirit and in truth" (John 4. 23–4). With the Messiah's coming the time had arrived when the worship of the Mosaic Law was to give way to another of a really universal nature. The dispute between the Jews and the Samaritans had no longer any justification. In instituting the New Law Christ inaugurated a new sacrifice which supplanted all those of the Old Law. It was to be celebrated throughout the whole world and in an entirely new spirit which was to form the very soul of all Christian worship. Fr Braun writes:

> The coming of this universalism coincided with the coming of the more spiritual religion which Christ came to teach us and which is given us not as the abolition of the old religion but as its fulfilment.... The Jews were too easily

[6] This quotation is taken from, and the page numbers refer to, the English translation of Dom Lambert Beauduin's booklet, *Liturgy: the Life of the Church*, translated from the French by Dom Virgil Michel, Collegeville, Minn., the Liturgical Press, 1926.

satisfied with their ritual practices. They had reduced the worship of God to a collection of gestures and attitudes deprived of any inward spirit.... The true adorers were careful not to reject external practices which will always be necessary since we are made up of body and soul. But they placed the principal emphasis on worship in spirit.... To adore and to pray to God in spirit means adoration of him and prayer to him with the whole heart, the whole soul, and with purity of intention. And to adore him thus in *spirit* is to adore him indeed in truth. Purely external worship, without interior devotion, is only counterfeit prayer.[7]

Our Lord did not dismiss vocal prayer since he taught his disciples the *Pater noster*. St Teresa mentions a nun who "enjoyed the purest contemplation while she said the Lord's Prayer"[8] and she herself found in saying this prayer an admirable means of union with God.

The Lord's Prayer sung or said aloud by the priest at the altar possesses great power with God when it emanates from a soul which makes its own all the aspirations and petitions contained in it.

St Thomas Aquinas in his *Summa Theologica* declares that even bodily adoration is made in spirit to the extent that it is derived from and leads to spiritual devotion: "He prays in spirit and in truth who comes to prayer at the instigation of the Holy Spirit. Prayer consists principally in the spirit and finds its expression only secondarily in words; in the same way also adoration consists principally in interior reverence towards God and secondarily in certain bodily signs."[9]

Our Lord in the Sermon on the Mount, which forms the code of the New Law, attacks the formalism of those who pray from motives of ostentation and vanity. "And when you pray, you are not to be like hypocrites, who love to

[7] *La sainte Bible*, Volume 10, pp. 344–5.
[8] *Way of Perfection*, Chapter 10.
[9] *Summa Theologica*, 2a 2ae, Qu. 83 and 84.

stand praying in synagogues or at street corners, to be a mark for men's eyes. . . . But when thou art praying, go into the inner room and shut the door upon thyself, and so pray to thy Father in secret, and then thy Father, who sees what is done in secret, will reward thee" (Matt. 6. 5–6). St John Chrysostom comments trenchantly: "Does he forbid us solemn public prayer, that public prayer which gathers together before God a whole people at one in humble supplication? He who made the promise of the efficacy of common prayer could not forbid it, but he desired to lay down the true conditions of public prayer."[10] What our Lord had in mind was the intention of those who pray; they must have in their thoughts the glory of God and not their own vain glory.

With public prayer, which requires the simultaneous activity of body and soul, praying in secret means entering into close contact with God in the secret of our hearts by means of external actions. *Sic stemus ad psallendum*, says St Benedict in the nineteenth chapter of his Rule, *ut mens nostra concordet voci nostrae* ("So let us take our part in the psalmody that mind and heart concord together").

The public prayer of the Church, which brings into play all man's powers, his understanding, will, emotions and bodily actions, is completer than any other. It is fully appropriate to our human nature. We should always carry it out under the impulsion of the Holy Spirit, dwelling in our souls by grace; in this way we shall avoid the reproach made by Jesus which had already been addressed by Isaias to superficial worshippers: "This people does me honour with its lips, but its heart is far from me" (Matt. 15. 8; Isaias 29. 13).

All our external acts of worship must be the sincere and heartfelt expression of our faith and love of God. "God", says St Augustine, "is honoured by the worship due to him,

[10] *Homily on Matthew*, n. 2.

especially by faith, hope and charity."[11] By the theological virtues which govern the virtue of religion and which in its turn produces actions to the glory of God, our soul, which is spiritual, has direct contact with God, who is a spirit, and our worship is thereby made in "spirit and in truth".

The rôle of our external acts of worship is to be the perceptible expression of our interior devotion, the homage that our body, in dependence on our soul, renders to God by placing itself completely at his service, and the spur that this externalization of worship supplies to our understanding and our will.

When a large congregation takes part in public prayer and with fervour proclaims the glory of God, this collective action exerts a strong influence on all. Rites, words, chants, all combine as a powerful source of unification of this prayer and endow its expression with an especially dynamic quality.

Our bodies are called to share for eternity in the infinite beatitude of God and in the adoration that all the elect pay to the Blessed Trinity. It cannot therefore remain a stranger to that prayer by which, here below, our soul is sanctified by coming into contact with the divine majesty. On the contrary, it must join in this prayer as closely as possible to derive benefit from it and to pay to God the complete and public worship which he expects of his creatures who are not pure spirits like the angels.

The Missal contains several collects which mention soul and body in conjunction. "May the sacrament of which we have partaken, Lord, be felt by us as a support for mind and body, so that having health in both, we may glory in the fullness of divine healing" (Postcommunion, eleventh Sunday after Pentecost). "Grant health of soul and body to thy people, Lord, so that by persevering in good works

[11] *Enchiridion* 3.

they may deserve always to be shielded by thy mighty power" (Prayer over the people, third Friday in Lent).

## *THE OFFICIAL WORSHIP OF THE CHURCH*

What is meant by the Church? A clear idea will help us to understand the nature of the worship that she pays officially to God. "The Church", says the Catechism, "is the union of all the faithful under one head." That one head is our Lord Jesus Christ and his vicar on earth is the pope, the bishop of Rome. The Church, therefore, is a hierarchical, visible society of a supernatural character whose purpose is to continue our Lord's work by labouring for the salvation of souls and their sanctification. Clearly this is the purpose intended by Jesus, and in establishing his Church he endowed her with the means enabling her to realize it.

He centred the whole life of the Church on the holy sacrifice by which Calvary was to be perpetuated and in instituting the eucharistic sacrificial meal on the day before his passion he said to his apostles: "Do this for a commemoration of me" (1 Cor. 11. 24). After his resurrection he appeared to them in the Cenacle and said to them: "I came upon an errand from my Father, and now I am sending you out in my turn. With that he breathed on them, and said to them, Receive the Holy Spirit; when you forgive men's sins, they are forgiven, when you hold them bound, they are held bound" (John 20. 1–3). He showed himself again to his disciples on the shores of the sea of Tiberias and after the miraculous draught of fishes said to Peter: "Feed my lambs. . . . Feed my sheep" (John 21. 15–17). St Matthew concludes his Gospel with these words: "Jesus came near and spoke to them; All authority in heaven and on earth, he said, has been given to me; you, therefore, must go out, making disciples of all nations, and baptizing them in the name of the Father, and of the Son, and of the Holy Ghost, teaching them to observe all the commandments which I have given you" (Matt. 28. 18–20).

In order to carry out these commands of our Lord's as fully and as effectively as possible the Church employed, and when circumstances enabled her to do so, developed her public worship. In it by preaching the Gospel, by celebrating the holy sacrifice, by administering the sacraments and by praying publicly she exercises the magisterial and ministerial powers given her by Christ.

Appropriately it was St Pius X, the great promoter of the liturgical movement, who also condemned the Modernists, whose assertion it was that the public worship of the Church was not instituted by our Lord. In their view, therefore, the Church, which arose outside our Lord's intentions and solely under the influence of circumstances and from sheer necessity, herself instituted the essential features of Christian worship. In his Encyclical on the mystical Body of Jesus Christ Pius XII stated once more the true teaching on the subject and with great clarity:

> Jesus Christ on the cross not only compensated the outraged justice of the eternal Father, but also merited for us, his kindred, an unspeakable abundance of graces. These graces he might himself, had he so chosen, have bestowed directly upon the whole human race; but he willed to do this by means of a visible Church in which men would be united.... As the Word of God vouchsafed to use our nature to redeem man by his pains and torment, in a somewhat similar way he makes use of his Church throughout the ages to perpetuate the work he had begun.... "Christ," says the Apostle, "is the head of the body, the Church".... By the very fact of being a body the Church is visible.... It is certainly true that those who possess the sacred power in this Body must be considered primary and principal members, since it is through them that the divine Redeemer

> himself has willed the functions of Christ as teacher, king and priest to endure throughout the ages....
>
> The Saviour of the human race in his infinite goodness has in like manner admirably equipped his mystical Body by endowing it with the sacraments, making available for its members a progressive series of graces to sustain them from the cradle to their last breath, and abundantly providing also for the social needs of the whole Body.
>
> When the apostles were about to begin their sacred work of preaching, Christ our Lord sent his Spirit from heaven to touch them with the tongues of fire and, like a divine finger, to indicate the supernatural mission and function of the Church....
>
> This Spirit of Christ is the invisible principle to which we must also attribute the union of all parts of the Body with one another and with their exalted head, dwelling as he does whole in the Head, whole in the Body, and whole in each of its members. It is he himself who is present in all the members and divinely acts in each, though he also acts in the lower members through the ministry of the higher.... The Church is far more excellent than all other associations of human beings.

This long quotation has been given because in showing us the true nature of the Church as the society endued with life by the Holy Spirit it enables us to conclude that her official prayer involves the whole mystical Body of Christ. This is borne out by what the same pope says in his Encyclical on the liturgy issued some few years after *Mystici Corporis*: "The sacred liturgy is the public worship which our Redeemer as Head of the Church renders to the Father as well as the worship which the community of the faithful renders to its founder, and through him to the heavenly Father. It is, in short, the worship rendered by the mystical Body of Christ in the entirety of its Head and members."[12]

[12] Encyclical *Mediator Dei et hominum* (November 20th, 1947), hereinafter quoted as *Mediator*.

The whole Church, constituting one mystical *Person*, the whole Christ (*Christus totus*) inspired by the Holy Spirit, renders this public worship to God. All who take part in it do so as members of Christ and the Church. Under the inspiration of the Holy Spirit and in union with the whole of Christendom, of which Jesus Christ is the invisible Head, and the pope, his vicar, is the visible head, all pursue the same end, each individual retaining his personality while exercising with the others the rôle assigned to him by the official liturgical books. To identify oneself fully with this worship, which to the highest degree is Catholic, means working individually and socially at the development of the mystical Body of Christ by intensifying our own incorporation with him, our divine Head.

To this end, in some sort, we must cast off our own immediate personal interests by putting in the forefront of our minds the general welfare of the Church. And we shall do this by allowing the Spirit of God, who acts through her, to imbue us ever increasingly with that love of God and of our neighbour of which the liturgy is redolent. In this way, far from being the losers we shall gain, for, by spiritual symbiosis, we shall benefit more extensively from the prayer of all our brethren in Christ and the links which bind us together as children of the Church will thereby be made the stronger. "Lord Jesus Christ", runs one of the prayers of the Ordinary of the Mass, ". . . look not upon my sins but upon thy Church's faith, and deign to give her peace and unity in accordance with thy will."

## *THE PRIESTHOOD OF CHRIST AND HIS MYSTERY OF REDEMPTION*

Of its essence the priesthood of the Church depends on the priesthood of Christ of which it forms the prolongation, for it is our Lord himself who acts through the ministry of his priests and who thus continues through them his work of redemption and sanctification in souls. It was to accomplish this work of salvation that "the only-begotten Son of God, born of the Father before all ages . . . was incarnate by the Holy Ghost from the virgin Mary, and was made man". Since Jesus, by virtue of the mystery of the Incarnation, is the Son of God in person, from the first moment of his existence he was anointed priest by the unction of the godhead itself. His priestly power was not conferred on him afterwards as with other men.

Christ is therefore, as this shows, the "anointed one" pre-eminently. In very truth he is the only priest, and he alone could offer to his Father, in entire justice, a sacrifice of expiation for all the sins of the human race.

This sacrifice, of infinite value, since it was effected by a Man-God who offered himself voluntarily as a victim to expiate the sin of mankind against the divine majesty, Christ accomplished by shedding his blood on the altar of the cross.

But as St Paul declares, quoting David the Psalmist, "As Christ comes into the world, he says, No sacrifice, no offering was thy demand; thou hast endowed me instead with a body. Thou hast not found any pleasure in burnt sacrifices, in sacrifices for sin. See then, I said, I am coming to fulfil what is written of me. . . . He must clear the ground first, so as to build up afterwards. In accordance with this divine will we have been sanctified by an offering made once for all, the body of Jesus Christ" (Ps. 39. 7–9; Heb. 10. 5–10).

And Cardinal de Bérulle explains: "The Son of God, from the first moment of his life in his mother dedicated himself to that life, to that cross, to that death which were to follow afterwards. And this oblation and primary will of Jesus is an action and a will which never ceased by day or night. . . . This interior and spiritual movement was perpetual in the heart and spirit of Jesus."[13]

Thus all the actions of his life, united in his thought with that final act that he was to accomplish on the cross, combined to merit for us the grace of being able to associate ourselves with his paschal mystery by dying to sin and rising to a new life, that of the children of God. "Golgotha", wrote A. Barrois, "is not the steep path on which Jesus would come at the end of his life to accomplish in his blood the redeeming sacrifice, but it is the culminating point of a sacrifice whose first act was the incarnation of the Word."[14]

The incarnation in a mortal body foreshadowed, by making it possible, the final sacrifice. Our Saviour's death, on the other hand, was the condition of his resurrection from the dead, which was the starting point of his glorious life and his lordship in heaven until he comes as a sovereign judge at the end of time. We should also notice that by instituting the Eucharist in the Upper Room on the day before his death Jesus conferred on his apostles the priestly dignity by commanding them to renew in memory of him what he had just done, that is, offer the holy sacrifice of the Mass as the memorial of his passion.

St Thomas states: "By his passion Christ inaugurated the rite of the Christian religion, offering himself in sacrifice as a victim to God."[15] Thus the apostles (and the same applies to all those ordained priests) share in the priesthood of Christ. This priesthood they exercise first and foremost by celebrating the eucharistic sacrifice of which the principal priest and the divine victim are the same as in the Upper Room and on the cross. Liturgical worship, centred on the Mass, like the whole existence of our Saviour, is

[13] *Vie de Jésus*, Chapter 26.

[14] In *Revue des Sciences philosophiques et théologiques*, April 1925, p. 155.

[15] *Summa Theol.* 3a, Qu. 62, art 5.

therefore concentrated on the last Supper and Calvary and their glorious consequences—the resurrection, the ascension and the sending of the Holy Spirit.

The Church, by commemorating daily in concise fashion, and as far as possible on their anniversary, the joyful, sorrowful and glorious mysteries by which our Saviour effected our salvation, applies their merits or virtue to the souls in her charge. Thus from year to year she continues, through the ministry of those who have received the sacrament of Order, the redemptive and sanctifying action of the High Priest of the New Law. The faithful too share in a certain fashion in the priesthood of Christ, for baptism and confirmation mark their souls with an ineffaceable though invisible character.

## *FORMULAS, RITES AND OTHER EXTERNAL SIGNS*

Since the Church is a visible society quickened by the Holy Spirit her official worship necessarily and always includes actions which can be perceived by the senses. These acts—for liturgy is essentially active—are the formulas, rites and other external signs by means of which God and mankind are brought into close touch.

As we have already pointed out, it is not a question merely of external actions, as it were a theatrical representation or mere formalism. These liturgical actions are the external expression of an internal spiritual attitude without which they would be like a body without a soul. By these external signs and the symbolism which belongs to them, or is attributed to them, men are brought into contact with a higher world wherein they are under the power of the Holy Spirit who sanctifies them and causes them to render worship to God in spirit and in truth.

By *formulas* are meant principally the scriptural readings

which form the didactic parts of the Mass and the divine Office. They are to be heard with respect for, as St Peter says: "Men gave it utterance . . . carried away as they spoke, by the Holy Spirit" (2 Peter 1. 21). And when the Church during a liturgical ceremony sings or recites these sacred texts, this proclamation of the word of God possesses a special virtue which encourages the action of the Holy Spirit in souls.

To these portions of Scripture must be added the Psalter which priests and other ministers of the Church, together with many religious, say right through every week. Many verses of the 150 Psalms are used at Mass for the introit, gradual, alleluia verse, offertory and communion anthems.

This prayer, which is both vocal and mental, is also the work of the Holy Spirit. In his *Motu Proprio* (March 24th, 1945) Pius XII stated that he had "ordered the preparation of a new Latin translation of the Psalms that should follow more closely and be more faithful to the original text, so that what the Holy Spirit desired to express by the mouth of the Psalmist may be more easily made out". And the pope goes on to say that he desires that men and women consecrated to God "should be stimulated to cherish in their souls those sentiments of love, undaunted perseverance and devout compunction that the Holy Spirit excites within them by the reading of the Psalms".

The other formulas of prayer—collects, prefaces, sequences, hymns, litanies, etc.—composed by the Church, which are to be found in the liturgical books (Missal, Breviary, Pontifical, etc.), should be regarded in the light of what St Paul said to the Christians of Ephesus in speaking of their meetings for worship: "Let your contentment be in the Holy Spirit; your tongues unloosed in psalms and hymns and spiritual music, as you sing and give praise to the Lord in your heart" (Ephes. 5. 18–19).

By *rites* are meant principally the eucharistic sacrifice

and the sacraments which, in their essential features, were instituted by Christ and for their administration entrusted by him to the Church. These sacramental rites belong to the category of sacred signs and effect what they signify—*significando causant*. This signification, which was very simple at the outset, has been amplified by the Church. Under the guidance of the Holy Spirit she has surrounded these essential rites with a great number of formulas and ceremonies with the purpose of making their administration still more instructive and of inducing the faithful to benefit more fully from them.

These ritual amplifications were at first termed the "lesser sacraments". Peter Lombard gave them the technical name, which has since been commonly accepted, of *sacramentalia*, "sacramentals". The sacramentals resemble the sacraments because like them they produce a specific effect. But whereas the sacraments in virtue of their institution by Jesus Christ, act *ex opere operato*, that is, of themselves directly they are administered, the sacramentals act *ex opere operantis Ecclesiae*, that is, in virtue of the fact that they are instituted by the Church whose prayers and holiness possess great efficacy. Thus their use is a means by which we can obtain divine grace. In addition to instructing us about the effects of the sacrament the sacramentals arouse in our souls dispositions beneficial for the reception of the sacrament itself by making us ready to receive it.

In her liturgical worship the Church avails herself of the priesthood of Christ and his mystery of redemption by means of formulas, rites and other external signs *through which the Christian community is mercifully sanctified by God and renders filially to God the Father, through his divine Son and by the impulsion of the Holy Spirit, all honour and glory*. When we were in our sins God, in his merciful goodness, called on us to share his divine and eternal life. To this end the Father sent us his own Son. "What has revealed the love of God, where we are concerned," says St John in the Epistle of the first Sunday after Pentecost, "is that he has sent his only-begotten Son into the world, so that we might have life through him. That love resides . . . in his shewing love for us first, when he sent out his Son to be an atonement for our sins" (1 John 4. 9–10). When by his death, resurrection and ascension Jesus reconciled us with his Father and obtained the sending of the Holy Spirit, he sent him to the Church which he had founded so that with the help of this divine Spirit she might apply to souls his own work of redemption and thus bring it to its fullest completion.

As a consequence it is under the direction of the Holy Spirit that the Church has organized her official public worship for the purification and sanctification of souls by uniting them by faith and the sacraments of faith to Christ in all his mysteries: "He saved us," says St Paul in the Epistle of the Mass at dawn on Christmas Day, "and it was not thanks to anything we had done for our own justification. In accordance with his own merciful design he saved us, with the cleansing power (baptism) which gives new birth, and restores our nature through the Holy Spirit, shed on us in abundant measure through our Saviour Jesus Christ" (Titus 3. 5–6). Therefore, it is by the Church and in the Church that the Holy Spirit sanctifies us by making of us the mystical Body of Christ of which he is the divine life-giver. Thus, united vitally to the Son of God and quickened by "the Spirit of his Son" (Gal. 4. 6), it is indeed as the adopted children of the Father that we share in the life of the Trinity. God the Father loves us united inseparably with his Son and in our turn, in union with Jesus, we love him with a truly filial love. Our Lord said to his apostles: "The Father himself is your friend, since you have become my friends, and have learned to believe that I came from God" (John 16. 27); and St Paul says: "The spirit you have now received . . . is the spirit of adoption which makes us cry out, Abba, Father" (Rom. 8. 15).

Thus the Church, that is, the whole of Christendom, whose Head is the Son of God and whose soul is the Spirit of Christ, is indeed able to give to the Father by the Son in the unity of the Holy Spirit all honour and glory. And this she does officially by the sacred liturgy.

CHAPTER II

# THE LITURGICAL YEAR AND THE HOLY SPIRIT

## *THE DIFFERENT PHASES OF THE DRAMA OF REDEMPTION*

The liturgical year, which can be called the Holy Spirit's masterpiece, in the light of the Scriptures, inspired by the same Holy Spirit, sets before us sacred history—the true history of humanity—in the form of a drama which began with the fall of Adam and the promise of a Redeemer. It is the drama or mystery of redemption in which there is perpetual opposition between the Spirit of God and the spirit of the world. This drama is made up of three phases which unfold in the course of the centuries. Our divine Redeemer is the principal character and the Spirit of God is made manifest with increasing power. This dramatic action concludes with the definitive victory over the powers of evil won by our risen Lord and his Church vivified by the "Spirit of our Lord Jesus Christ".

The first phase of this drama shows us Yahweh's continual watching over his chosen people whose deeds and activities foreshadowed, heralded and prepared the advent of the Saviour, the deliverance wrought by him and the coming of the kingdom of God. In this phase, known as the Old Testament, the gift of the Spirit is merely a personal gift. It is bestowed on certain prominent persons (the High Priest of the Mosaic Law, kings, prophets) for the benefit of the community over which they preside.

In the second phase of the drama of redemption the chief character is Christ in person whose hidden and public life is described for us by the evangelists. This comes to a sudden conclusion with the tragedy of Calvary soon to be followed by the appearances of the risen Lord and his ascension into heaven. The meaning of this earthly existence of Jesus was lost on the world. While his enemies rejoiced in their triumph revelation shows that actually it meant their defeat. The sacred writers, inspired by the Holy Spirit, tell us in fact that the Son of God took flesh to effect our salvation. Having proclaimed his divine message he accomplished our redemption for ever by the expiation of our sins on the cross. And, since his resurrection, which has made him "life-giving spirit", throughout the whole world he is the source of all grace and the primary cause of all spiritual life. It is from the humanity of Christ, completely spiritualized and glorified in heaven, that the graces of the Holy Spirit, whose fullness our divine Saviour possesses, flow into our souls. The parallelism and the antithesis between the two persons called by Scripture the old Adam and the new Adam, who is the Son of God made man and risen from the dead, fall naturally into place here: "If there is such a thing as a natural body, there must be a spiritual body too. Mankind begins with the Adam who became, as Scripture tells us, a living soul; it is fulfilled in the Adam who has become a life-giving spirit . . . the man who came first came from earth, fashioned from dust, the man who came afterwards came from heaven, and his fashion is heavenly" (1 Cor. 15. 44–9). In both cases, but on different levels, Adam and the Man-God are heads of humanity, the first of fallen humanity, the second of redeemed humanity.

By Adam's sin, and without our collaboration, we have all contracted original sin. Likewise, in the person of the new Adam, and entirely independent of any action of ours, our liberation was effected. By taking on mortal flesh in the Virgin's womb the incarnate Word intended in advance to undergo the death which is the punishment due to Adam's disobedience. Personally united to a flesh "in the likeness of our guilty nature" (Rom, 8. 3) the Son of God took upon himself the responsibility of original sin and of all the sins which are its consequence. These sins he crucified, in a certain manner, with him on the cross. And thus he merited that we should be delivered from what stood in the way of the divine life in our souls.

On the other hand, by rising from the dead to a new and immortal life, Jesus abolished in his person all that was perishable and earthly. Under the entire dominion of the Holy Spirit his humanity was, we repeat, completely spiritualized as befitted a Man-God, and this Man-God was henceforth in a position to pour forth in abundance into souls the graces of the Holy Spirit which he possesses in fullness.

Adam's taint affected us when by our birth we became members of fallen humanity of which he is the head. Similarly, with our rehabilitation we must be inserted into the mystical Body of Christ, the Head of the new humanity. When we are bound up in this way with Jesus his Spirit flows into us and supernaturalizes our whole lives, for he is the soul of all the members of this mystical Body.

This brings us to the third phase of the drama of redemption, that of the life of the Church in which the Holy Spirit plays a leading rôle. After the passing of Jesus from this world to his Father it is in fact the function of the Church, guided and endued with life by the Holy Spirit, to bring us into contact with our risen Lord and thus to ensure for us those graces which will cause us to die to sin and to live as true members of Christ. This phase began on the day of Pentecost and will last until the day of the second and glorious coming of the Son of God as sovereign Judge and divine rewarder.

The coming down of the Holy Spirit on the apostles on the fiftieth day after Christ's resurrection marks an important stage, therefore, in the unfolding of the divine plan whose purpose is to establish the kingdom of God among men. The reign of the Holy Spirit, an entirely spiritual one to follow that of Jesus, has sometimes been mentioned. This far too obsolute conception is erroneous. Of course, in this third phase it is the Holy Spirit who sanctifies souls interiorly by uniting them by spiritual bonds to the risen Lord. But ordinarily it is through the Church and in the Church that the Holy Spirit acts. "Where the Church is", says St Irenaeus, "there is the Spirit of God, and where the Spirit of God is there is the Church and every grace. . . . Separation from the Church means rejecting the Spirit."[1]

The Church referred to in this quotation is the visible Church on which the Holy Spirit came down in the discernible form of tongues of fire. It is the apostolic Church to which Jesus, in order to extend to the whole world the benefits of redemption, entrusted the powers of *magisterium*, ministry and government as was pointed out above (Chapter I).

The Holy Spirit, the life-giver of this Church, of which the glorified Christ is the invisible Head and the pope, the successor of Peter, the visible head, never ceases to work through her and in her for the growth of the kingdom of God throughout the world.

This kingdom which is both a spiritual and an external one is no different from that which Jesus instituted in this world by founding the Church on Peter and the apostles. The Holy Spirit does not therefore substitute his own reign

[1] *Adversus Haereses*, Bk 3, Chapter 24.

for that of our Saviour; on the contrary he ensures its full development and does so patently, in particular by the intermediary of the members of the ecclesiastical hierarchy. "Some he has appointed to be apostles," says St Paul, "others to be prophets, others to be evangelists, or pastors, or teachers. They are to order the lives of the faithful, minister to their needs, build up the frame of Christ's body (that is, the Church) until we all realize our common unity through faith in the Son of God, and fuller knowledge of him. So we shall reach perfect manhood, that maturity which is proportioned to the completed growth of Christ" (Ephes. 4. 11–13).

This growth of the Church, the mystical Body of Christ, is therefore the characteristic feature of the third phase of the drama of redemption. And it is in this connection that the liturgy, the official worship of the Church and the principal instrument for the sanctification of souls by the Holy Spirit, plays its indispensable rôle. It will be sufficient proof of this to show what the Church, in the celebration of the liturgical festivals, tells us of the Holy Spirit, the soul of the mystical Body, and what by means of this celebration the Holy Spirit and the Church effect in the souls of those who take an active part in it.

## *LITURGICAL USE OF SCRIPTURE AND TRADITION*

In order properly to understand the liturgical year it must be considered in the context of the entirety of the mystery of redemption of which Scripture and tradition provide us with the fundamental data. The Breviary and Missal, in fact, are chiefly made up of extracts from the books inspired by the Holy Spirit and of commentaries on them by the Fathers of the Church. Thus each year the history of the salvation of the human race, as it is described in the Bible, from Genesis to the Apocalypse, is set before us by the cycle of liturgical festivals.

The official proclamation of these passages of Scripture by the ministers of the Church, and especially the reading or chanting of the Epistle and Gospel in the presence of the Christian community, endow them with a new reality and thus place within our grasp the principal truths of revelation.

The formulas, rites, ceremonies (sacraments, sacramentals, etc.) and all the sacred signs mentioned in the first chapter of this book, increase this reality by their particular virtuality. As a consequence, by taking our part we have a real rôle in the drama of redemption.

In this drama which continues down the centuries there is unity of action and constant moving forward. Generally speaking, the Old Testament is used as the prelude, as an adumbration of the New Testament which forms its prolongation accomplished in the most perfect way. On the other hand, it is by careful examination of the revelation made by our Lord and shown in all its clarity by the Holy Spirit that we can understand the real significance of the Old Testament.

This comparison between the different phases of the mystery of redemption is to be found in the liturgy. In it the Church contemplates simultaneously, in the sequence of the different liturgical seasons, and even every day, the divine plan for the salvation of men in its four dimensions —before the coming of Christ, during this coming, after it and then the whole mystery in relation to the glorious coming of our Saviour and the final apotheosis of this drama in heaven.

Enlightened and spurred on by the Holy Spirit the Church sets before us, then, the economy of redemption in its fullness. She does not do so by a method of historical reconstruction, according to the rules of the theatre, but by the entirety of the ceremonies, prayers and rites of her official worship.

Biblical history, the history of Jesus Christ, the history of the Church, is therefore something far different from the liturgical dramatization in which the Church presents them and in which the action of our risen Saviour and that of the Holy Spirit combine to make us not mere spectators but active participants in the work of salvation in its present phase.

This dramatization in the form that the Church sets it before us at the present time is divided into two parts which are termed the Christmas cycle and the Easter cycle.

It is no part of our plan to show here how this dramatization has gradually developed in the course of centuries. We can confine ourselves to pointing out that the Easter cycle, centred on the mystery of the death and resurrection of Jesus Christ, was the first to take form. The paschal mystery, the cause of our salvation (Easter), is completed by that of the coming of the Holy Spirit on the Church (Pentecost). The Christmas cycle was added afterwards; its principal festivals are the birth of our Lord and the Epiphany.

This cycle was therefore made the beginning of the liturgical year in order to follow the unfolding of the mysteries of our Saviour. But it is obvious, in spite of the fundamental importance of the mystery of the Incarnation, that Easter surpasses Christmas. The Son of God became man, but mortal man, for the purpose of our redemption which he achieved by dying and rising again and the benefits of which he applied to us by the action of his Spirit through and in the Church.

Easter, which reaches its final completion in the outpouring of the Holy Spirit at Pentecost, stands at the summit of the history of salvation, and therefore at the very apex of the liturgical cycle which is its carrying into effect. It is by the paschal mystery indeed that the union of man and God, realized in Jesus at the Incarnation, attains in him its full perfection. And it is in this way, also, that our sharing in the mystery of the Incarnation (Christmas) is increasingly intensified every year by a renewal of our spiritual resurrection to the life of grace (Easter) and by an ever greater outpouring of the gifts of the Holy Spirit (Pentecost).

We are now in a position to see how the Church by means of the masterpiece formed by the arrangement of the Christian festivals sets before us the unceasing action of the Holy Spirit of God to whom we owe our sanctification.

## *CHRISTMAS CYCLE: ADVENT, CHRISTMAS, EPIPHANY*

### *Advent and Christmas seasons*

The season of Advent forms a prelude to the liturgical year during which the Church sets before us the different mysteries of the life of Christ and celebrates the feasts of saints who by their fidelity to the grace of the Holy Spirit have fought the good fight and now share the glory of our risen Lord in heaven.

The coming of the Messiah into this world formed for many centuries the object of the hope of the people of God. This hope is now shared by Christian people who for the four weeks of Advent prepare to commemorate the birthday of our Lord and then to celebrate the feasts of the liturgical year which concludes with the twenty-fourth Sunday after Pentecost when we are reminded of the last judgement. Thus the Church contemplates simultaneously our Lord's first and second coming—that which happened nearly two thousand years ago and that which will come to pass in God's good time.

*Our Saviour's first coming*

The first coming of Jesus, commemorated at Christmas, has already taken place historically, consequently the purpose of this feast is liturgically to make real this mystery so that we may benefit ever more intensely from the special grace belonging to it.

The Church speaks of an *admirabile commercium* (a "wonderful exchange") in the Vespers of the Circumcision (1st antiphon). God takes on our humanity in order to make us share in his divinity. In the secret prayer of the Midnight Mass we pray: "May the offering of today's feast be acceptable to you, Lord, so that by the bounty of your grace and through this holy exchange of gifts we may be found in the likeness of him in whom our human substance has been made one with you." It is for us, therefore, to confess our faith in the Incarnation and to be born ever increasingly to that divine life which the Son of God came to bring us by taking flesh in the womb of the Virgin Mary at Nazareth and by being born in the city of David at Bethlehem.

*The Annunciation to Mary and Joseph*

The Gospel of the Wednesday in the Advent Ember week is that of the annunciation of the mystery of the Incarnation made by an angel to Mary. This wonderful scene is the opening of the time of salvation; the blessed Virgin assents and the mysterious union between God and man is accomplished in her by the almighty power of the Holy Spirit. "The Holy Spirit will come upon thee," said the angel, "and the power of the most High will overshadow thee. Thus this holy offspring of thine shall be known for the Son of God" (Luke 1. 35). "His mother Mary", says the Gospel for Christmas Eve, "was espoused to Joseph, but they had not yet come together, when she was found to be with child, by the power of the Holy

Ghost" (Matt. 1. 18). "She conceived", St Augustine explains, "not by concupiscence of the flesh but by obedience of mind."

The angel of the Lord then appeared to Joseph to reveal this mystery to him. This account, given in the Gospel on Christmas Eve, brings out very clearly the virginal motherhood of Mary by the action of the Holy Spirit: "Joseph, son of David, do not be afraid to take thy wife Mary to thyself, for it is by the power of the Holy Ghost that she has conceived this child; and she will bear a son, whom thou shalt call Jesus, for he is to save his people from their sins" (Matt. 1. 20–1).

### *The Visitation: of Mary to Elizabeth and of Christ to John the Baptist*

The Advent Ember Friday is devoted to consideration of Mary's visitation of Elizabeth. The action of the Holy Spirit emerges even more clearly: "In the days that followed, Mary rose up and went with all haste to a town of Juda, in the hill country where Zachary dwelt; and there entering in she gave Elizabeth greeting" (Luke 1. 39–40). "Mary", explains St Ambrose in the first lesson of Matins read on this day, "desired to carry out a duty of friendship by visiting Elizabeth, and she left in haste because she was beside herself with joy. . . . The grace of the Holy Spirit is never slow in those efforts that it inspires. . . . Mary came to Elizabeth, Christ to John." At the meeting with Mary and the child that she bore in her womb Elizabeth was inspired by the Holy Spirit. The child who leaped in her womb revealed to her, together with the Holy Spirit, the presence of the Messiah and Saviour: "No sooner had Elizabeth heard Mary's greeting, than the child leaped in her womb; and Elizabeth herself was filled with the Holy Ghost; so that she cried out with a loud voice, Blessed art thou among women, and blessed is the fruit of thy womb" (Luke 1. 41–2).

The Fathers of the Church have commented on this passage: "Just as it was only after being inspired by the Holy Spirit that the prophets uttered their prophecies," says Theophylactus, "so it was only after leaping with joy under the influx of divine grace that John prophesied by the mouth of his mother. And what did he proclaim? He said, 'Blessed art thou among women, and blessed is the fruit of thy womb'."[2]

At this first meeting with the infant God the Precursor was sanctified by the Holy Spirit even as the angel had said when he appeared to Zachary in the temple and told him that Elizabeth his wife would bear a child: "And from the time when he is yet a child in his mother's womb he shall be filled with the Holy Ghost" (Luke 1. 15). On June 24th, the feast of the Birthday of St John the Baptist, the Gospel is the account of the birth and circumcision of the Precursor. In his commentary on this Gospel, read at Matins on the feast, St Ambrose says that Elizabeth would not agree to her child being called by his father's name, but wished him to bear the name John, "because she knew through a revelation of the Holy Spirit the name that the angel had previously told to Zachary". And the Gospel concludes with the following sentence: "Then his father Zachary was filled with the Holy Ghost, and spoke in prophecy: Blessed be the Lord, the God of Israel; he has visited his people, and wrought their redemption" (Luke 1. 67–8).

*Presentation of Jesus in the Temple*

At the presentation of Jesus in the Temple, Simeon, an old man, was inspired by the Spirit of God and he too spoke like the prophets: "Simeon . . . an upright man of careful observance, who waited patiently for comfort to be brought to Israel. The Holy Spirit was upon him; and by the Holy Spirit it had been revealed to him that he was

[2] Migne, *Patrologia Graeca*, 123. 707–14. (Hereafter quoted as Migne, *P.G.*, followed by volume and column number.)

not to meet death, until he had seen the Christ whom the Lord had anointed. He came now, led by the Spirit, into the Temple; and . . . Simeon too was able to take him in his arms. And he said, blessing God: Ruler of all, now dost thou let thy servant go in peace . . ." (Luke 2. 25–9).

*Prophecies inspired by the Spirit of God*

In another way, too, the Church places us under the guidance of this same Holy Spirit during the Christmas cycle of the liturgical year. In the Breviary the daily reading of Scripture during Advent and on the feast of Christmas and Epiphany is taken from Isaias, a prophet inspired by the Spirit of God. St Paul, quoting a passage from this prophet which the Church repeats for us during Advent, writes: "It was true utterance the Holy Spirit made to our fathers through the prophet Isaias" (Acts 28. 25). And St Peter also declares: "Yet always you must remember this, that no prophecy in scripture is the subject of private interpretation. It was never man's impulse, after all, that gave us prophecy; men gave it utterance, but they were men whom God had sanctified, carried away, as they spoke, by the Holy Spirit" (2 Peter 1. 20–1).

Therefore it was under the inspiration of the Spirit of God that the prophets uttered their messages and that these were recorded in Scripture. Guided by this same Holy Spirit, whose revelation has shown her that these prophecies obtained their full meaning at the time of the Messiah, the Church has directed that they should be read in the course of the liturgical offices. Indeed it is striking that by means of this harmonization of the Old and the New Testaments the liturgy recalls and celebrates what the prophecies foretold.

*Prophecies concerning the Messiah*

Isaias foretold the twofold coming of the Messiah, his coming as Redeemer and King, his birth of a virgin mother. Born of the tribe of David he is to be filled with the Spirit of God and his glorious reign will know no end.

These texts light up the whole liturgy of the Christmas cycle, for the precise object of this section of the liturgical year is to commemorate the successful realizations of the prophecies in Christ so that, under the action of the Holy Spirit, it may be effected also and ever increasingly in his mystical Body.

"Behold, the King is coming, the Lord of the world, and he will take from us the yoke of our captivity" (Magnificat antiphon, second Monday in Advent: Isaias 10. 27). "Behold, the virgin shall be with child, and shall bear a son, says the Lord, and he shall be called Wonderful, God the Mighty. He will sit on David's kingly throne for ever" (Seventh responsory, first Sunday of Advent: Isaias 7. 14; 9. 6, 7). "From the stock of Jesse a scion shall burgeon yet; out of his roots a flower shall spring. One shall be born, on whom the spirit of the Lord will rest; a spirit wise and discerning, a spirit prudent and strong, a spirit of knowledge and of piety, and ever fear of the Lord shall fill his heart" (Second lesson, second Sunday of Advent: Isaias 11. 1). "Yes, the day of the Lord is coming, pitiless, full of vengeance and bitter retribution, ready to turn earth into a wilderness, ridding it of its sinful brood. The stars of heaven, its glittering constellations, will shed no ray; sunrise will be darkness, and the moon refuse her light. I will punish the world's guilt . . . crushing the haughtiness of tyrants" (Second lesson, Monday of second week of Advent: Isaias 13. 9–11). "Behold, our Lord will come with power, and he will give light to the eyes of his servants" (Fifth antiphon at Lauds, second Sunday of Advent: Isaias 40. 10).

The Breviary quotes passages from many other prophets during Advent: Jeremias, Ezechiel, Daniel, Osee, Joel, Michaeas, Habacuc, Aggaeus, Sophonias, Zacharias and

Malachias. Thus the Church by their means places us under the guidance of the Holy Spirit whose organs they are.

*Prophecies concerning the Precursor*

Of these prophets, Isaias and Malachias also foretold the coming of the Precursor of the Messiah, that is, John the Baptist, into this world. Indeed the latter asserted: "I am what the prophet Isaias spoke of, the voice of one crying in the wilderness, Straighten out the way of the Lord" (John 1. 23; cf. Isaias 40. 3). And Christ, speaking of John the Baptist, quoted the following prophecy from Malachias: "This is the man of whom it was written, Behold, I am sending before thee that angel of mine, who is to prepare the way for thy coming" (Matt. 11. 10; Mal. 3. 1). Jesus announced himself to John's disciples as the Messiah by quoting the miracles, foretold by Isaias, which were to indicate that the time of salvation had arrived. At the synagogue in Nazareth, again, Jesus applied to himself this prophecy of Isaias: "The Lord has anointed me, on me his spirit has fallen; he has sent me to bring good news to men that are humbled, to heal broken hearts" (Isaias 61. 1). During the Christmas festival the Church recalls the following prophecy of Isaias: "For our sakes a child is born, to our race a son is given, whose shoulder will bear the sceptre of princely power. What name shall be given him? Peerless among counsellors, the mighty God, Father of the world to come, the Prince of peace" (Isaias 9. 6; read at Matins on Christmas Day).

*The Second coming of our Lord in the Christmas and Advent liturgy*

The collect after the anthem of the Blessed Virgin *Alma Redemptoris Mater*, which is proper to the Advent season, shows that the Church, by placing us at the outset of the ecclesiastical year in contact with the mystery of the Incarnation, desires to associate us with everything that Jesus accomplished for our salvation, particularly by his passion and resurrection: "Pour forth thy grace into our hearts, we pray thee, Lord, so that we, to whom the Incarnation of Christ, thy Son, was made known by the angel's message, may by his passion and cross be brought to the glory of his resurrection." This glory in its fullness will be given to the elect when the last judgement takes place at the end of time. Thus it is finally and necessarily the second coming of the Son of God that the Church has in mind when in her official worship she makes real all the mysteries of Christ. And this worship is celebrated during that phase of the drama of redemption which immediately precedes our Lord's return in glory: "O God, who year by year dost gladden us with the prospect of our redemption, grant that we who joyfully welcome thy only-begotten Son as our Redeemer may look with confidence on the same Jesus Christ, thy Son, our Lord, when he comes as judge." So we pray in the collect on Christmas Eve.

*The Holy Spirit prepares us for this second coming*

In the Epistles of the Advent season St Paul prepares us for this second coming. He calls on us especially to be watchful and to practise the virtue of hope by surrendering our souls in all gladness to the action of the Holy Spirit: "Already it is high time for us to awake out of our sleep; our salvation is closer to us now than when we first learned to believe" (Rom. 13. 11; Epistle, first Sunday of Advent). "May God, the author of our hope, fill you with all joy and peace in your believing; so that you may have hope in abundance, through the power of the Holy Spirit" (Rom. 15. 13). "Joy to you in the Lord at all times; once again I wish you joy. Give proof to all of your courtesy. The Lord is near" (Phil. 4. 4–5).

In the Epistle for Christmas Eve the Apostle of the

Gentiles refers to the good news which was foretold in God's name by the prophets and which is recorded in the Scriptures. "It is Paul who writes; a servant of Jesus Christ, called to be his apostle, and set apart to preach the gospel of God. That gospel, promised long ago by means of his prophets in the holy scriptures, tells us of his Son, descended, in respect of his human birth, from the line of David, but, in respect of the sanctified spirit that was his, marked out miraculously as the Son of God by his resurrection from the dead; our Lord Jesus Christ" (Rom. 1. 1–5).

This Epistle deals with the mystery of the Incarnation by which the Son of God took on mortal flesh, in descent from the tribe of David, and with the mystery of the resurrection which made this flesh immortal by the profoundly spiritual action of the Holy Ghost.

On the feast of Christmas the Apostle shows us Christ in all his glory: "A Son, who is the radiance of his Father's splendour, and the full expression of his being; all creation depends, for its support, on his enabling word. Now, making atonement for our sins, he has taken his place on high, at the right hand of God's majesty" (Heb. 1. 3–4). So it is with Jesus in glory, with our divine risen Lord, that we are united in every one of the feasts of the Church. As we take part in them, what the Holy Spirit effected in the humanity of Jesus is extended to our souls and prepares us for the glorious resurrection of our bodies which will occur when Christ comes to judge the living and the dead. "It is to heaven that we look expectantly", says the Apostle, "for the coming of our Lord Jesus Christ to save us; he will form this humbled body of ours anew, moulding it into the image of his glorified body, so effective is his power to make all things obey him" (Phil. 3. 20–1). This confident expectation is in us the work of the Holy Spirit: "In accordance with his own merciful design he saved us, with the cleansing power which gives new birth, and restores our nature through the Holy Spirit, shed on us in abundant measure through our Saviour, Jesus Christ. So, justified by his grace, we were to become heirs, with the hope of eternal life set before us" (Titus 3. 5–6; Christmas Day, Mass at dawn). This hope will be fulfilled when Christ returns in glory as the divine Rewarder of those souls faithful to the inspirations of the Holy Spirit: "And then they will see the Son of Man coming in a cloud, with his full power and majesty. When all this begins, look up, and lift up your heads; it means that the time draws near for your deliverance" (Luke 21.27–8; Gospel, first Sunday of Advent).

*The Epiphany: the coming of the Wise Men*

On the feast of the Epiphany the coming of the Magi is also set before us as the awe-inspiring realization of a vision of Isaias in which this prophet contemplated all nations flocking to Jerusalem, a type of the Church. St Leo comments on it thus:

> In the Magi adoring Christ we must see, then, the first fruits of our vocation and our faith and with joyful hearts celebrate the beginnings of this wonderful hope. For from this moment we have begun to enter into our heavenly inheritance. Henceforth the mysterious passages in holy Scripture which refer to Christ have been discovered by us and the truth that the blindness of the Jews did not accept has spread its light abroad among all nations. Let us do honour, then, to this most holy day on which the Author of our salvation made himself known and let us adore as almighty in heaven him whom the Magi adored as a little child in the manger.[3]

*The manifestation of Jesus at the Jordan*

On January 13th, the feast of the Commemoration of the Baptism of our Lord, the Church places before us the

[3] 6th lesson at Matins on the feast of the Epiphany.

scene at the manifestation of Jesus when he came to be baptized by John the Baptist. "John", we read in the Gospel of that day, "also bore witness thus, I saw the Spirit coming down from heaven like a dove, and resting upon him. Till then, I did not know him; but then I remembered what I had been told by the God who sent me to baptize with water. He told me, The man who will baptize with the Holy Spirit is the man on whom thou wilt see the Spirit come down and rest. Now I have seen him, and have borne my witness that this is the Son of God."

Jesus, having taken on himself the responsibility for our sins, desired to be baptized with water as if he were himself a sinner. St Gregory Nazianzen writes:

> His purpose was to bury the old Adam in the waters and principally by his baptism to sanctify the waters of the Jordan in order that, as he was spirit and flesh, so those who were baptized subsequently, should be sanctified by the virtue of the Spirit and the element of water. Jesus came out of the water, so to say, drawing after him and raising up with himself the world which hitherto had been sunk in the depths. I see the opening of heaven which the first Adam had of old closed to himself and to us. The Holy Spirit bears witness: this witness comes from heaven, for there came down from heaven he concerning whom the Spirit bears witness.[4]

John the Baptist had shown the true nature of Jesus' mission when he said: "I am baptizing you with water . . . he will baptize you with the Holy Ghost, and with fire" (Matt. 3. 11). It is Christ's function to merit for us the Holy Spirit and to spread him lavishly abroad in the world of souls by the baptism whose administration he has entrusted to his Church. "The holiness of baptism", explains St Augustine, "must be attributed to Jesus alone for on him came down the dove and of him it was said to John

[4] January 13th, 5th and 6th lessons at Matins.

that he would baptize with the Holy Spirit. If Peter baptizes it is Jesus who baptizes, if Paul baptizes it is Jesus who baptizes, if Judas baptizes it is Jesus who baptizes."[5]

The coming down of the Holy Spirit on Jesus at his baptism in the Jordan heralds the irruption of the Holy Spirit on the Church on the day of Pentecost. It was after being baptized in the Holy Spirit who came down upon them in the form of tongues of fire that the apostles baptized the crowds.

Speaking of the Messiah, Isaias had prophesied: "And now, here is my servant, to whom I grant protection; the man of my choice, greatly beloved. My spirit rests upon him, and he will proclaim right order among the Gentiles. . . . He will not snap the staff that is already crushed" (Isaias 42. 1–3). In their account of the baptism of Jesus the synoptic Gospels use similar terms to those of the prophet. Thus St Luke says: "It was while all the people were being baptized that Jesus was baptized too, and stood there praying. Suddenly heaven was opened, and the Holy Spirit came down upon him in bodily form, like a dove, and a voice came from heaven, which said, Thou art my beloved Son, in thee I am well pleased" (Luke 3. 21–2).

Jesus began his earthly life by being conceived by the Holy Spirit. He inaugurated his public ministry after what may be called his official investiture as prophet, high priest and king, anointed with the chrism of the Holy Spirit. On his return to Galilee he declared in the synagogue of Nazareth that in him was fulfilled this prophecy of Isaias: "The Lord has anointed me, on me his spirit has fallen" (Isaias 61. 1; cf. Luke 4. 18). And on the day of Pentecost St Peter also declared: "You have heard . . . about Jesus of Nazareth, how God anointed him with the Holy Spirit and with power, so that he went about doing good" (Acts 10. 37–8).

[5] January 13th, 8th lesson at Matins.

*The manifestation of Jesus at Cana*

The Gospel of the second Sunday after Epiphany is that of the wedding feast at Cana. In order to understand it the literary form used by St John must be borne in mind: "John, the last evangelist," says St Clement of Alexandria, "seeing that whatever was of the corporeal order was brought out clearly enough by the other evangelists, divinely inspired by the Spirit wrote his spiritual Gospel." In his account, therefore, the literal sense is accompanied by a mystical sense which refers to the mystery of the union of Christ and his Church. There is a comparison between the divine wedding feast and the human wedding feast which is its symbol. Mary's approach to her Son. "They have no wine left", can be understood in two ways as Jesus' answer implies :"Nay, woman, why dost thou trouble me with that? My time has not come yet" (John 2. 4).

The expression "my time" occurs as many as seven times in St John's Gospel and always in reference to the paschal mystery. "The time" of his being raised up is to be when, by his death on the cross, he will merit his resurrection, his glorification in heaven and our sharing in these mysteries by his sending us the Holy Spirit. "Why dost thou trouble me with that?" says Jesus. But Mary's request was to be granted and she knew that it was to be so since she said to the servants: "Do whatever he tells you." In fact her divine Son told them to fill with water six large water-pots and to take to the master of the feast for tasting the water that he changed into wine, better wine than that which had been served beforehand. "So", says the evangelist, "Jesus . . . made known the glory that was his, so that his disciples learned to believe in him" (John 2. 11).

This miraculous action possesses a spiritual significance which refers, as we pointed out, to the paschal mystery designated by the "time" mentioned by Jesus. By his passion, resurrection, ascension and the sending down of the Holy Spirit on the Church, which was its blessed outcome, the Son of God substituted the New for the Old Testament. The people of God, the vine of Israel, hitherto fruitful, no longer bore fruit: "They have no wine left."

At the messianic wedding feast Christ will provide a new wine in profusion and of high quality. The wine which spiritually inebriates souls was lacking to the Mosaic dispensation for it is the Holy Spirit, as St Paul explains in his letter to the Ephesians: "Do not besot yourself with wine. . . . Let your contentment be in the Holy Spirit" (Ephes. 5. 18). And to those who on the day of Pentecost railed at the apostles as having "had their fill of new wine" St Peter replied: "These men are not drunk, as you suppose; it is only the third hour of the day. This is what was foretold by the prophet Joel: In the last times, God says, I will pour out my spirit upon all mankind" (Acts 2. 14–16). And St Gaudentius adds this comment :"It would appear, according to Jesus' answer, that Mary's request went much further than obtaining a merely material beverage; she was asking for that outpouring of the Holy Spirit which was to fill souls with spiritual inebriation and which Jesus was not to grant until after his passion and resurrection."[6]

## *EASTER CYCLE: SEPTUAGESIMA, LENT AND PASSIONTIDE*

The second cycle of the liturgical year leads up to the festival of Easter which is continued until Pentecost. This cycle is divided into the seasons of Septuagesima (three Sundays), Lent (four Sundays) and Passiontide (two Sundays). Then comes the period of fifty days, from Easter to Pentecost, for the Paschal mystery includes not only the triumph of Jesus and his glorious passage from this world

[6] Sermon 9.

to his Father, but also the sending of the Holy Spirit on the apostles according to the promise made to them by our Lord.

Thus the whole work of the redemption leads to the official promulgation of the Church whose mission it is to extend the kingdom of God and his Christ by bringing souls under the ascendancy of the Holy Spirit. It was at Pentecost, when the Holy Spirit took possession of the infant Church, that he began through her his victorious struggle against the spirit of evil, and from this moment, too, he spreads abroad in souls by her agency spiritual and divine life.

*Septuagesima*

At Septuagesima the Church begins with Genesis, followed by Exodus, etc., the course of Scripture reading (the *lectio continua*) lasting throughout the year. Thus it is the whole of sacred history, in its main features, that liturgy places before us and explains its symbolic or typical meaning. On several occasions our Lord asserted that Scripture spoke of him. The apostles, in the light of the Holy Spirit, and then the Fathers of the Church, established clearly the continuous connection between the first phase of the drama of redemption and that of the life of Christ and his Church, all of which fulfil the figures, promises and prophecies, recapitulating them in a far more perfect form.

The story of the creation and the fall (Septuagesima), of Noe and the flood (Sexagesima), of Abraham and the Covenant (Quinquagesima), of Jacob (second week of Lent), of Joseph (third week of Lent) and of Moses leading the people of God through the desert to the promised land (fourth week of Lent) are all so many events which refer to messianic times. Thus in the Epistle of Septuagesima Sunday, and in that of the ninth Sunday after Pentecost, which forms its continuation, St Paul compares the exodus of the Jews with the conduct of Christians: "Our fathers were hidden, all of them, under the cloud, and found a path, all of them, through the sea; all alike, in the cloud and in the sea, were baptized into Moses' fellowship. They all ate the same prophetic food, and all drank the same prophetic drink, watered by the same prophetic rock which bore them company. . . . And for all that God was ill-pleased with most of them. . . . When all this happened to them it was a symbol; the record of it was written as a warning to us, in whom history has reached its fulfilment" (1 Cor. 10. 1–5, 11–12).

Christians have the use of the sacraments of baptism and the Eucharist which were prefigured by the pillar of cloud and the passage over the Red Sea, by the manna and the water gushing from the rock. But to ensure our salvation we have to be careful not to fall into the same sins as the Israelites.

There is no need to develop at greater length this parallelism between the two "economies" of the old and the new people of God. It will be referred to again only in connection with the commentary on liturgical texts which treat formally of the Holy Spirit; for example, in Chapter III, where is shown the action that this divine Spirit exerts through the Church by means of the sacraments.

*Season of Lent: Ash Wednesday*

The Church begins Lent by placing ashes on the heads of the faithful and praying that they may be filled with the spirit of compunction. The celebrant concludes this rite with the following collect which emphasizes the spiritual combat of these holy forty days: "Grant us, Lord, to begin with holy fasts our Christian warfare; that as we do battle with the spirits of evil we may be protected by the help of self-denial." And on this same Ash Wednesday, in the Gospel of the Mass which is an extract from the Sermon on the Mount, Jesus speaks to us of the spirit which should animate us for us to be pleasing to God and to lay up treasure in heaven: "Do thou, at thy times of fasting, anoint thy head and wash thy face, so that thy fast may not be known to men, but to thy Father who dwells in secret; and then thy Father, who sees what is done in secret, will reward thee. . . . Lay up treasure for yourselves in heaven. . . . Where your treasure is, there your heart is too" (Matt. 6. 17–18, 20–1).

It is characteristic of the New Law that it allows to the Mosaic Law its full development by perfecting the spirit informing it. For it is our own interior dispositions, our intention, our affection made supernatural by the Holy Spirit which endows our external practices with their true value in the eyes of God. For this reason, in the collect for the Friday after Ash Wednesday, the Church prays to God "to look with gracious favour on the fasts we have undertaken; so that the abstinence which we keep with our bodies may have its counterpart in the sincerity of our souls."

*Sundays of Lent*

The proper observance of Lent, which involves both body and soul, is a result of divine grace; thus, in the Epistle read on the first Sunday of Lent, St Paul exhorts us "not to offer God's grace an ineffectual welcome"; he himself, as God's minister, allows himself to be led by the Holy Spirit and, endowed with the "power of God", he fights the good fight "armed with innocence" (2 Cor. 6. 1, 6–7). But our model above all others, and especially during the holy forty days which prepare us every year for the festival of Easter, is Jesus tempted by the devil in the desert and triumphantly repulsing him, as the Gospel of the first Sunday in Lent shows.

Adam's fall and that of the whole human race was occasioned by the devil whom Christ calls "the prince of this world" and whom he came to vanquish in order to re-establish the kingdom of God in the souls of men. "The man who lives sinfully", we read in St John, "takes his character from the devil; the devil was a sinner from the first. If the Son of God was revealed to us, it was so that he might undo what the devil had done" (1 John 3. 8). It is for this reason that St Matthew says, "Jesus was led by the Spirit away into the wilderness, to be tempted there by the devil" (Matt. 4. 1).

Three times Christ answered the tempter, "It is written", quoting against him a text from Deuteronomy referring to the sojourn of the Israelites in the desert. In this way he showed that he desired to efface the threefold disobedience of the people of Israel during its exodus in the desert and that the word of God, recorded in the Scriptures with the assistance of the Holy Spirit, is powerful beyond compare. "Christ", says St Thomas, "desired to be tempted that he might be an example and a help to us in temptations and teach us how we should overcome them."[7]

The Gospel of the third Sunday in Lent once more shows us Jesus at grips with the devil: "He had just cast out a devil, which was dumb; and no sooner had the devil gone out than the dumb man found speech. The multitudes were filled with amazement" (Luke 11. 14). This was a case of diabolical possession together with systematic opposition on the part of some scribes and Pharisees. These opponents of Jesus went so far as to accuse him of being in league with Beelzebub, the prince of the devils, in order to free the man possessed. "But he could read their thoughts, and said to them . . . How do you suppose that Satan's kingdom can stand firm if he is at war with himself?" No, Satan is not at war with himself; he gives way only to a stronger than himself: "When a strong man, fully armed, mounts guard over his own palace, his goods are left in peace; but

[7] *Summa Theol.* 3a, Qu. 41, art 1, ad 4.

when a man comes who is stronger still, he will take away all the armour that bred such confidence, and divide among others the spoils of victory" (Luke 11. 21–2).

The strong man armed mentioned by our Lord is none other than Satan who dominated the world unmolested. But a stronger than he comes to put an end to his domination over mankind, enslaved to him by their passions and vices: "If I by the finger of God cast out devils, doubtless the kingdom of God is come amongst you" (Luke 11. 20, Douay version). The expression "finger of God" means the "Spirit of God" as is shown by a parallel text of St Matthew (12. 28). The Vesper hymn for Pentecost (*Veni, Creator Spiritus*) also speaks of the Holy Spirit as "the finger of the right hand of the Father". Moreover, in explaining the passage from St Luke quoted above St Gregory says: "What else is signified by the fingers of the Redeemer but the gifts of the Spirit?"[8]

The Word incarnate whose soul was entirely filled with the "Spirit of God", with the "Holy Spirit", possessed divine power far mightier than the devil's and he gave evidence of it by delivering the unfortunate man held in tyrannical possession by Satan.

Two spiritual kingdoms confronted each other: that of the Spirit of evil, of the "impure Spirit" as the Gospel of this Sunday calls him, and that of the Spirit of God, of the Spirit of holiness which, in Jesus, could be sure of victory.

In this struggle between Christ and Satan mankind cannot therefore remain indifferent, for "he who is not with me is against me; he who does not gather his store with me, scatters it abroad" (Luke 11. 23). In the Mass of the Wednesday of the fourth week of Lent in the first lesson, Ezechiel foretells the pouring out of living waters and of the Holy Spirit. In the waters the Church sees an allusion

[8] 7th lesson, Matins, 11th Sunday after Pentecost.

to baptism which effects the spiritual transformation of souls: "I will pour cleansing streams over you, to purge you from every stain you bear. . . . I will give you a new heart, and breathe a new spirit into you" (Ezech. 36. 25). At Easter the catechumens were baptized "in water and the Holy Spirit". They were born thus to the life of grace, to a spiritual life in which the Holy Spirit plays the preponderant rôle.

In Scripture the term "spirit" (*pneuma*) designates the Holy Spirit directly (it is then written with a capital) or indirectly, for it is he who supernaturalizes the *spirit* of man by making him share in the fullness of graces which he showered on the soul of Jesus when the mystery of the Incarnation took place.

### *Passiontide*

During the two weeks of Passiontide the daily reading from Scripture in the Breviary is taken from Jeremias. Once again, therefore, the Church places us under the guidance of the Holy Spirit "who spoke through the prophets". And indeed there is more than one striking resemblance between our Saviour's passion and the sufferings of Jeremias. Thus the Church sees in the persecutions endured by this prophet, which he described for us in striking terms, a prefiguration and prediction of what the Messiah had to suffer from his persecutors: "I had been unsuspecting as a cade lamb that is led off to the slaughterhouse. . . . They whispered . . . let us rid the world of him, so that his very name will be forgotten" (Jer. 11. 19). Isaias prophesied even more clearly various events of our Lord's passion. The Church quotes him during Holy Week. The Gospel of the Monday in Passion Week relates an attempt to arrest Jesus when he was in Jerusalem for the feast of Tabernacles. "Both chief priests and Pharisees sent officers to arrest him. Then Jesus said, For a little while I am still with you, and then I go back to him that sent me" (John 7. 33). This attempt on the part of the Jewish religious leaders, who wished to get rid of Jesus, failed; his "time", the time of his passion and glorification, that is, of his return to his Father, had not yet come.

The feast of Tabernacles reminded the Jews of their sojourn in the desert. During it there took place a rite of sprinkling with water drawn from the spring of Siloe. This water was poured out at the foot of the altar of holocausts in commemoration of the water with which Yahweh had miraculously quenched the thirst of his people in the desert of Pharan.

There are a great number of passages in the prophets showing God as a spring overflowing with living water. For example, Isaias says: "They did not go thirsty when he led them through the desert; he could bring water out of the rock for them, cleave the hard rock and make the water flow" (Isaias 48. 21). This rock, as St Paul wrote, was a figure of Christ: "All drank the same prophetic drink, watered by the same prophetic rock which bore them company, the rock that was Christ" (1 Cor. 10. 4). The water springing up symbolizes the spiritual life of which Christ is the source whence flow into souls the graces of the Holy Spirit. The living water is especially the emblem of this life-giving Spirit. Indeed, as St John recounts, on the most solemn day of the feast of Tabernacles, Jesus cried aloud: "If any man is thirsty, let him come to me, and drink; yes, if a man believes in me, as the scripture says, Fountains of living water shall flow into his bosom. He was speaking here of the Spirit, which was to be received by those who learned to believe in him" (John 7. 37–9). Thus, six months before his passion Christ proclaimed his mission as the sender of the Holy Spirit which he fulfilled after his return to his Father.

The Gospel of the Friday in Passion Week shows us the

chief priests and Pharisees gathered in council against Jesus after hearing that he had raised Lazarus from the dead.

> What are we about? they said. This man is performing many miracles, and if we leave him to his own devices, he will find credit everywhere. Then the Romans will come, and make an end of our city and our race. And one of them, Caiphas, who held the high priesthood in that year, said to them, . . . it is best for us if one man is put to death for the sake of the people, to save a whole nation from destruction. It was not of his own impulse that he said this; holding the high priesthood as he did in that year, he was able to prophesy that Jesus was to die for the sake of the nation; and not only for that nation's sake, but so as to bring together into one all God's children, scattered far and wide. From that day forward, then, they plotted his death. (John 11. 47–53.)

The use of the word prophesy by St John implies the intervention of the Holy Spirit. St Augustine explains it as follows: "From this we learn that even wicked men may foretell the future by the spirit of prophecy; this, however, the evangelist ascribes to a divine sacrament, for this man was the pontiff, that is, the high priest."[9]

On Palm Sunday the Church, commemorating our Lord's triumphant entry into Jerusalem, causes us to acclaim him as king: "The multitude goes out to meet the Redeemer with flowers and palms, and pays the homage due to a triumphant conqueror. Hail our King, Son of David, Redeemer of the world, whom the prophets foretold would come as the Saviour of the house of Israel."

Our Lord always complied with the predictions made about him by the prophets under the inspiration of the Holy Spirit. Thus in the Gospel read at the blessing of Palms St Matthew quotes one of these prophecies: "All this was so ordained, to fulfil the word spoken by the

[9] *Treatise 49 on John*; 3rd lesson at Matins, Friday after Passion Sunday.

prophet (Zacharias): Tell the daughter of Sion, Behold, thy king is coming to thee, humbly riding on an ass, on a colt whose mother has borne the yoke" (Matt. 21. 4–5). And in the Gospel of the Saturday in Passion Week St John says: "The disciples did not understand all this at the time; only after Jesus had attained his glory did they remember what they had done, and how it fulfilled the words written of him" (John 12. 16). It was therefore when our risen Lord had given them understanding of the Scriptures and had sent them the Holy Spirit that the apostles understood all the implications of this prophecy.

In this same passage from his Gospel St John tells us that Jesus foretold his approaching death, the definitive victory that he would win over the devil and the salvation he would bring to the world by his exaltation on the cross: "I have only reached this hour of trial that I might undergo it. . . . Now is the time when the prince of this world is to be cast out. Yes, if only I am lifted up from the earth, I will attract all men to myself. (In saying this, he prophesied the death he was to die.)" (John 12. 27, 31–3).

### *The Paschal triduum: Maundy Thursday, Good Friday, Holy Saturday*

"I will attract all men to myself." This universal nature of the salvation announced by Jesus is the theme of the solemn collects on Good Friday. Here we notice the third which is concerned with the action of the Spirit of God in the whole Church: "Almighty, everlasting God, by whose Spirit the whole body of the Church is sanctified and guided, heed our petition on behalf of all its orders and degrees, that by the gift of thy grace, all in their several stations may give thee faithful service."

### *The commemoration of the Lord's Supper*

On Maundy Thursday the Church celebrates the commemoration of the Last Supper which recalls especially the institution by our Lord of the eucharistic sacrifice and of the Catholic priesthood. The Gospel of the day states: "Before the paschal feast began, Jesus already knew that the time had come for his passage from this world to the Father. He still loved those who were his own, whom he was leaving in the world, and he would give them the uttermost proof of his love." In all humility and charity he washed their feet. Then, having eaten with them the paschal lamb, he took bread and wine and changed them into his body and blood. Jesus, a priest according to the order of Melchisedech, thus by a rite without the shedding of blood anticipated the offering, with blood shedding, that he was to effect the next day on the cross for the salvation of all men. "He offered to God his Father", says the Council of Trent, "his body and blood under the species of bread and wine, distributed them under these same symbols to the apostles whom thereby he ordained as priests of the New Testament and gave to them and to their successors in the priesthood the order to offer them by the words 'Do this in memory of me'."[10]

St Paul, regarding the Mass as a sacrificial meal at which we are united with the divine Victim of Golgotha made present at the "Lord's feast", declares in the passage read as the Epistle on Maundy Thursday: "So it is the Lord's death that you are heralding, whenever you eat this bread and drink this cup, until he comes" (1 Cor. 11. 26).

The offering of the "Blood of the New Testament", ever renewed down the centuries on the altars of the whole world, ensures for all Christians the graces of which Calvary is the source and which the Holy Spirit pours out lavishly in the souls of men. In his sermon to his disciples after the Last Supper our Lord showed them in fact the whole action that this Spirit of love and of truth would exercise in the Church and, through her, in the world. We

[10] Session 22, c. 1.

return to this below, for this sermon recurs in the Gospels between Easter and Pentecost.

*The arrest and condemnation of Jesus*

We must call attention here how in certain parts of the passion narratives there appears clearly Jesus' concern to comply in all things with the will of his Father as it was revealed by the Holy Spirit to the prophets and recorded by them in the Scriptures of which St Paul said that everything in them "has been divinely inspired" (2 Tim. 3. 16).

When, led by Judas, the cohort and the Temple guards came to arrest Jesus at Gethsemani, Simon Peter struck Malchus, the high priest's servant, with his sword. But our Lord said: "Put thy sword back into its place; all those who take up the sword will perish by the sword. Dost thou doubt that if I call upon my Father, even now, he will send more than twelve legions of angels to my side. But how, were it so, should the scriptures be fulfilled, which have prophesied that all must be as it is? . . . All this was so ordained, to fulfil what was written by the prophets" (Matt. 26. 52–6).

When, shortly afterwards, Jesus appeared before the Sanhedrin, the high priest questioned him. Finally, having exhausted all other arguments, he asked him: "Art thou the Christ, the Son of the blessed God? Jesus said to him, I am. And you will see the Son of Man sitting at the right hand of God's power, and coming with the clouds of heaven" (Mark 14. 61–2). The expression "sitting at the right hand of God's power" is an allusion to the Psalm of David (Ps. 109. 1) *Dixit Dominus*: "Sit here at my right hand while I make thy enemies a footstool under thy feet," which is a messianic prophecy. The "coming with the clouds of heaven" recalls the vision of the prophet Daniel who saw "how one came riding on the clouds of heaven, that was yet a son of man" (Dan. 3. 13–14) and receiving from the Judge crowned with age (God) power and sovereignty over all peoples.

Our Lord's declaration before the Sanhedrin that he was the Son of God, which amounted to a public claim to divine kingship, meant the signing of his death warrant. The religious leaders of the Jews exclaimed that he was blaspheming and declared that he had incurred the penalty of death. But since they had no power to carry out this sentence they had recourse to Pilate who governed Judaea in the name of the Romans.

Before this civil authority they accused him of a crime of a political nature: "We have discovered . . . that this man is subverting the loyalty of our people . . . and calls himself Christ the king" (Luke 23. 2). Questioned about this by the governor, Jesus answered: "My kingdom . . . does not belong to this world. If my kingdom were one which belonged to this world my servants would be fighting to prevent my falling into the hands of the Jews." To Pilate's further question whether he were a king Jesus answered: "It is thy own lips that have called me a king. What I was born for, what I came into the world for, is to bear witness of the truth. Whoever belongs to the truth listens to my voice" (John 18. 36–7).

This is the spiritual kingdom that the "Spirit of truth", promised by Christ in his sermon after the Last Supper, will extend to the whole world; it was of a nature entirely different from that with which Jesus had been charged, and consequently the case was not one that concerned the Roman governor. Thus he stated, "I can find no fault in him." The Jews then cried out: "We have our own law, and by our law he ought to die, for pretending to be the Son of God" (John 19. 6–7).

We are here at the very heart of the drama of redemption for it was as Son of God, and to establish his kingship over souls by right of conquest, that Jesus voluntarily gave himself up to death. To Pilate's further questions he answered nothing that might have saved his life. And in the end as the outcry made by those who required him to be crucified increased in violence the governor declared: "I have no part in the death of this innocent man; it concerns you only" (Matt. 27. 24). "He handed over Jesus to their will" (Luke 23. 25). And finally: "Jesus went out, carrying his own cross, to the place named after a skull; its Hebrew name is Golgotha. There they crucified him" (John 19. 17–18).

*Death of Jesus on the cross*

At about the sixth hour (midday) our Lord's agony began. It lasted three long hours and was extremely painful. At the ninth hour (that is, three hours after midday) Jesus gave a great cry: "My God, my God, why hast thou forsaken me?" (Matt. 27. 46). The twenty-first Psalm begins with this phrase; in it David recalls the persecutions he has suffered in the past and expresses his hope of approaching victory. Our Lord, on the cross, by making his own these words inspired by the Holy Spirit, showed that they were prophetic and that they achieved their perfect fulfilment in him. Other verses of this Psalm, which were accomplished at this time, prove this clearly: "They offered him a draught of wine, mixed with gall" (Matt. 27. 34; Ps. 21. 8); they divided "his garments among them by casting lots" (Matt. 27. 35); "The chief priests, with the scribes and elders, mocked him in the same way. He saved others, they said, he cannot save himself. If he is the king of Israel, he has but to come down from the cross. . . . He trusted in God; let God, if he favours him, succour him now" (Matt. 27. 41–3; Ps. 21. 8–9).

Of all the physical sufferings connected with crucifixion thirst is probably the most acute. It was the only one of which Jesus complained and he did so precisely in order that all the prophecies made about him under the inspiration of the Holy Spirit should find their complete fulfilment. "Jesus knew well that all was achieved which the scripture demanded for its accomplishment; and he said, I am thirsty.[11] There was a jar there full of vinegar; so they filled a sponge with the vinegar and put it on a stick of hyssop, and brought it close to his mouth. Jesus drank the vinegar, and said, It is achieved. Then he bowed his head and yielded up his spirit" (John 19. 28–30; Ps. 21. 16; Ps. 68. 22). St Luke writes: "Jesus said, crying with a loud voice, Father, into thy hands I commend my spirit; and yielded up his spirit as he said it" (Luke 23. 46; Ps. 30. 6). Here again it is from the book of Psalms, whose principal author is the Holy Spirit, that our divine Saviour took this verse. Thus it was under the influence of this divine Spirit that he ended his earthly life by giving up to the Father his spirit, his soul, a breath issuing from the mouth of God.

In the Epistle of Passion Sunday and the seventh lesson of Matins on Holy Saturday, St Paul speaks of the sacrifice offered by Jesus in shedding his blood for our salvation. One of the reasons why this offering surpasses all the sacrifices of the Old Law is because Jesus, high priest of the New Law, accomplished it under the movement of the Holy Spirit who inspired all his actions: "The blood of bulls and goats . . . have power to hallow them for every purpose of outward purification; and shall not the blood of Christ, who offered himself, through the Holy Spirit, as a victim unblemished in God's sight, purify our consciences, and set them free from lifeless observances, to serve the living God?" (Heb. 9. 13–14).

In the order of Mass the second prayer preparatory to

[11] This verse may also be construed, "Jesus knew well that all was achieved, and he said, I am thirsty, in order that the scripture might be accomplished". Footnote to this verse in the Knox version quoted above.

Holy Communion gives expression to the same idea: "Lord Jesus Christ, Son of the living God, who by the Father's will and *the cooperation of the Holy Spirit* didst by thy death bring life to the world. . . ."

*Our sharing in the passion of Jesus*

On the other hand, if it was through the Holy Spirit that our Lord effected our redemption it is also through the guidance of this same Spirit of God that the Church commemorates and celebrates this mystery in order to associate the faithful with it, by exhorting them to greater generosity during the whole of Lent. She prays, speaking of the fast which mortifies our body, that our soul should "abstain from sin", *a culpa jejunet* (Saturday, 3rd week in Lent). St Leo says on this subject: "Taught by the Holy Ghost, the holy apostles ordained a strict fast to be kept upon these days; that by sharing together in the cross of Christ, we too may take our part in some way in what he did for us, as the Apostle says: 'We must share his sufferings, if we are to share his glory'."[12]

## *EASTER CYCLE: EASTER, ASCENSION AND PENTECOST*

*Eastertide*

Easter is the "solemnity of solemnities" because on it is celebrated the anniversary of our Lord's resurrection and because by this festival the Church places this mystery so to say within our reach for us to share increasingly in the new life of our risen Lord. "Christ our passover was sacrificed", says the Easter Preface, ". . . by dying he has brought our death to naught, and by rising again has restored us to life."[13] The paschal mystery has therefore a twofold aspect corresponding with the passion of Christ

[12] 4th lesson, Passion Sunday.

[13] Cf. also Rom. 4. 25.

and his resurrection. This mystery is one both of death and of life.

By his expiatory death our Lord overcame the obstacle that in his mortal humanity prevented his being wholly under the dominion of the Holy Spirit. The obstacle was sin for which the Son of God, made man and exempt from all sin, had taken upon himself the responsibility, that sin instigated by the devil when he tempted Eve and through her Adam, the punishment of which was death.

*Jesus' victory on the cross*

The Word incarnate, whose soul was temporarily separated from his body by voluntarily undergoing this punishment of death in our name and by then allowing himself to be buried in the tomb, annihilated in some sort the "old man". Confronting the "Prince of this world" he deprived him of his gain by paying to God in strict justice all our debt, that is, by offering to him in love a just expiation for our sins. Death henceforth assumes for us, as it had for Jesus, the character of a deliverance. "Christ the undefiled", runs the Easter sequence, "hath sinners to his Father reconciled. Death with life contended; combat strangely ended! Life's own Champion slain, yet lives to reign."

The drama of redemption, which during our Lord's passion on Calvary was of a tragic nature, concluded in the glorious victory of Christ over the devil. The latter, to all appearances the victor, was definitively vanquished, for the new Adam, by his complete obedience repairing Adam's disobedience, won for himself the right of conquest over mankind, redeemed at the cost of his blood. All those who in the bonds of love, the bonds of the Holy Spirit, cleave to the risen Lord, as the members to their head, will share in his victory over the powers of evil.

*The negative side of the mystery of redemption*

This deliverance from the dominion of the devil, sin and its consequences, forms the negative side of the work of salvation. The Son of God accomplished it by freeing himself through his death of what, during the whole of his earthly existence, formed an obstacle to the glorious development of the mystery of the Incarnation, for he had to endow himself with a human nature subject to suffering and death in order to accomplish this redemption. By this means, we repeat, he was able, by offering his life in sacrifice, to merit that we could deliver ourselves from whatever opposed in us the action of grace, the action of the Spirit of Christ in our souls.

*The positive side of the mystery of salvation*

The positive side and the culminating point of the paschal mystery is the complete possession by divine life of the humanity of our Lord and its springing up in our hearts. By his resurrection from the dead the Son of God possesses a humanity that is henceforth immortal for it is completely under the influence of the Holy Spirit. This humanity is essentially the same as that which hung upon the cross and was transfixed by the lance, as Jesus showed Thomas by saying to him: "Let me have thy finger; see, here are my hands. Let me have thy hand; put it into my side" (John 20. 27).

But this risen humanity has all the qualities of glorified bodies (impassibility, agility, subtlety). And so he was able to come out of the sealed tomb and appear in the Cenacle where the apostles were gathered *januis clausis*, behind "closed doors". And as they thought they were seeing a ghost and were afraid Jesus said to them: "What . . . are you dismayed? Whence come these surmises in your hearts? Look at my hands and my feet, to be assured that it is myself; touch me, and look; a spirit has not flesh and bones, as you see that I have" (Luke 24. 38–9).

The body of our crucified Lord, embalmed by Joseph of Arimathea and Nicodemus with myrrh and aloes and buried in the tomb, had therefore really risen. His humanity had taken on a quite new mode of existence. Wholly "spiritualized", by the action of the Holy Spirit, henceforward it was perfectly fitted to make all souls share in the fullness of his spiritual life. Indeed, Jesus began to exercise this power for the benefit of the apostles on the very day of his resurrection. At his first appearance in the Upper Room in Jerusalem he declared to them: "I came upon an errand from my Father, and now I am sending you out in my turn. With that he breathed on them, and said to them, Receive the Holy Spirit; when you forgive men's sins, they are forgiven, when you hold them bound, they are held bound" (John 20. 21–3). The rôle of the apostles and their successors was to associate mankind with Christ's death and resurrection. Thus, by the power of the Spirit of God who upheld Jesus in his struggle against the devil on Calvary and who breathed a new life into him after his death, souls will die to sin and live supernaturally for God. The Spirit of Christ dwelling in them will be the pledge of the resurrection of their bodies when Christ comes at the end of time. St Paul, the apostle of the risen Lord, explaining this mystery, writes: "And if the Spirit of him who raised up Jesus from the dead dwells in you, he who raised up Jesus Christ from the dead will give life to your perishable bodies too, for the sake of his Spirit who dwells in you" (Rom. 8. 11–12).

*Third phase of the drama of redemption*

Since our Lord's resurrection the drama of redemption unfolds in a new manner. The history of Christ according to the flesh has come to an end and it is that of the Church, his mystical Body, which begins. Our risen Lord, freed from the material conditions of his earthly life, leaves this world to be glorified by his Father in heaven and from on high he sends down upon his apostles and disciples the Holy Spirit whom he promised.

But before this it was necessary for them to be fully assured of the resurrection of their divine Master, for Peter to be invested, as Christ's Vicar, with the charge of supreme Pastor over the lambs and sheep of Christ's flock, and for the apostolic college—understanding in the light of the Scriptures the real meaning of the messianic times—to prepare for the coming of the Holy Spirit and the accomplishment of the mission for which Jesus Christ, "by the Holy Spirit", would furnish them with guidance: "All authority in heaven and on earth . . . has been given to me; you, therefore, must go out, making disciples of all nations, and baptizing them in the name of the Father, and of the Son, and of the Holy Ghost, teaching them to observe all the commandments which I have given you" (Matt. 28. 18–20).

St Luke, in the Acts of the Apostles, the daily reading of which is begun in the Breviary on the Monday after Low Sunday, declares:

> The first book which I wrote,[14] Theophilus, was concerned with all that Jesus set out to do and teach, until the day came when he was taken up into heaven. He then laid a charge, by the power of the Holy Spirit, on the apostles whom he had chosen. He had shewn them by many proofs that he was still alive, after his passion; throughout the course of forty days he had been appearing to them, and telling them about the kingdom of God; and now he gave them orders, as he shared a meal with them, not to leave Jerusalem, but to wait there for the fulfilment of the Father's promise. You have heard it, he said, from my own lips; John's baptism, I told you, was with water, but there is a baptism with the Holy Spirit which you are to receive, not many days from this. . . . Enough for you that the Holy Spirit will come upon you, and you will receive strength from him; you are to be my witnesses in Jerusalem and throughout Judaea, in Samaria, yes, to the ends of the earth. (Acts 1. 1–8.)

[14] That is, the Gospel according to St Luke.

*Rôle of the Holy Spirit in the Church*

The rôle to be played by the Holy Spirit in the Church and in the world was described by Jesus in his sermon after the Last Supper. The liturgy repeats this in the Gospel of some of the Sundays after Easter, on the Sunday after the Ascension and on the vigil and feast of Pentecost.

Speaking to his apostles our Lord told them: "I will ask the Father, and he will give you another to befriend you, one who is to dwell continually with you for ever. It is the truth-giving Spirit, for whom the world can find no room, because it cannot see him, cannot recognize him. But you are to recognize him; he will be continually at your side, nay, he will be in you. . . . So much converse I have held with you, still at your side. He who is to befriend you, the Holy Spirit, whom the Father will send on my account, will in his turn make everything plain, and recall to your minds everything that I have said to you" (John 14. 16–17, 25–6).

The Holy Spirit is to be sent by the Father at the request made to him by Jesus, and by means of the enlightenment of this Spirit of God the apostles and their successors will understand the full significance of the words said by Jesus and taught in the Scriptures: "When the truth-giving Spirit, who proceeds from the Father, has come to befriend you, he whom I will send to you from the Father's side, he will bear witness of what I was. And you, too, are to be my witnesses, you who from the first have been in my company" (John 15. 26–7).

It is not only in Christ's name but also through Christ that the Father is to send the Holy Spirit. This Spirit is the Spirit of both the Father and of the Son, he proceeds from both and, like them, is truth itself. His coming will bear witness to the Godhead of Jesus and to his divine mission. And of this witness the apostles, who lived with Christ and saw him after the resurrection, are to be the ambassadors throughout the world. Their witness will be the more effective since through them the Holy Spirit will cause Christians to live the life of our risen Lord himself: "It is better for you I should go away; he who is to befriend you will not come to you unless I do go, but if only I make my way there, I will send him to you. He will come, and it will be for him to prove the world wrong, about sin, and about rightness of heart, and about judging. About sin; they have not found belief in me. About rightness of heart; I am going back to my Father, and you are not to see me any more. About judging; he who rules this world has had sentence passed on him already" (John 16. 7–11).

As Christ's upholder, the Spirit of God will show by means of the witness of the apostles how great is the sin of those who, imbued with the spirit of the world, refuse to believe in Jesus and condemn him. And this Spirit will show, too, always by means of the apostles and their successors, how God will emphasize the injustice of men by glorifying Christ in heaven. As the defender of Christ the Holy Spirit will put to shame those who under the inspiration of the Prince of this world consider that their sentence is irrevocable. For through his death Jesus became the victor over Satan and, by the action of the Holy Spirit, the Church shows forth this victory of her Lord by her triumphant resistance to persecutions.

Our Lord told his apostles: "When they hand you over thus, do not consider anxiously what you are to say or how you are to say it; words will be given you when the time comes; it is not you who speak, it is the Spirit of your Father that speaks in you" (Matt. 10. 19–20). And on another occasion: "I have still much to say to you, but it is beyond your reach as yet. It will be for him, the truth-giving Spirit, when he comes, to guide you into all truth. He will not utter a message of his own; he will utter the message that has been given to him; and he will make plain to you what is still to come. And he will bring honour to me, because it is from me that he will derive what he makes plain to you" (John 16. 12–14).

Jesus, who proceeds from the Father, has revealed to the world what he has received from the Father (John 8. 26). In the same way the Spirit who proceeds from the Father and the Son leads souls to the knowledge of the divine truths that the Father revealed to his Son in begetting him and that both communicate to him whom the Scriptures call the "Spirit of the Father" and the Spirit of the Son. And St Augustine explains that he is the Spirit of the Son because he does not speak of himself but announces what he has received from the Son.[15] As indeed our Lord himself said: "And he will bring honour to me, because it is from me that he will derive what he makes plain to you" (John 16. 14).

### *The Ascension*

St Luke concludes his Gospel by the account of the Ascension and begins the Acts of the Apostles by showing that this event took place forty days after our Lord's resurrection. Forty days after the festival of Easter, therefore, the Church celebrates the feast of the Ascension. The pericope from St Mark's Gospel, sung on that day, concludes with this sentence: "And so the Lord Jesus, when he had finished speaking to them, was taken up to heaven, and is seated now at the right hand of God; and they went out and preached everywhere, the Lord aiding them, and attesting his word by the miracles that went with them" (Mark 16. 19–20). The aid given them by the Lord recalls his promise: "I will not leave you friendless; I am coming to you" (John 14. 18). And in fact he did not leave friendless those to whom in his sermon after the Last Supper he had said, "It is only for a short time that I am with you,

[15] Migne, *P.L.*, 38. 1888.

my children" (John 13. 33). After his resurrection and his return to heaven he came back to them by his Holy Spirit who is the bond of love by which all the members of the mystical Body of Christ are united to their divine Head and are, with him, children of the Father. As he had explained to them: "When that day comes, you will learn for yourselves that I am in my Father, and you are in me, and I am in you. . . . He who loves me will win my Father's love, and I too will love him, and will reveal myself to him" (John 14. 20–1).

In the Epistle read on the feast of the Ascension St Luke tells how our Lord after giving instructions to the apostles "by the power of the Holy Spirit" was "taken up into heaven". And further on in the same passage: "They saw him lifted up, and a cloud caught him away from their sight" (Acts 1, 2, 9). The body of the risen Lord, since it was no longer subjected to the laws of matter, but was a spiritual body bearing the stamp of heaven (cf. 1 Cor. 15. 44, 49), being lifted up into the sky entered the heavenly kingdom where the angels adore the Godhead. Indeed he himself had said that at the resurrection the "dead are as the angels in heaven are" (Matt. 22. 30). Placed high in heaven where he sits "at the right hand of the Father" (*Credo*) Jesus, the "King of glory" (*Te Deum*), there exercises his universal kingship: "That was why Christ died and lived again," says St Paul, "he would be Lord both of the dead and of the living" (Rom. 14. 9). "Power is given to him in heaven and on earth," explains St Jerome, "that he who before had reigned in heaven, might now reign also on earth, through the faith of them that believe" (1st lesson, Friday in Easter Week).

Wholly "Eastered", it can be said, by his return to his Father, Christ in his superterrestrial mode of existence is no longer subject to the laws of blood or race. His relations with men are sublimated and he reigns from the highest heaven not over Israel according to the flesh but according to the spirit, that is, over all those who, Jews or Gentiles, are by their faith and love children of Abraham.

*Jesus in heaven and the Church on earth ask for the sending of the Holy Spirit*

Our Lord, showing his Father his glorious wounds, the trophies of his triumph, asks for the Holy Spirit to be sent, and this he does himself on the day of Pentecost in the name of his Father: "I will ask the Father, and he will give you another to befriend you, one who is to dwell continually with you for ever" (John 14. 16). And his apostles, with Mary the Mother of Jesus with them, echoing his words on earth, "with one mind, gave themselves up to prayer". In this way they prepared for the coming of the Holy Spirit.

And it is this that the Church continues to do in her liturgical and priestly prayer which is always performed in dependence on the priesthood of Christ, "this high priest of ours . . . ministering, now, in the sanctuary" (Heb. 8. 2) in heaven. Moreover, our Lord, speaking of the efficacy of confident, persevering prayer, said on one occasion: "Why then, if you . . . know well enough how to give your children what is good for them, is not your Father much more ready to give, from heaven, his gracious Spirit to those who ask him?" (Luke 11. 13). At Vespers on the feast of the Ascension the Church makes this prayer to our Lord: "O King of glory . . . who today ascended in triumph above all the heavens! . . . Send upon us the Spirit of truth promised by the Father" (Antiphon at Magnificat, 2nd Vespers).

## *PENTECOST*

*The coming of the Holy Spirit on the new-born Church*

The feast of Pentecost commemorates for us the coming down of the Holy Spirit on our Lady, the apostles and disciples gathered together in the Cenacle. For a whole week both Missal and Breviary describe this coming, show its wonderful consequences and combine effectively, by their use of various passages both of Scripture and the Fathers read in the churches of the whole world, to keep all Christendom under the power of this same Spirit. For the mystery of Pentecost, to which the Church owes her existence, never ceases to exert its influence over all the souls who, from one generation to another and to the end of time, ensure the constant development of the mystical Body of Christ.

All the members of the visible Church, invisibly united to their divine Head in the bonds of love of the Holy Spirit, constitute a magnificent Temple wherein this Spirit of God constantly dwells. His presence is continually shown forth by the works of holiness which the Church never ceases to produce down the ages. The kingdom of God is therefore already established in this world thanks to the combined purifying (*gratia sanans*) and sanctifying (*gratia elevans*) action of the Spirit of Christ.

It is impossible to make full use here of all the treasures contained in the liturgy of Pentecost and its octave; we must confine ourselves to indicating some of them.

The Scripture readings (the *lectio continua* already referred to) appointed for the Pentecostal liturgy are taken from the Acts of the Apostles which have aptly been called "the Gospel of the Holy Spirit". "The Gospels", says St John Chrysostom, "are the story of what Christ said and did; the Acts of what the other Comforter said and did."[16]

The Epistle read at the Mass of Pentecost, a passage from the Acts of the Apostles, is an account of the triumphal coming of the Holy Spirit, "Lord and life-giver" (*Credo*): "When the day of Pentecost came round, while all the disciples were gathered together in unity of purpose,

[16] Migne, *P.G.*, 60. 21.

all at once a sound came from heaven like that of a strong wind blowing, and filled the whole house where they were sitting. Then appeared to them what seemed to be tongues of fire, which parted and came to rest on each of them; and they were all filled with the Holy Spirit, and began to speak in strange languages, as the Spirit gave utterance to each" (Acts 2. 1–4). Not only external phenomena (strong wind, tongues of fire) testified to the coming of the Spirit of God on the apostles, but also, and more especially, the effects that his presence produced among them.

An immense crowd of people belonging to different countries—St Luke mentions sixteen—hastened to the place at the noise accompanying the coming of the Spirit. "So when the noise of this went abroad, the crowd which gathered was in bewilderment; each man severally heard them speak in his own language. . . . So they were all beside themselves with perplexity, and asked one another, What can this mean? There were others who said, mockingly, They have had their fill of new wine" (Acts 2. 6–13). Peter then stood up and told them: "These men are not drunk, as you suppose; it is only the third hour of the day. This is what was foretold by the prophet Joel: In the last times, God says, I will pour out my spirit upon all mankind, and your sons and daughters will be prophets" (Acts 2. 15–18). This event, then, was the fulfilment of what the Spirit of God had inspired one of the seers of the Old Testament to foretell. And its fulfilment showed that the messianic times had come.

The apostles had themselves witnessed that Christ had really risen and they had been present at his ascension. But the coming of the Paraclete was needed to show them the Son of man in glory sitting at the right hand of the Father and the power that from above he would exercise over the earth in the Church and by the Church.

The work of redemption accomplished by Christ had

been accepted by the Father since the Holy Spirit had come to shower on the new-born Church the graces merited for her by our Saviour through his victory on the cross. Made ready by this Spirit, which is the Spirit of Jesus, the apostolic college could then undertake its mission of conquest and on the very day of Pentecost they bravely began to speak to the people and preach the Gospel. "The power of the apostles", says St Gregory, "is taken from the Holy Ghost: for they would not have dared to withstand the powers of this world, if the Holy Ghost had not confirmed them with his fortitude. We know what these doctors of the holy Church were before the coming of that Spirit, and we see how they were endowed with that fortitude, after he had descended upon them."[17] And the hymn sung at Matins on the feast of Pentecost and during its octave gives emphasis to the same ideas:

> Forthwith a tongue of fire
> Alights on every brow;
> Each breast receives the Father's light,
> The Word's enkindling glow.
>
> The Holy Ghost on all
> Is mightily outpoured;
> Who straight in divers tongues declare
> The wonders of the Lord.

The Preface for Pentecost makes us give thanks to God through Christ our Lord "who ascended above all the heavens and taking his seat at the right hand (of the Father), sent down the Holy Spirit, as he had promised, upon his adopted children. Therefore it is that the whole round world exults with overflowing joy."

*The action of the Holy Spirit in the primitive Church*

God sent his Son to proclaim to us the good news of salvation and effect our redemption and return to his

[17] 5th lesson, Common of Apostles.

Father by his bloody and triumphant sacrifice on the cross and by his glorious resurrection and entry into heaven where he was received as a victor. The Father and the Son then sent the Holy Spirit to perfect the work of Christ by the agency of the sacred hierarchy. To this end the apostles and their successors share in the powers of Jesus, prophet, priest and king.

The Man-God was invested with this threefold teaching, priestly and royal function from the very first moment of his incarnation, for then, together with the fullness of the Holy Spirit, he received this ample consecration, but he did not begin to exercise it officially until after the descent upon him of the Holy Spirit in the form of a dove at the time of his baptism in the Jordan. In the same way the Church, invested by Jesus with teaching, priestly and governing powers, did not begin their exercise until after being baptized with the Holy Spirit (cf. Acts 1. 5).

The following is what the liturgy tells us of the action of this divine Spirit in the primitive Church.

*The election of Matthias*

"Peter stood up and spoke before all the brethren. . . . Brethren, he said, there is a prophecy in scripture that must needs be fulfilled; that which the Holy Spirit made, by the lips of David, about Judas. . . . In the book of Psalms the words are written, . . . Let another take over his office. . . . They gave them lots; and the lot fell upon Matthias, and he took rank with the eleven apostles" (Acts 1. 15).

*The lame man at the Beautiful Gate*

"Peter and John were going up to the temple at the ninth hour, which is the hour of prayer, when a man was carried by who had been lame from birth. Every day he was put down at what is called the Beautiful Gate of the temple, so that he could beg alms." He asked Peter and John for alms, but Peter said to him: "Silver and gold are not mine to give, I give thee what I can. In the name of Jesus of Nazareth, rise up and walk." The man was healed immediately. But Annas and Caiphas and all those who belonged to the high-priestly race caused Peter and John to appear before them: "Peter was filled with the Holy Spirit, and said to them, Rulers of the people, elders of Israel, listen to me. . . . You crucified Jesus Christ, the Nazarene, and God raised him from the dead; it is through his name that this man stands before you restored. . . . Salvation is not to be found elsewhere" (Acts 3. 1–6; 4. 8–12).

*Ananias and Sapphira*

The first Christians in Jerusalem shared all their possessions in common. They sold their lands, brought the price obtained to the apostles and a share was given to each according to his needs.

> But there was a man called Ananias who, with his wife Sapphira, sold an estate, and kept back some of the money, with his wife's knowledge, only bringing a part of it to lay at the feet of the apostles. Whereupon Peter said, Ananias, how is it that Satan has taken possession of thy heart, bidding thee defraud the Holy Spirit by keeping back some of the money that was paid thee for the land? . . . It is God, not man, thou hast defrauded. At these words Ananias fell down and died. . . . It was about three hours later that his wife came in, knowing nothing of what had happened. . . . Peter said to her, What is this conspiracy between you, to put the Spirit of the Lord to the test. . . . And all at once she fell at his feet and died. (Acts 5. 1–10.)

Peter, filled with the Holy Spirit, who knows all things, was not deceived by this double lie. He could not allow the Holy Spirit to be tempted or put to the test to see if he would reveal this deceit to the apostles. Ananias and

Sapphira resisted the Holy Spirit and the punishment which was visited upon the guilty pair in their bodies was beneficial to the infant Church. Moreover St Augustine observes that God in his great mercy spared them the punishment of eternal death.

*St Stephen, deacon and martyr*

The apostles, desiring to devote themselves with greater freedom to the ministry of the word, chose seven deacons to come to the help of the Christian community. "So the twelve called together the general body of the disciples, and said, . . . You must find among you seven men who are well spoken of, full of the Holy Spirit and of wisdom" (Acts 6. 3–4). Among those chosen St Luke mentions Stephen in the first place and speaks of his martyrdom:

> They chose Stephen, a man who was full of faith and of the Holy Spirit. . . . And Stephen, full of grace and power, performed great miracles and signs among the people. There were those who came forward to debate with him . . . but they were no match for Stephen's wisdom, and for the Spirit which then gave utterance. . . . Stiff-necked race [Stephen concluded] your heart and ears still uncircumcised, you are for ever resisting the Holy Spirit, just as your fathers did. There was not one of the prophets they did not persecute; it was death to foretell the coming of that just man, whom you in these times have betrayed and murdered. . . . At hearing this, they were cut to the heart, and began to gnash their teeth at him. But he, full of the Holy Spirit, fastened his eyes on heaven, and saw there the glory of God, and Jesus standing at God's right hand; I see heaven opening, he said, and the Son of Man standing at the right hand of God. Then they cried aloud, and put their fingers into their ears; with one accord they fell upon him, thrust him out of the city, and stoned him. . . . He, meanwhile, was praying; Lord Jesus, he said, receive my spirit; and then, kneeling down, he cried aloud, Lord do not count this sin against them. And with that he fell asleep in the Lord. (Acts 6. 5–10; 7. 51–60.)

*Peter and John in Samaria: Simon Magus*

One of the seven deacons chosen at the same time as Stephen went to Samaria to preach the kingdom of God and the name of Jesus. His name was Philip. So great was his influence that many men and women left a certain Simon, who had misled them with sorcery, and asked for baptism. It was the privilege of the apostles, as it is still that of the bishops their successors, to give the Holy Spirit by the laying on of hands—what we know as the sacrament of confirmation. St Luke tells us this in the following passage:

> And now the apostles at Jerusalem, hearing that Samaria had received the word of God, sent Peter and John to visit them. So these two came down and prayed for them, that they might receive the Holy Spirit.... Then the apostles began to lay their hands on them, so that the Holy Spirit was given them.... Simon, seeing that the Holy Spirit was granted through the imposition of the apostles' hands, offered them money; Let me, too, he said, have such powers that when I lay my hands on anyone he will receive the Holy Spirit. Whereupon Peter said to him, Take thy wealth with thee to perdition, thou who hast told thyself that God's free gift can be bought with money. There is no share, no part for thee in these doings; thy heart is not true in the sight of God. (Acts 8. 14–22.)

For Simon to demand for himself the same power as the apostles and to liken the laying on of hands to a magical rite, the secret of which he desired to purchase for money in order to derive from it profit and renown, showed that he entirely misunderstood the work of the Holy Spirit in the souls of men. This divine power cannot be acquired for money. And in the Church, inspired by the Spirit of Pentecost, simony has always been regarded as a very serious sin.

*Philip and the Queen of Ethiopia's steward*

On the road leading from Jerusalem to Gaza an Ethiopian, a eunuch, a courtier of Candace, queen of

Ethiopia, with charge of all her wealth, "was now on his way home, driving along in his chariot and reading the prophet Isaias. The Spirit said to Philip, Go up to that chariot and keep close by it" (Acts 8. 26–9). The passage that the Ethiopian was reading foretold our Lord's passion. Philip explained it to him, and touched by grace, this Gentile asked the deacon, sent by the Holy Spirit, to baptize him. "He answered, I believe that Jesus Christ is the Son of God. So he had the chariot stopped, and both of them, Philip and the eunuch, went down into the water, and Philip baptized him there. But when they came up from the water, Philip was carried off by the spirit of the Lord, and the eunuch did not see him any longer; he went on his way rejoicing" (Acts 8. 37–9).

By making Philip and the eunuch encounter each other the Holy Spirit showed very clearly that the Church from the very beginning was to be universal in character.

*Saul's conversion*

The miraculous conversion of Paul shows also that in bringing down the great persecutor of the infant Church in order to make him into the especial apostle of the Gentiles our risen Lord was no respecter of persons. Indeed Paul was, and still remains by his Epistles which are officially read in all Churches, the especial instrument of the Holy Ghost for the spreading abroad of the kingdom of God and of his Christ throughout the whole world. This conversion is the object of the feast observed on January 25th each year. In its Epistle we read: "The Lord said to [Ananias], Rise up and go to the road called Straight Street; and enquire at the house of Judas for a man of Tarsus, named Saul. . . . This is a man I have chosen to be the instrument for bringing my name before the heathen and their rulers, and before the people of Israel too. . . . So Ananias set out; and as soon as he came into the house he laid his hands upon him, and said, Brother Saul, I have been sent by that Lord Jesus who appeared to thee on thy way as thou camest here; thou art to recover thy sight, and be filled with the Holy Spirit" (Acts 9. 11–17).

*Peter's preaching*

> Thereupon Peter began speaking. . . . Men, brothers, [the Lord] gave us a commission to preach to the people and to bear witness that he, and none other, has been chosen by God to judge the living and the dead. All the prophets bear him this testimony. . . . Before Peter had finished speaking to them thus, the Holy Spirit fell on all those who were listening to his message. The faithful who had come over with Peter, holding to the tradition of circumcision as they did, were astonished to find that the free gift of the Holy Spirit could be lavished upon the Gentiles, whom they heard speaking with tongues, and proclaiming the greatness of God. Then Peter said openly, Who will grudge us the water for baptizing these men, that have received the Holy Spirit just as we did? And he gave orders that they should be baptized in the name of the Lord Jesus Christ. (Acts 10. 34, 42–8.)

The head of the Church himself clearly shows that the salvation brought by the Messiah and comprising the gift of the Holy Spirit and baptism for the remission of sins would, as was foretold by the prophets, spread beyond the frontiers of Judaism.

*Saul and Barnabas in Cyprus*

> The Church at Antioch had as its prophets and teachers Barnabas, and Simon who was called Niger, and Lucius of Cyrene, and Manahen, foster-brother of Herod the tetrarch, and Saul. These were offering worship to God and fasting, when the Holy Spirit said, I must have Barnabas and Saul dedicated to the work to which I have called them. . . . And they, sent on their travels by the Holy Spirit . . . took ship for Cyprus. . . . And when they had been through

the whole island up to Paphos [they encountered] Sergius Paulus a man of good sense, who had sent for Barnabas and Saul and asked if he might hear the word of God. And Elymas, the magician, ... opposed them, trying to turn the governor away from the faith. Then Saul, whose other name is Paul, filled with the Holy Spirit, fastened his eyes on him, and said: Child of the devil. ... See, then, if the hand of the Lord does not fall upon thee now. (Acts 13. 1–11.)

Elymas was stricken with blindness and the governor, greatly impressed by the Lord's teaching and by what had happened, embraced the faith.

*The Council of Jerusalem*

Some believers who belonged to the party of the Pharisees came forward and declared, They [the Gentiles] must be circumcised; we must call upon them to keep the law of Moses. When the apostles and presbyters assembled to decide about this matter there was much disputing over it, until Peter rose and said to them, ... God, who can read men's hearts, has assured them of his favour by giving the Holy Spirit to them as to us. He would not make any difference between us and them; he had removed all uncleanness from their hearts when he gave them faith. How is it, then, that you would now call God in question, by putting a yoke on the necks of the disciples, such as we and our fathers have been too weak to bear? (Acts 15. 5–10.)

The apostles and priests thereupon sent delegates, among whom were Paul and Barnabas, to the Gentile converts in Antioch, Syria and Cilicia to inform them that it was the Holy Spirit's pleasure and theirs that no burden should be laid upon them save what was necessary (cf. Acts 15. 28). This passage shows that the Church was indeed under the guidance of the Holy Spirit—the "Spirit of truth" promised by Jesus and sent by him who inspired the heads of the infant Church to come to this first decision in council.

This Spirit continues to enlighten the Church, particularly in the general Councils in which the pope and the bishops issue decrees concerning dogma, morals and discipline.

*Paul at Ephesus*

On his third missionary journey St Paul went to Ephesus.

> He met some disciples there and asked them, Was the Holy Spirit given to you when you learned to believe? Why, they said, nobody even mentioned to us the existence of a Holy Spirit. What baptism, then, did you receive? Paul asked; and they said, John's baptism. So Paul told them, John baptized to bring men to repentance; but he bade the people have faith in one who was to come after him, that is, in Jesus. On hearing this, they received baptism in the name of the Lord Jesus; and when Paul laid his hands upon them, the Holy Spirit came down on them, and they spoke with tongues, and prophesied. (Acts 19. 1–6.)

*Paul leaves again for Jerusalem*

After a missionary journey in Greece St Paul took ship and set off for Jerusalem where he was eager to celebrate the feast of Pentecost. Off Ephesus he summoned the heads of the local Church and said to them: "Now, a prisoner in spirit, I am going up to Jerusalem, knowing nothing of what is to befall me there; only, as I go from city to city, the Holy Spirit assures me that at Jerusalem bondage and affliction await me. . . . Keep watch, then, over yourselves, and over God's Church, in which the Holy Spirit has made you bishops; you are to be shepherds of that flock which he won for himself at the price of his own blood" (Acts 20. 22–8).

*Paul on his way to Rome*

In Jerusalem the Apostle of the Gentiles was taken to task by the Jews who sought to put him to death. Arrested by the captain of the garrison Paul took advantage of his status as a Roman citizen. He was then taken to Caesarea where Festus, who was governor of Judaea from A.D. 60

to 62, said to him: "Hast thou appealed to Caesar? To Caesar thou shalt go" (Acts 25. 12). Taken to Rome, Paul found occasion to make contact with an influential group of Jews living in the capital of the Empire. He spoke to them of the kingdom of God, awaited by every Israelite, "trying to convince them from Moses and the prophets of what Jesus was" (Acts 28. 24). The majority of them refused to believe and Paul declared to them: "It is a true utterance of the Holy Spirit made to our fathers through the prophet Isaias: . . . The heart of this people has become dull, their ears are slow to listen, and they keep their eyes shut, so that they may never see with those eyes, or hear with those ears, or understand with that heart, and turn back to me, and win healing from me. Take notice, then, that this message of salvation has been sent by God to the Gentiles, and they, at least, will listen to it" (Acts 28. 25–8).

*St Peter's Epistles*

To the Acts of the Apostles must be added the Epistles of St Peter and of St John which bear witness to the action of the Holy Spirit. In this context the following passage is very relevant:

> Peter, an apostle of Jesus Christ, to the elect. . . . chosen in the foreknowledge of God the Father, to be sanctified by the Spirit, to give their allegiance to Jesus Christ and be sprinkled with his blood; Grace and peace be yours abundantly. . . . Salvation was the aim and quest of the prophets, and the grace of which they prophesied has been reserved for you. The Spirit of Christ was in them, making known to them the sufferings which Christ's cause brings with it, and the glory that crowns them; when was it to be, and how was the time of it to be recognized? It was revealed to them that their errand was not to their own age, it was to you. And now the angels can satisfy their eager gaze; the Holy Spirit has been sent from heaven, and your evangelists have made the whole mystery plain, to you instead. . . . Your lot will be a blessed one, if you are reproached for the name

of Christ; it means that the virtue of God's honour and glory and power, it means that his own Spirit, is resting upon you. (1 Peter 1. 1–3, 10–12; 4. 14.)

*St John's Epistles*

In his first Epistle St John insists on the necessity of discerning which are the agents of the Spirit of God and which those of the spirit of the world.

> Not all prophetic spirits, brethren, deserve your credence; you must put them to the test, to see whether they come from God. Many false prophets have made their appearance in the world. This is the test by which God's Spirit is to be recognized; every spirit which acknowledges Jesus Christ as having come to us in human flesh has God for its author; and no spirit which would disunite Jesus comes from God. . . . We belong to God, and a man must have knowledge of God if he is to listen to us; if he does not belong to God, he does not listen to us at all. That is the test by which we distinguish the true Spirit from the false spirit. . . . He alone triumphs over the world, who believes that Jesus is the Son of God. He it is, Jesus Christ, whose coming has been made known to us by water and blood; water and blood as well, not water only; and we have the Spirit's witness that Christ is the truth. . . . We have a threefold warrant on earth, the Spirit, the water and the blood, three witnesses that conspire in one. (1 John 4. 1–6; 5. 5–8.)

In St John's day the godhead of Jesus was denied by the Gnostics. This heretical sect asserted that Christ, a heavenly, spiritual and impassible being, sent from heaven by the Father, was only united to Jesus after the baptism in the Jordan (water) and left him at Calvary (blood). St John, and the Holy Spirit through his agency, declares that Jesus came "by water and blood as well, not water only". The manifestation of Jesus at his baptism (water) is inseparable from that which took place on Calvary (blood).

In addition we should bear in mind the literary form adopted by St John in his Gospel; he has been called a "great sacramentalist". "The blood and the water", writes Fr Lebreton, "seem in verse 6 to indicate Christ's baptism and passion and, at the same time, the shedding of the blood and water which issued from Jesus' side on the cross. In verse 8 the Christian sacraments of baptism and the Eucharist come to the forefront. Their witness agrees with that of the Spirit and all three tend to this same end which is to bear testimony to the incarnation of the Son of God. Here the rôle of the Spirit is therefore what Christ declared it to be after the Last Supper; he must bear witness to the Son of God."

This witness is borne in a special manner by the Church, and through her by the Holy Spirit, whenever she administers the sacraments of baptism and the Eucharist. Baptism, the sacrament of faith, and the Eucharist, the "mystery of faith", necessarily include firm belief in the resurrection of Jesus and in the real presence of our risen Lord under the species of bread and wine consecrated respectively into his body and blood.

* * *

Having shown in this chapter how the Holy Spirit was in very truth the soul of the new-born Church, we now go on to see the use made by the sacred hierarchy of the sacraments so that the Spirit of Christ may exert his influence on Christians in all the circumstances of their life.

CHAPTER III

# THE SACRAMENTAL LITURGY AND THE HOLY SPIRIT

It is principally by means of the sacraments, liturgical acts in the highest sense of the word, that the Church pours out in souls the graces of the Holy Spirit.

The sacraments, centred round the paschal mystery—three of them, baptism, confirmation, the Eucharist, were administered to the neophytes during the Easter festival—enable souls to have a share in our Lord's passion and resurrection. St Paul, speaking to the baptized and, in general, to all those who have received the sacraments of Christian initiation, writes, referring to Christ: "You, by baptism, have been united with his burial, united, too, with his resurrection, through your faith in that exercise of power by which God raised him from the dead" (Col. 2. 12). And again: "Our sins had made dead men of us, and he, in giving life to Christ, gave life to us too; . . . raised us up too, enthroned us too above the heavens, in Christ Jesus" (Ephes. 2. 6).

In order to accentuate this fundamental relationship of all the sacraments with Christ's paschal mystery this chapter devoted to them is inserted here. It comes, therefore, immediately after that dealing with the rôle played by the Holy Spirit in the mysteries of the death and resurrection of our Saviour which were closely followed by the coming of the Comforter who sanctified the infant Church.

It is as well to point out that this chapter deals only with those texts of the sacramental liturgy in which there is mention of the Holy Spirit, since other volumes of this series are concerned with the sacraments in general and in detail.[1]

In the economy of salvation the sacraments play an essential part. "Among the mystical and sacred signs instituted by our Lord Jesus Christ to be for the faithful channels of his grace," says the Council of Trent, "there is none that can be compared to the august sacrament of the Eucharist."[2] Whether it is envisaged as a sacrifice offered to God or as a sacrament given to men, the Eucharist stands at the centre of the whole sacramental system. In one way or another the six other sacraments are connected with it.

The part played by the Holy Spirit, the gift of the Father and the Son, his action through these sacred signs, is expressed in the rites themselves, and to understand this clearly we have only to refer to the liturgical texts.

## *BAPTISM*

Our Lord, speaking to Nicodemus, explained to him that to enter the kingdom of God it was necessary to be reborn to a new life, a spiritual life, infused by the Holy Ghost: "Believe me, no man can enter into the kingdom of God unless birth comes to him from water, and from the Holy Spirit. What is born by natural birth is a thing

[1] See volumes 49–55 inclusive.

[2] *On the Sacraments*, Chapter XVIII.

of nature, what is born by spiritual birth is a thing of spirit. . . . The wind breathes where it will, and thou canst hear the sound of it, but knowest nothing of the way it came or the way it goes; so it is, when a man is born by the breath of the Spirit" (John 3. 5–8). Jesus compares the entirely spiritual action of the Holy Ghost to that of the wind (*spiritus*) whose effects can be perceived without itself being seen. In the book of Genesis the wind which blew at the origin of the world is called the breath (*spiritus*) of God: "Over its waters stirred the breath of God" (Gen. 1. 2).

In his account of the coming of the Holy Spirit on the day of Pentecost St Luke says that it was accompanied by the sound of a strong wind blowing (*spiritus vehementis*) which filled the whole house where the apostles were sitting (Acts 2. 2). Thus the comparison made by our Lord between the invisible element of wind and the invisible action performed by the Holy Spirit is easy to understand.

*Baptismal water*

Water was appointed by Christ as the matter of the sacrament by which we are born to spiritual life through the infusion of the Holy Spirit. The Church, therefore, blesses the baptismal water at the time when formerly solemn baptism was administered to the catechumens, that is, during the holy night of Easter. In this ceremony there is constant mention of the Holy Spirit. The celebrant prays:

> Almighty and eternal God . . . send forth the spirit of adoption to regenerate those who are born anew of the baptismal waters, so that the work of our humble ministry may be perfected by the operation of thy power. (*1st Collect.*)
>
> O God, whose Spirit in the very first beginnings of the world did brood over the waters, giving the element of water, even in its origin, the power to sanctify. . . . May this water,

> prepared for the rebirth of men, be rendered fruitful by the secret inpouring of his divine power; may a heavenly offspring, conceived in holiness and reborn into a new creation, come forth from the stainless womb of this divine font; and may all, . . . be brought forth into one new infancy by the motherhood of grace. (*Preface.*)

After breathing three times on this water the priest continues :"(May the power of the Holy Ghost) make the whole substance of this water fruitful in regenerative power." Then, pouring chrism into the water, he adds: "Let the inpouring of the chrism of our Lord Jesus Christ and of the Holy Ghost take place in the name of the holy Trinity."

*Ceremonies of baptism*

In the baptism of adults the priest breathes three times on the face of the catechumen and says: "Go out of him, thou unclean spirit, and give place to the Holy Ghost, the Comforter." He breathes once more in the form of a cross, saying: "N., by this breath receive the Spirit of goodness and the blessing of God." (Breath is here the symbol of the Holy Spirit.)

In the baptism of infants the priest says: "I exorcize thee, unclean spirit, in the name of God the Father almighty and in the name of Jesus Christ his Son and in the power of the Holy Ghost, that thou depart from the creature of God N. whom our Lord has vouchsafed to call to his holy temple, that he may become the temple of the living God, and that the Holy Ghost may dwell in him."

Having baptized the infant or adult the priest anoints him with the chrism saying: "May almighty God, the Father of our Lord Jesus Christ, who has caused thee to be born again by water and the Holy Spirit, and granted thee remission of all thy sins, himself anoint thee with the chrism of salvation in the same Christ Jesus, our Lord."

## *CONFIRMATION*

This sacrament is pre-eminently that which confers the Holy Spirit in order to enable the baptized to confess their faith with proper courage and to defend the Church as true soldiers of Christ. Thus the bishop, with those to be confirmed kneeling before him, prays as follows: "May the Holy Spirit come down upon you and may the strength of the Most High keep you from sin." Stretching out his hands, he adds: "Almighty, everlasting God, who hast vouchsafed to regenerate these thy servants by water and the Holy Ghost . . . send forth upon them from heaven thy sevenfold Holy Spirit, the Comforter." The bishop then anoints each candidate with chrism and lays his hands upon them; he then concludes with this collect: "O God, who didst give thy Holy Spirit to thy apostles, and hast willed that through them and their successors the same gift should be delivered to all the faithful; look graciously on the service we humbly render thee; and grant that the same Spirit coming down upon those whose foreheads we have anointed with holy chrism and signed with the sign of the holy cross, may by his gracious indwelling make them a temple of his glory."

## *PENANCE*

Our Lord himself showed what is the relationship between this sacrament and the Holy Spirit. After his resurrection Jesus appeared to his apostles gathered together in Jerusalem. He breathed on them, saying: "Receive the Holy Spirit; when you forgive men's sins they are forgiven, when you hold them bound, they are held bound" (John 20. 22–3). Here, once again, breath is a symbolic gesture signifying the infusion of the Holy Spirit in the souls of the apostles. The Council of Trent points out on the subject of the sacrament of penance that, unlike baptism, it does not remit all the punishment due to sin by which the baptized Christian has banished the Holy Spirit from his heart and that in consequence the need arises for some satisfaction to be made: "Divine justice seems to require that the reconciliation should be granted in a different manner to those who, delivered from sin and the slavery of the devil after receiving the gift of the Holy Spirit, nevertheless do not fear knowingly to profane the temple of God and to sadden the Holy Spirit."[3]

## *THE EUCHARIST*

At the offertory of the Mass the priest invokes the Holy Spirit saying: "Come, thou sanctifier, almighty everlasting God, and bless these sacrificial gifts, prepared for the glory of thy holy name." The Mozarabic liturgy is even more explicit: "Come, Holy Spirit, the sanctifier." Many medieval Missals use similar terms.

It is, of course, the priesthood of Christ which is brought into operation at the altar, for it is as Christ's minister and by repeating the consecratory formulas used by him at the Last Supper that the priest re-enacts sacramentally the sacrifice of Calvary. But the Holy Spirit cooperates in this work as he cooperated in the sacrifice made by Jesus of himself on Calvary. Thus in one of the prayers before the celebrant's communion we find these words: "Lord Jesus Christ, Son of the living God, who, by the Father's will and the cooperation of the Holy Spirit, didst by thy death bring life to the world, deliver me by this most holy Body and Blood of thine from all my sins." At the moment of the consecration the action of the Holy Spirit coincides with that of our risen Lord performed by the ministry of the priest.

In the oriental liturgies a special prayer, the epiclesis,

[3] *Catechism of the Council of Trent*, Chapter 24.

invokes the intervention of the Holy Spirit. Said after the consecration, it gives expression to what has already been done and attributes it, like every sanctifying action, to the operation of him whom the ancient liturgy of St Mark calls "the Spirit, the all holy, the Lord and life-giver". This fully justifies the statement often repeated by the Greek Fathers: "Every creative act of God's comes from the Father, through the Son and is completed in the Holy Spirit."

## *THE SACRAMENT OF THE SICK*

When a priest administers this sacrament, whose proper name is the anointing of the sick, once again it is to the Holy Spirit that are attributed its beneficial effects both on soul and body. "The effect of this anointing", says the Council of Trent, "is the grace of the Holy Spirit which . . . comforts the soul of the sick person . . . and even restores health to the body when it is expedient for the salvation of the soul."[4]

In administering this sacrament the priest anoints the sick person on the eyes, ears, nostrils, lips, hands and feet with the oil of the sick and prays to our Lord as follows: "Lord God, thou didst say by the mouth of thy apostle St James: Is one of you sick? Let him send for the presbyters of the Church, and let them pray over him, anointing him with oil in the Lord's name. Prayer offered in faith will restore the sick man, and the Lord will give him relief; if he is guilty of sins they will be pardoned. Heal, then, our Redeemer, the infirmities of this sick person by the grace of the Holy Spirit."

The anointing made with oil, which is a soothing substance, and the sacramental formula which gives expression to the effects of the anointing, inform us what Christ, by

[4] *Of extreme unction*, Chapter 2.

the external ministry of his priest, and the Spirit of Christ, directly by his invisible action, perform for the benefit of the sick person. This sacrament, therefore, like all the others, is a visible sign and an efficacious grace by which we can understand what the God of love and mercy does for our benefit and his glory.

Our Lord by his death earned for us an abundant outpouring of the Holy Spirit, of the Spirit of Christ, and Christians seriously afflicted with illness owe to this the graces mentioned in the prayers said in the course of the administration of this sacrament and designated by the eloquent symbolism of the soothing, pervasive oil.

The motherly care with which the Church performs these anointings to relieve the moral and physical sufferings of her children contributes also to the efficacy of these remedies which are of both divine and ecclesiastical institution.

## *ORDERS*

Here again we mention only those formulas and rites by which the action of the Holy Spirit is brought to our notice by the Church.

### *Exorcists*

Addressing those who are to receive this minor order the bishop says to them: "By ordination as an exorcist you receive the power to lay hands on the possessed and, by this imposition of your hands, with the grace of the Holy Spirit, together with the words of the exorcism, you drive out unclean spirits from the bodies of the possessed. But in driving out the devil from the body of your brothers, take care to cast out from your own soul and body every stain and every iniquity, lest you yourselves become slaves of him from whom you deliver others. May God grant you this by his Holy Spirit."

*The subdiaconate*

With the candidates for the subdiaconate before him the bishop prays to God as follows: "May there rest upon them the Spirit of wisdom and understanding, the Spirit of counsel and strength, the Spirit of knowledge and piety, and may they be pervaded with the Spirit of fear."

*The diaconate*

The bishop stretching out his hands over the candidates for the diaconate, recites a preface. Then, interrupting it temporarily, he places his right hand on each of the ordinands, saying: "Receive the Holy Spirit that you may be strong and resist the devil and his temptations: in the name of the Lord." He then continues the preface and, with his right hand stretched out over the deacons, he says the essential formula of ordination to the diaconate: "Send on them, Lord, the Holy Spirit to strengthen them by the grace of the seven gifts so that they may faithfully perform the work of thy service." In a final collect the bishop prays to God for the deacons: "Be pleased to pour spiritual love into thy servants so that . . . they may remain worthy to belong to the order of the seven first deacons chosen by the apostles under the inspiration of the Holy Spirit with blessed Stephen as their leader and model."

*The priesthood*

Addressing the ordinands the bishop says to them: "In requiring Moses to choose for his assistants from among the people of Israel seventy men on whom he would pour forth the gifts of the Holy Spirit the Lord enjoined him thus: Choose those whom you know to be capable of being elders of the people. You will of a certainty have been prefigured by these seventy elders if, with the help of the Holy Spirit, keeping the law of the ten commandments, you give proof of wisdom and maturity by your service and your works." During the ceremony the bishop says this prayer: "Hear us, Lord our God, and pour forth on your servants here present the blessing of the Holy Spirit and the strength of the priestly grace."

In a solemn preface he says these words which constitute the essential formula of priestly ordination: "Grant, we beseech thee, almighty Father, to these thy servants the dignity of the priesthood, renew in their hearts the spirit of holiness. . . ."

While the hymn *Veni Creator Spiritus* is being sung the bishop anoints the hands of the ordinands with the holy oil, asking that "whatever they consecrate may be consecrated and sanctified". This anointing, made with the oil of the catechumens, symbolizes the graces with which the Holy Spirit imbues the souls of priests, and it is to this divine Spirit that are attributed the works of sanctification and consecration.

Before the final prayers of the Mass, which the new priests concelebrate with the bishop, a responsory is chanted with this refrain: "Receive in you the Holy Spirit, the Defender. He it is whom the Father will send you. Alleluia." Then the bishop lays his hands on each of the priests and says to them: "Receive the Holy Spirit; when you forgive men's sins they are forgiven, when you hold them bound, they are held bound." This is a repetition of what our risen Lord said long ago to his apostles gathered together in the Cenacle.

*The episcopate*

The ceremony of the consecration of a bishop begins with an examination concerning the different mysteries of faith which must be publicly professed by the bishop-elect. About the Holy Spirit the consecrating bishop asks him: "Do you believe that the Holy Spirit is fully, perfectly and truly God; that he proceeds from the Father and the Son, is their equal in essence, power, eternity and in all things?" The bishop-elect answers: "I do believe."

The essential rite conferring the episcopate is the laying-on of hands. The consecrating bishop and his two assistant bishops together lay their hands on the head of the bishop-elect, saying the sacramental formula which is absolute (whereas for deacons and priests limitations are added): "Receive the Holy Spirit." Then come the anointings with the chrism, the first on the head and the other on the hands. They are made with chrism and not with the oil of catechumens (as with priests) because the bishop enjoys the fullness of the priesthood. And chrism, which is a mixture of olive oil with balm, designates more clearly the taking possession of the soul by the Holy Spirit whose grace is a spiritual perfume for the soul. The Hebrew word *reah* (perfume, odour) is very like the word *ruah* which means spirit, breath, wind, all of which are words used of the Holy Spirit. As in the case of the other ordinations these anointings take place during the singing of the *Veni Creator*.

The solemn invocation of the Holy Spirit falls naturally into place in a ceremony in which that Spirit with his abundant gifts is given so fully to the bishop-elect. The words of the second verse *Et spiritalis unctio* were the cause of this moment being chosen for the anointing. We can also see the fullness of grace and of the Holy Spirit in this holy oil which, poured on the head, seems as if it were to impregnate the whole body of the bishop, as the continuation of the preface would appear to show: "Grant, Lord, that this anointing poured copiously upon his head, may extend to his face and run down over his whole body, that the power of thy Spirit filling him interiorly and outwardly may entirely cover him. May a constant faith, pure charity and sincere peace shine in him."

## *CONSECRATION OF THE HOLY OILS ON MAUNDY THURSDAY*

This solemn consecration brings out clearly what has just been said of those sacraments in which the Church makes use of holy oil to signify the supernatural effects that the Holy Spirit, proceeding from the Father and the Son, produces in souls.

In each diocese the bishop presides over this ceremony on Maundy Thursday in his cathedral. Assisted by seven deacons and seven subdeacons, as at a papal Mass, and surrounded by twelve priests, in memory of the twelve apostles, he celebrates pontifically the Mass of Chrism with the blessing of the Holy Oils which begins with this passage from Exodus: "Thou shalt make the oil to be used for anointing" (30. 25).

*Blessing of the oil of the sick* (*before the Paternoster*)

During this blessing the bishop asks in a prayer: "Send down from heaven thy Holy Spirit, our protector, upon this juice of the olive, which thou hast caused the green tree to bring forth for the refreshment of man's body and soul."

*Blessing of the chrism* (*after the communion*)

In a solemn preface the bishop begins by giving thanks to God for the creation of the olive tree and recalls that a dove returned to the ark with a green olive branch, a token of peace restored to the earth. This dove foreshadowed that other which, as a symbol of the Holy Spirit, came down over Jesus at the time of his baptism in the waters of the Jordan. The bishop adds:

"We entreat thee, Lord, holy Father, almighty everlasting God, to hallow this rich substance with thy blessing. Charge it with the power of the Holy Spirit, and let Christ thy Son give his own mighty aid: he whose holy name taught us to call it the chrism with which thou hast anointed priests and kings, prophets and martyrs. To all who shall be born anew of water and the Holy Spirit, may it be a saving chrism, making them heirs of eternal life and partakers in the glory of heaven."

*Blessing of the oil of catechumens* (*after the communion*)

"God . . . who strengthenest the efforts of our weak wills with the power of the Holy Spirit, we pray thee, Lord, to send forth thy blessing upon this oil. . . . When thy servants come to the threshold of the faith and are ready to be cleansed by the working of thy Holy Spirit, let this anointing help them to the salvation they are to receive in the sacrament of baptism, with its divine gift of new birth."

From this rapid examination of the different rites of the sacramental liturgy and the ceremonies connected therewith it can be seen that the action of the Holy Spirit therein is preponderant. Consequently it is also especially through the sacraments that this action is exerted, for each one of them is a channel of graces in accordance with the needs of souls in the different states and circumstances of their lives. In fact it was for this purpose that Christ instituted the sacraments and entrusted their administration to the Church. This she does with maternal care and these sacramental rites form for her the principal means of countering the wicked action of the powers of evil or of the spirit of the world by opposing to them the insuperable power of the Spirit of God.

In the hands of the Church the sacraments are principally a wonderful means for the sanctification of souls. Through them Christians are increasingly incorporated in Christ in his mystery of death to sin and of life to God under the movement of the Holy Spirit, "Lord and life-giver", who himself inspired and animated our divine Saviour.

To sum up, the liturgy is entirely centred on the paschal mystery of the death and resurrection of our Lord celebrated at the altar. There, when priests, the ministers of the one High Priest of the new Law, aided by the Holy Spirit, offer in sacrifice of praise to God and give as food to the faithful the eucharistic Christ, it is then indeed that the combined action of this divine Spirit of our risen Lord and of the Church is especially effective. We are then at the very heart of the whole sacramental system and of the yearly and daily implementation of the mystery of Redemption.

The Eucharist is the sacrament of the incorporation of Christians into the risen Christ. Assimilation of this bread of life means for us to be quickened by the Spirit who animates both our divine Head and all the members of his mystical Body. In the unity of this Spirit we can all say with St Paul: "I am alive; or rather, not I; it is Christ that lives in me" (Gal. 2. 20). And again: "The man who unites himself to the Lord becomes one spirit with him" (1 Cor. 6. 17).

In the postcommunion of the Friday after Ash Wednesday the Church puts on our lips this prayer which shows the effects of the combined action of Christ present in the Eucharist and of the Holy Spirit: "Pour into our hearts, Lord, the Spirit of thy love, so that we who have eaten our fill of one and the same heavenly bread may, through thy goodness, come to be of one mind." There is very little difference between this prayer and the postcommunion of Easter which has already been quoted, but it recalls more explicitly this thought from St Paul: "Is not the bread we break a participation in Christ's body? The one bread makes us one body, though we are many in number; the same bread is shared by all" (1 Cor. 10. 17). And on the feast of Corpus Christi the Church sings at Matins: "Let us adore Christ the King, of all the nations overlord, who gives to those who feed on him the richness of his spirit."

CHAPTER IV

# THE SEASON AFTER PENTECOST

The season after Pentecost is composed of a long series of from twenty-four to twenty-eight Sundays when the Church, having celebrated for the first half of the liturgical year (about six months) the mysteries of the life of Jesus, draws more deeply on the teaching of the divine Master (in the Gospels) so that we may live increasingly by it. She does so with the powerful assistance of the Holy Spirit and by making her own the profound teaching of St Paul (in the Epistles) on the subject of the mystical Body of Christ which is the Church.

The Gospels of this second part of the year do not mention the Holy Spirit directly or at least by name[1]; consequently in this chapter we shall examine among other things the rôle attributed by the Apostle to the Holy Spirit in the life of the Church. Obviously this can only be a partial treatment here; in addition to the Epistles of St Paul in the Missal for the season after Pentecost we shall draw on the letters of this same Apostle as they are appointed

[1] Except on one occasion: see the Gospel of the 17th Sunday after Pentecost where Jesus explains the messianic meaning of Psalm 109 whose author, he says, is "David . . . moved by the Spirit" (Matt. 22. 43).

in the Breviary from December 26th to Septuagesima Sunday. These were not referred to in connection with that liturgical season since they do not directly concern it. We shall draw also on the Epistles of the Masses of the season after Epiphany because most of them (3rd to 6th Sundays) are frequently transferred to the end of the long series of Masses of the season after Pentecost.

The Epistles of St Paul are concerned particularly with the phase of the drama of redemption which followed Pentecost. Their use in this chapter devoted to the development of the Church in the course of the centuries will help us to a better understanding in this liturgical season after Pentecost of what the Apostle reveals to us on the action of the Holy Spirit through whom the mystical Body of Christ ever grows and increases.

## *THE HOLY SPIRIT EVER ACTIVE IN THE CHURCH*

The Holy Spirit who came down on the day of Pentecost on the apostles at Jerusalem was sent both by God the Father and by his divine Son as Jesus himself had foretold to his apostles at the Last Supper. By this sending of the Holy Spirit, which continues to be realized by the work of grace in souls and by the sacraments, God the Father extends the effects of his Fatherhood to the whole Church and God the Son, gloriously risen, makes all Christians share in his divine Sonship.

All those who have been baptized "in water and the Holy Spirit" are incorporated in Christ by faith and love. By him and in him they become children of God, for he adopts them as brothers and with himself makes them the object of the Father's especial love. St Paul writes: "Those who follow the leading of God's Spirit are all God's sons" (Rom. 8. 14). St John, speaking of the incarnate Word, says: "But all those who did welcome him, he empowered to become the children of God" (John 1. 12). And in his first Epistle he writes: "See how the Father has shewn his love towards us; that we should be counted as God's sons, should be his sons" (1 John 3. 1). And again: "This is our proof that we are dwelling in him, and he in us; he has given us a share of his own Spirit . . . and where a man acknowledges that Jesus is the Son of God, God dwells in him and he in God. . . . God is love; he who dwells in love dwells in God, and God in him" (1 John 4. 13–16).

Since the Holy Spirit is that divine love which proceeds from the Father and the Son and unites them among themselves in the bonds of an infinite affection the importance of his action in the Church can easily be understood. The Father and the Son by ceaselessly communicating to us this Spirit of truth and love cause us to share in that loving knowledge that they have of each other. They also cause us to enter increasingly into their intimate life as adopted members of the divine family. This then is the mystery of Pentecost which is extended from century to century in the Church, the Christian community of the brothers of Jesus and the children of God.

This mystery, which is the especial work of the Holy Spirit, can be stated shortly as the sharing of all the faithful of Christ and of his Church in the life of the Trinity even in this world until this participation is made perfect in heaven, the "Father's house" (John 14. 2).

St Paul, converted by our risen Lord and inspired by the Spirit of God, spoke very clearly of this mystery in his Epistles. We can now examine, in the extracts appearing in the liturgy, the extent to which the Apostle attributes to the Holy Spirit the unity and the universality of the Church of Christ, the great family which the divine Spirit vivifies and causes to live even here below in the society of the Father and the Son.

## *THE MYSTERY OF CHRIST AND THE CHURCH*

On several occasions St Paul speaks of a "mystery", or something hidden, which our risen Lord and the Holy Spirit disclosed to him and which he in turn is charged to reveal to the Gentiles. This "mystery", present from all eternity in the mind of divine Wisdom, he calls the "mystery of God", the "mystery of Christ", the "mystery of the Gospel" and the "mystery of faith". He makes it concrete in Christ who died and rose again to ensure salvation and eternal life to all men without exception: "Christ died for us all, so that being alive should no longer mean living with our own life, but with his life who died for us and has risen again" (2 Cor. 5. 15).

This mystery, then, encompasses all races and all peoples so that Jews and Gentiles are called to form part of the Church founded by Jesus and to profit by the graces and gifts of the Holy Spirit merited for them by our Saviour. It is this that we termed the mystery of Pentecost since that was the moment at which it began to be carried into effect.

Among the metaphors used by the Apostle to explain this mystery of the union of all Christians throughout the whole world we find the "Kingdom of God", the "Temple of God", the "House of God" which is the "Church of the living God", the "Kingdom of Christ" and so on. He uses particularly the metaphor of the Church as the mystical Body of Christ and in this connection says: "A man's body is all one, though it has a number of different organs; and all this multitude of organs goes to make up one body; so it is with Christ. We too, all of us, have been baptized into a single body by the power of a single Spirit, Jews and Greeks, slaves and free men alike; we have all been given drink at a single source, the one Spirit" (1 Cor. 12. 13–14).

This mystery of God, of Christ, of his Church was

revealed to the Apostle when our risen Lord appeared to him and converted him on the road to Damascus. The Holy Spirit also revealed this mystery to Paul on different occasions for he had many visions.[2] This is what St Paul, who understood so well the action of the Spirit of God in the Church and in the soul of each of the faithful, said of this mystery:

> When I came to you and preached Christ's message to you, I did so without any high pretensions to eloquence, or to philosophy. I had no thought of bringing you any other knowledge than that of Jesus Christ, and of him as crucified. It was with distrust of myself, full of anxious fear, that I approached you.... What we make known is the wisdom of God, his secret, kept hidden till now; so, before the ages, God had decreed, reserving glory for us. (None of the rulers of this world could read his secret, or they would not have crucified him to whom all glory belongs.)... To us, then, God has made a revelation of it through his Spirit; there is no depth in God's nature so deep that the Spirit cannot find it out.... So no one else can know God's thoughts, but the Spirit of God. And what we have received is no spirit of worldly wisdom; it is the Spirit that comes from God, to make us understand God's gifts to us; gifts which we make known, not in such words as human wisdom teaches, but in words taught us by the Spirit, matching what is spiritual with what is spiritual. (1 Cor. 2. 1–13.)

In his first letter to the Thessalonians St Paul writes in the same strain: "Brethren, God loves you, and we are sure that he has made choice of you. Our preaching to you did not depend on mere argument; power was there, and the influence of the Holy Spirit, and an effect of full conviction. . . . And on your side you followed our example, the Lord's example. There was great persecution, and yet you welcomed our message, rejoicing in the Holy Spirit;

[2] Cf. Epistle, January 25th (Acts 9. 4–5) and Epistle, June 30th (Gal. 1. 11–12).

and now you have become a model to all the believers throughout Macedonia and Achaia" (1 Thess. 1. 4–7).

In his first letter to Timothy, the Apostle emphasizes the universality of the Church, for the mystery of Christ, the object of Christian faith and devotion, is preached throughout the whole world. He bases his argument on the quotation of a small part of a liturgical hymn probably used at the meetings for worship of the first Christians. It possesses a marked rhythm with the phrases in pairs referring alternately to what happens in heaven and what on earth. The incarnation is mentioned together with the resurrection in which our Lord's humanity was fully spiritualized by the Holy Ghost, the ascension at which the angels were present to celebrate the triumph of Christ glorified in heaven and the preaching of the Gospel to arouse faith in these mysteries throughout the world: "So much I tell thee by letter . . . so that, if I am slow in coming, thou mayest be in no doubt over the conduct that is expected of thee in God's household. By that I mean the Church of the living God, the pillar and foundation upon which the truth rests. No question of it, it is a great mystery we worship.

Revelation made in human nature,
justification won in the realm of the Spirit;
a vision seen by angels,
a mystery preached to the Gentiles;
Christ in this world, accepted by faith,
Christ, on high, taken up into glory."

(1 Tim. 3. 14–16.)

## *THE BLESSINGS PROMISED TO ABRAHAM*

To understand the full implications of the blessings promised by God to Abraham there must be discerned in them the mystery of Christ and of the Church to which they look forward when they are interpreted in the light of the revelation made by Jesus, the Son of God, and spread abroad by the apostles under the impulsion of the Holy Spirit.

It must be borne in mind, also, that the promises were made to Abraham long before the promulgation of the Law of Moses which, far from superseding them, on the contrary itself gave way, in those parts in which it was provisional or imperfect, before the Law of the Gospel and the action of our risen Lord and of the Holy Spirit in the new people of God which is the Church.

Now the Jews interpreted the promises made to Abraham and the prescriptions of the Law in a sense in which the letter only too often prevailed over the spirit. In addition, they claimed for themselves alone, as faithful observers of the Law and as children of Abraham by descent, the blessings promised by God to this Patriarch. And the Jewish party among the first Christians required the Gentiles to observe certain prescriptions of the Mosaic Law (circumcision, for example) if they were to benefit from these promises, because they were made to Abraham and his people.

In his letters, especially those to the Romans and to the Galatians, but also to the Corinthians, Ephesians and Colossians, St Paul makes the whole matter plain, basing his argument on texts inspired by the Holy Spirit. To the Christians at Rome he writes "(The Gospel) is an instrument of God's power, that brings salvation to all who believe in it, Jew first and then Greek. It reveals God's way of justifying us, faith first and last; as the scripture says, It is faith that brings life to the just man" (Rom. 1. 16–17; Hab. 2. 4). And again: "What does scripture tell us? Abraham put his faith in God, and it was reckoned virtue in him. . . . It was not through obedience to the law, but through faith justifying them, that Abraham and his posterity were promised the inheritance of the world" (Rom. 4. 3, 13; Gen. 18. 18; 22. 17–18).

The Apostle also wrote to the Galatians: "Remember how Abraham put his faith in God, and it was reckoned virtue in him. You must recognize, then, that Abraham's real children are the children of his faith. There is a passage in scripture which, long beforehand, brings to Abraham the good news, Through thee all the nations shall be blessed; and that passage looks forward to God's justification of the Gentiles by faith" (Gal. 3. 6–9; Gen. 18. 18; 12. 3).

Nevertheless, it is through Christ that these blessings of a spiritual nature have been merited and are shared out among believers. This is why St Paul goes on to speak of the death of Jesus on the cross which brought to an end the Law of Moses as the means of salvation. This Law cursed him who was hung from a gibbet, and our divine Saviour, in the name of all sinners, voluntarily took this curse on himself, thus obtaining for them the messianic blessings promised to Abraham under the figure of temporal goods (the Promised Land, etc.). "From this curse invoked by the law Christ has ransomed us, by himself becoming, for our sakes, an accursed thing; we read that, There is a curse on the man who hangs on a gibbet. Thus, in Christ Jesus, the blessing of Abraham was to be imparted to the Gentiles, so that we, through faith, might receive the promised gift of the Spirit" (Gal. 3. 13–14).

As the Galatians were allowing themselves to be indoctrinated by the Jewish party the Apostle enjoined caution on them:

> Senseless Galatians, who is it that has cast a spell on you, that you should refuse your loyalty to the truth, you, before whom Jesus Christ has been exposed to view on his cross? Let me be content with asking you one question. Was it from observance of the law that the Spirit came to you, or from obeying the call of faith? Are you so far out of your right senses? You dedicated your first beginnings to the spirit; and can you now find your completion in outward

> things? . . . When God lavishes his Spirit on you and enables you to perform miracles, what is the reason for it? Your observance of the law, or your obedience to the call of faith? (Gal. 3. 1–5.)

Only those who are united to Christ by faith are in a position to profit by the inheritance promised to Abraham: so was it declared by the Holy Spirit in the Scriptures: "The promises you know of were made to Abraham and his offspring; (it does not, by the way, say, To thy descendants, as if it meant a number of people; it says, To thy offspring, in the singular, meaning Christ)" (Gal. 3. 16).

Adherence to Jesus, our risen Lord, by a living faith, full of confidence and love, means the assurance of salvation by drawing on the Holy Spirit at his source and by placing oneself completely under his entirely spiritual dominion: "Now you have been washed clean, now you have been sanctified, now you have been justified in the name of the Lord Jesus, by the Spirit of the God we serve" (1 Cor. 6. 11). And again: "You are an open letter from Christ, promulgated through us; a message written not in ink, but in the Spirit of the living God, with human hearts, instead of stone, to carry it" (2 Cor. 3. 3).

The position of the Gentiles is quite different from what it formerly was. By becoming Christ's followers and children of the Church by baptism in "water and the Spirit" they have absolute right of entry to the house of God and its privileges are theirs: "You are no longer exiles, then, or aliens; the saints are your fellow citizens, you belong to God's household. Apostles and prophets are the foundation on which you were built, and the chief cornerstone of it is Jesus Christ himself. In him the whole fabric is bound together, as it grows into a temple, dedicated to the Lord; in him you too are being built in with the rest, so that God may find in you a dwelling-place for his Spirit" (Ephes. 2. 19–22).

In this Temple of living stones (cf. postcommunion, Mass for dedication of a church) in which the Spirit dwells (1 Cor. 3. 16) the prayer of all Christians is to go up to God: "You have received . . . the spirit of adoption, which makes us cry out, Abba, Father," explains St Paul (Rom. 8. 15). Elsewhere he says: "Never cease praying. Give thanks upon all occasions; this is what God expects of you all in Christ Jesus. Do not stifle the utterances of the Spirit" (1 Thess. 5. 16–18).

## *FRATERNAL CHARITY*

Jesus laid great emphasis on the love that we should have not only for God but also for our neighbour. In her official prayer the Church continually reminds us of this teaching of our Lord's. We have but to read the Gospels of the fifth, twelfth and seventeenth Sundays after Pentecost to see the truth of this statement. In the last-mentioned our divine Master declares that the greatest commandment of the Law is: "Thou shalt love the Lord thy God with thy whole heart and thy whole soul and thy whole mind. This is the greatest of the commandments and the first. And the second, its like, is this, Thou shalt love thy neighbour as thyself. On these two commandments, all the law and the prophets depend" (Matt. 22. 37–40).

Far from abrogating these two fundamental points of the Law of Moses the Law of the Gospel ensures their more perfect performance. This is shown clearly by the parable of the Good Samaritan and the command to be at peace with our neighbour if we wish God to accept the sacrifice which we offer to him on the altar. The extracts from the first Epistle of St John (read on the first and second Sundays after Pentecost) bring out clearly the need to love our neighbour for our love of God to be sincere. Once again readers are referred to the Missal to receive this teaching from the mouth of the evangelist of whom the Church tells us (in the Mass for his feast day, December 27th): "the Lord moved him to speech before the assembled people, filling him with the spirit of wisdom and discernment" (Introit: Ecclus. 15. 5).

St Paul is no less explicit and he shows the preponderant rôle played by the Holy Spirit in the exercise of the virtue of charity which must be the characteristic of the members of the mystical Body of Christ:

> All our hope of justification lies in the spirit; it rests on our faith; once we are in Christ, circumcision means nothing, and the want of it means nothing; the faith that finds its expression in love is all that matters. . . . You must be servants still, serving one another in a spirit of charity. After all, the whole of the law is summed up in one phrase, Thou shalt love thy neighbour as thyself. . . . Let me say this; learn to live and move in the spirit. . . . The spirit yields a harvest of love, joy, peace, patience, kindness, generosity, forbearance, gentleness, faith, courtesy, temperateness, purity. (Gal. 5. 5–6, 13–16 and 22–3.)

Writing to the Colossians St Paul tells them: "Your teacher was Epaphras, for us, a well-loved fellow bondsman, and for you a loyal minister of Jesus Christ; and it is he who has told us of this love which you cherish in the Spirit" (Col. 1. 7). And to the Corinthians he declares: "As God's ministers, we must do everything to make ourselves acceptable . . . we have to rely on the Holy Spirit, on unaffected love, on the truth of our message, on the power of God" (2 Cor. 6. 4–7).

## *HOLINESS IN THE CHURCH*

St Paul often encourages the Churches to which he sends his letters to practise virtue and to avoid the excesses habitual with the Gentiles who are not under the sanctifying influence of the Holy Spirit of God. Thus he writes to the Thessalonians: "What God asks of you is that you should sanctify yourselves and keep clear of fornication. . . . The life to which God has called us is not one of incontinence, it is a life of holiness, and to despise it is to despise, not man, but God, the God who has implanted his Holy Spirit in us" (1 Thess. 4. 2–8; and cf. Gal. 5. 24–5 and Ephes. 3. 16–19). St Paul tells the Ephesians, "May you be filled with all the completion God has to give" (3. 19). Now this completion of God, this fullness in men's souls, is derived from the Holy Spirit, the "Power of the Most High" who unites them to Christ by arousing in them faith and love. They are thus united in great measure to the life of their divine Head in whom resides the fullness of grace. Our Lord penetrates them with the strength of his Spirit which is also that of his Father and they are thereby sanctified and protected against their enemies. "The Spirit of the Lord fills the whole earth," sings the Church every year at Pentecost in the introit, "the whole frame of created things recognizes the accents of his voice. Let God bestir himself and rout his enemies" (Wisdom 1. 7; Ps. 67. 2). The Holy Ghost the Comforter never forsakes the Church. And so we see in the Proper of Saints a continual procession of apostles, martyrs, confessors, virgins and all the holy men and women whom, from century to century, the Holy Spirit, in very various ways and according to the needs of the Church, has enriched with his graces, gifts, fruits and charismata.

A volume twice as long as the present one would be needed to bring out this point clearly. Here we must be content with applying to them what St Paul says on the subject of the charismata enjoyed by the infant Church:

> There are different kinds of gifts, though it is the same Spirit who gives them. . . . The revelation of the Spirit is imparted to each, to make the best advantage of it. One learns to speak with wisdom, by the power of the Spirit;

another to speak with knowledge, with the same Spirit for his rule; one, through the same Spirit, is given faith; another, through the same Spirit, powers of healing; one can perform miracles, one can prophesy, another can test the spirit of the prophets; one can speak in different tongues, another can interpret the tongues; but all this is the work of one and the same Spirit, who distributes his gifts as he will to each severally. (1 Cor. 12. 4–11.)

To this may be added three quotations from the Breviary. The first two concern our Lady: "Blessed Mary, Mother of God, ever a virgin, temple of the Lord, sanctuary of the Holy Ghost, as none other thou alone hast pleased our Lord Jesus Christ: pray for the people, intercede for the clergy, pray for women vowed to God" (Antiphon to *Benedictus*, Office of our Lady on Saturday). The sermon of St Jerome, read at the second nocturn of Matins on the feast of the Immaculate Conception, brings out the same point very clearly:

The nature and the greatness of the glorious and blessed Mary ever Virgin were revealed by God in the message of the angel who said: "Hail, thou who art full of grace; the Lord is with thee; blessed art thou among women." It was fitting that the Virgin should be endowed with such gifts as to be full of grace.... Showered with the gifts of the Holy Spirit she shows in all things the simplicity of a dove because all that is accomplished in her is purity and simplicity, all is truth and grace, all is mercy and justice, that justice which comes from heaven; she is immaculate because there is in her no stain.

The third extract is from a homily of St Robert Bellarmine on the doctors of the Church; it is read on May 13th, the feast day of this saint.

Consider the apostles. What could be better or more sublime than the apostles' way of life? Next, consider those holy men whom we call Fathers and doctors, those most shining lights which God has willed should shine in the

> firmament of the Church, that all the darkness of heresy might be dispersed, such as Irenaeus, Cyprian, Hilary, Athanasius, Basil, the two Gregories, Ambrose, Jerome, Augustine, Chrysostom, and Cyril.... How the manifold working of the Holy Spirit, who dwelt in their hearts, reveals itself in their pages! ... The writings of the saints breathe religion, chastity, integrity, and charity.... Since the apostles, holy Church has thriven by such planters, waterers, builders, shepherds, and nurses.

The Holy Spirit, the soul of the Church, never forsakes her therefore, and ensures her continuing supernatural vitality.

## *THE FINAL APOTHEOSIS*

The first and last Sunday of the liturgical year, that is, the first Sunday of Advent and the twenty-fourth Sunday after Pentecost, have as their Gospel the prophecy of the second coming of our Saviour. And every day the Missal and Breviary, in one way or another, allude to eternal life, that is, to the definitive and perfect union of the elect with God in heaven. This is the ultimate purpose of every truly Christian life.

Thus the liturgy places before us considerations concerning our last end. We are travellers journeying towards the heavenly fatherland. The people of God, set free from the captivity of Egypt or Babylon, yearned only to possess the Promised Land and to come to the holy city of Jerusalem. In the same way, the Christian people, delivered by Christ from the captivity of sin, on a final analysis, aspires only to realize the paschal mystery of its divine Head. It was for our benefit that Jesus went from this world to his Father in order to prepare a place for us in heaven. He told his apostles: "And though I do go away, to prepare you a home, I am coming back; and then I will take you to myself, so that you too may be where I am" (John 14. 3).

Once again it is the office of the Holy Spirit to sustain Christians in this hope, and for this purpose the Father, through his Son, showers them with the graces of the Spirit of adoption who ensures for them the heavenly patrimony as the children of God and the brothers of Christ: "In accordance with his own merciful design [God] saved us, with the cleansing power which gives us new birth and restores our nature through the Holy Spirit, shed on us in abundant measure through our Saviour, Jesus Christ. So, justified by his grace, we were to become heirs, with the hope of eternal life set before us, in Christ Jesus our Lord" (Titus 3. 5–7). And St John in the Apocalypse says: "I heard a voice from heaven telling me: Write thus: Blessed are the dead who die in the Lord. Yes, for ever henceforward, the Spirit says; they are to have rest from their labours; but the deeds they did in life go with them now" (Apoc. 14. 13).

## CHAPTER V

# DEVOTION TO THE HOLY SPIRIT IN THE LITURGY

### *IN THE UNITY OF THE HOLY SPIRIT*

In conclusion we can examine the place given to the Holy Spirit by the Church in the formulas of her official prayer, the liturgical worship that she offers to this third person of the Blessed Trinity and the favours that she expects from him.

At first sight it may seem astonishing that no collect, secret or postcommunion of the Roman Missal is addressed directly to the Holy Spirit. Even on the feast of Pentecost, its vigil, during the octave or in the votive Mass of the Holy Spirit, as well as in the prayers in honour of the Holy Spirit (*Deus qui corda* and *Deus, cui omne cor patet*), it is God the Father who is addressed through our Lord Jesus Christ, his Son, to obtain the help, the illumination and the graces of the divine Comforter. And these prayers conclude usually as follows: "Through our Lord Jesus Christ, thy Son, who is God, living and reigning with thee, in the unity of the (same) Holy Spirit, for ever and ever."

The Church, taking her stand on the Gospels and Tradition, teaches that in God, the one infinitely perfect being, there are three distinct Persons who are called the Father, the Son and the Holy Spirit. The Father possesses the Godhead of himself (*a se*). The Son possesses it because he receives it in all its fullness from his Father (*ab alio*). The Holy Spirit possesses it also because the Father and the Son give it to him in its entirety (*ab utroque*).

The one divine nature is thus possessed by three Persons really distinct from each other. This is the mystery of the Blessed Trinity. It was revealed to us by our Lord and the Church gives expression to it in her liturgical prayer.

In the words for the sign of the cross, in the *Gloria* and the *Credo*, in the collects and in the great eucharistic prayer of the Canon, in the other ceremonies of the sacramental liturgy (baptism, confirmation, penance, etc.), in the *Gloria Patri* which concludes the Psalms in the divine Office, in the blessings before the lessons and in the final *Te Deum* at Matins the three divine Persons are named in the order of their original differentiation which we have just mentioned.

Since the Father is the principle of the Trinity omnipotence is attributed to him (*Credo*). He is named the first. To the Son, begotten of the Father by way of knowledge, is attributed Truth and Wisdom. He is named after the Father. The Holy Spirit, proceeding from the Father and the Son, is called "the power of the most High" (Luke 1. 35) and "the truth-giving Spirit" (John 14. 17). He is named third. There is a special reason for calling him the "Spirit of love" for he is in person the bond of love uniting the Father and the Son.

On the other hand, it is by reason of their dependence of origin that the Son was sent into this world by the Father, as is celebrated by the Church at Christmas, and that the Holy Spirit was then sent by the Father and the Son, as the feast of Pentecost, celebrated after the Ascension, shows very clearly.

The whole liturgical cycle by its arrangement and the content of its formulas forms a reflection as in a mirror of the life of the Trinity. Its purpose is to enable us to share in this life. And thus the three divine Persons, possessing the one and the same nature, for there are not three Gods, work together to effect our salvation and sanctification, doing so in accordance with that which characterizes them as Father, as Son and as Holy Spirit. All the actions of God in us are trinitarian. "Everything", says St Cyril of Alexandria, "is done by the Father through the Son in the Holy Ghost."[1]

Between the Father and the Son there is unity of love in the Spirit. Both Father and Son, by giving us all this Spirit of love, from which they are inseparable, dwell in our souls. They thus enable us to share by grace, of which the Holy Spirit is the agent, in that divine love which unites them. As a result, the Spirit of God, sent by the Father and the Son, draws us to the Father and the Son and causes us to live closely united to them by inflaming our hearts with love for them. We are really united to the Father and the Son in the unity of the Holy Spirit who is their bond of love and our bond too with them. In the Gospel for the feast of Pentecost our Lord says: "If a man has any love for me, he will be true to my word; and then he will win my Father's love, and we will both come to him, and make our continual abode with him" (John 14. 23).

Even as the Son, receiving all things from his Father, never ceased here below to refer all things to him, in the same way the Holy Spirit, receiving all from the Father and the Son, never ceases to bear witness to them and to be our indispensable link with them. And it is in this way that the Church presents him to us in her prayer.

## *PRAYERS ADDRESSED TO THE HOLY SPIRIT*

Since the Holy Spirit is a divine Person, equal in all things to the two others, the Church addresses him directly

[1] Migne, *P.G.*, 76. 17.2.

in prayer and honours the three Persons of the Blessed Trinity with the same worship.

The solemn profession of faith, the *Credo* of the Mass, declares: "I believe too in the Holy Spirit, Lord and life-giver, who proceeds from the Father and the Son; who together with the Father and the Son is adored and glorified."

At the second Alleluia of the Mass of Pentecost and in the first verse of the hymn at Vespers the whole body of Christians, kneeling, addresses this prayer to the Holy Spirit :"Come, Holy Spirit, fill the hearts of thy faithful and kindle in them the fire of thy love" (*Veni, Sancte Spiritus*).

Come, Holy Ghost, Creator, come
From thy bright heavenly throne,
Come, take possession of our souls,
And make them all thy own.

(*Veni, Creator Spiritus*)

Every day all priests and religious bound to the recitation of the Breviary say this hymn at Terce (the hour at which the Holy Spirit came down upon the apostles gathered together in the Cenacle).

O Holy Spirit, thou who art
One with the Father and the Son,
We beg thee at this hour impart
Thy grace to each and every one.

Let lips, tongue, mind and all our might
Combine thy praises to proclaim,
May fire of love burn ever bright,
Enkindling others with its flame.

O loving Father, hear our cry,
And thou, the Father's only Son,
With whom the Spirit reigns on high,
Eternal, equal, Three in one. Amen.

In the sequence for Pentecost the Church turns directly to the Holy Spirit:

Holy Spirit, Lord of light,
From the clear celestial height,
Thy pure beaming radiance give.

The *Veni Sanctificator* of the offertory of the Mass is probably a direct appeal to the Holy Spirit. All the doxologies directly honour the three Persons of the Blessed Trinity; thus that of the hymn for Vespers on the feast of Corpus Christi, which is also sung at Benediction of the Blessed Sacrament, runs:

Unto God, divine Begetter,
With his sole begotten Son,
Glory, strength and benediction,
Laud and honour e'er be done;
Equal praise to God the Spirit
Who proceeds from both as one. Amen.

There is also the verse added on some occasions to the *Te Deum*: "Let us bless the Father, the Son and the Holy Spirit." The Church, as has already been mentioned, so to say baptizes each Psalm by concluding it with the *Gloria Patri*: "Glory be to the Father and to the Son and to the Holy Ghost." The preface of the Blessed Trinity states that it is our duty to give thanks everywhere and always to God the Father who with his only Son and the Holy Spirit is one God. It adds: "In acknowledging the true, eternal Godhead, we adore in it each several Person, and yet a unity of essence, and a co-equal majesty."

## *GRACES ASKED OF THE HOLY SPIRIT OR GRANTED BY HIM*

These petitions and graces are too numerous for them to be enumerated here. We mention merely certain prayers which show us the effects of the Holy Spirit in the souls of men.

Heal our wounds, our strength renew;
On our dryness pour thy dew;
Wash the stains of guilt away:
. . .
Thou, on us who evermore
Thee confess and thee adore,
With thy sevenfold gifts descend.

(*Veni, Sancte Spiritus*)

Far from us drive our deadly foe;
True peace unto us bring;
And through all perils lead us safe
Beneath thy sacred wing.

Through thee may we the Father know,
Through thee th'eternal Son,
And thee, the Spirit of them both,
Thrice-blessed Three in One.

(*Veni, Creator Spiritus*)

"May the Holy Spirit heal our souls with the divine sacrament . . . for he is himself the remission of all sins" (Postcommunion, Whit Tuesday). "May the Holy Spirit deign to come and dwell in us, so making us the temple of his glory" (collect, Whit Wednesday). "May the Holy Spirit inflame us with that fire which our Lord Jesus Christ sent down to earth, desiring that it should be kindled into a burning flame" (collect, Ember Saturday of Pentecost). "May the Comforter who proceeds from thee bring light into our minds . . . and guide us to all truth, as thy Son promised" (collect, Whit Wednesday). In brief, the Holy Spirit effects in the world of souls a new creation: "Send forth thy Spirit, and there will be fresh creation; thou wilt repeople the earth" (1st Alleluia, Whit Sunday).

The liturgy, therefore, is a school in which, under the guidance of the Church, can be learned, among other things, the rôle played by the Holy Spirit in the great drama of redemption, what we all owe to him and how we should honour and invoke him.

# CONCLUSION

In the first chapter we endeavoured to state, using a definition that is both descriptive and explanatory, what are the essential elements of the official worship of the Church. This was a necessary preliminary to describing and explaining as clearly as possible what the liturgy tells us of the Holy Spirit and of the rôle that he plays in it in order to ensure, through the priestly ministry of the sacred hierarchy, the glory of God and the sanctification of souls.

Then, following the course of the liturgical year, we showed how the different phases of the drama of redemption are employed and made present so that, under the guidance of the Holy Spirit and of the Church, all Christians may be yearly associated with them more closely.

By thus setting out the main features of a theology and spirituality of the liturgy, of which the Spirit of love is the life-giving power, we hope to have proved, at least summarily, that active participation in the sacred mysteries and the prayer of the Church is "the primary and indispensable source of the true Christian Spirit" (Pius X and Pius XI).

The liturgy, the supreme means of a fruitful and dynamic pastoral method, furnishes to the Church, by placing her under the inspiration of the Spirit of God, the most powerful arms against the enemies of God. It also provides for Christians, by the power of the same Spirit and under the guidance of the Church, the most efficacious means of living in ever closer union with Christ and with the Father. "Eternal life", said our divine Master, "is knowing thee, who art the only true God, and Jesus Christ whom thou hast sent" (John 17. 3). And St John writes: "It is as eye-witnesses that we give you news of that life, that eternal life, which ever abode with the Father and has dawned, now, on us. This message about what we have seen and heard we pass on to you, so that you too may share in our fellowship. What is it, this fellowship of ours? Fellowship with the Father, and with his Son Jesus Christ" (1 John 1. 2–3).

It is by the exercise of the powers of ministry and *magisterium* that the sacred hierarchy effects this union of all the faithful with the life of the Trinity. Every Sunday in the churches of the whole world the reading of the sacred Scriptures, divinely inspired by the Spirit of God, and the recitation or singing of the formulas of the official prayer of the Church, sustains this supernatural life.

To this liturgy of the word is added that of the eucharistic action, giving glory to God and supernatural graces to all the baptized. The holy sacrifice of the Mass, the renewal of the Last Supper and the efficacious sign of Calvary, places within our grasp the graces of the Holy Spirit which Jesus merited for us on the cross.

It is therefore by taking part in this sacrifice and by communicating at it sacramentally that Christian souls strengthen the bonds of faith, hope and love which unite them with their divine Head. And he, with ever greater bounty, fills them with his life-giving Spirit. So is fulfilled the prayer made by Jesus to his Father after he had instituted this sacred meal: "That they may be all one; that they too may be one in us, as thou, Father, art in me, and I in thee; so that the world may come to believe that it is thou who hast sent me" (John 17. 22–3).

With the love of the Father for his Son, a love which extends to the humanity of Jesus and to his mystical Body, corresponds the love of the Word and of his Church for the Father. It is a fatherly love on the one side and a filial love on the other and its centre is the Holy Spirit.

This union in love will achieve its consummation in heaven. Eucharistic union is its prelude here on earth. It prepares souls for what the Apocalypse calls the wedding feast of the Lamb with the Church his bride. "Let us rejoice and triumph and give him the praise. . . His bride has clothed herself in readiness for it. . . . And now the angel said to me, . . . blessed are those who are bidden to the Lamb's wedding-feast" (Apoc. 19. 7, 9). "The Spirit and my bride bid me come. Let everyone who hears this read out say, Come. . . . Be it so, then; come, Lord Jesus" (Apoc. 22. 17, 20). With this appeal, which the Spirit of Christ has inspired in his Church, the last book of the Scriptures concludes. St John adds this greeting: "May the grace of our Lord Jesus Christ be with you all" (Apoc. 22. 21).

# SELECT BIBLIOGRAPHY

(An asterisk denotes works by non-Catholics)

*In this series:*

Daniel-Rops: *What is the Bible?* Bernard Piault: *What is the Trinity?* François Amiot: *History of the Mass.*

BEAUDUIN, Dom Lambert: *Liturgy, the Life of the Church,* Collegeville, Minn., The Liturgical Press, 1926.

CABROL, Dom Fernand: *Liturgical Prayer: Its History and Spirit,* London, Burns Oates, 1932, and Westminster, Md, Newman Press, 1950.

GARDEIL, Ambroise: *The Holy Spirit in Christian Life,* London and St Louis, Mo, Herder, 1953.

GUARDINI, Romano: *Sacred Signs,* London and New York, Sheed and Ward, 1931: *Spirit of the Liturgy,* London and New York, Sheed and Ward, 1935.

LEFEBVRE, Dom Gaspar: *Catholic Liturgy: Its Fundamental Principles,* London, Sands, and St Louis, Mo, Herder, 1954.

LUBAC, Henri de, S.J.: *Splendour of the Church,* London and New York, Sheed and Ward, 1956.

PUNIET, Dom Pierre de: *The Roman Pontifical,* London and New York, Longmans, 1932.

SCROGGIE, W. Graham, D.D.: *The Unfolding Drama of Redemption,* two Volumes, London, Pickering and Inglis, n.d.

VONIER, Dom Anscar: *The Spirit and the Bride,* in Volume I of the *Collected Works,* London, Burns Oates, and Westminster, Md, Newman Press, 1952.

*Mediator Dei et Hominum: On the Sacred Liturgy* (Encyclical Letter of Pius XII). Edited with notes by Gerard Ellard, S.J., New York, America Press, 1949. Another edition, by Mgr G. Smith, London, Catholic Truth Society, 1949.